GERMAN
IN RECORD TIME
WITHOUT A TEACHER

by RUDOLPH F. LERCH

AUTHENTIC PUBLICATIONS, INC
636 Eleventh Avenue, New York 36, N. Y.

CONTENTS

	pages
Introduction	3-4
German pronunciation	4
Phonetic representation of german sounds	4-7
The german alphabet and it's pronunciation	7-8
Accentuation	8
Syllabication	9
Capitalization	9
Punctuation	9-10
Grammar	10
Nouns	11-12
Number and case	12
The articles	12-13
Pronouns	13-19
The plural of nouns	19-20
Declension of nouns	20-23
Adjectives, declension	23-25
Adjectives, comparison	25-27
List of adjectives	27-29
Numerals	29-33
The verb	33-43
Irregular verbs	44-45
List of regular verbs	46-47
Verbs, mental activity	47
Verbs to events and circumstances	48-51
Several common expressions	51-52
Prepositions	53-55
Adverbs	55-56
Conjunctions	56-57
Construction of sentences	57-58
Measures and weights	58-59
Days of the week	59
The months	59-60
The seasons	60
The time	60-61
CLASSIFIED VOCABULARY	62-117
Common courtesy - expressions	62-63
Arithmetical expressions	63
Weather	63-64
Colors	64
Geographical terms	64-66
Metals and minerals	66
Precious stones	67
Trees, vegetables, fruits and flowers	67-69
Animals, birds & fishes	69-71
The human body	71-73
The senses	73-74
Circumstances of life	75-76
The family	76-77
Accidents and diseases	77-78
First aid, Medicine	78-79
In the house	79-81
In school	81-82
Tableware	82-83
In the kitchen	83
In the restaurant	83-85
Men's clothing	85
Ladies' garments and accessories	85-86
At the dressmaker	86
Toilet articles	86-87
Traveling	87
At the railway station	88-89
The arrival	89-90
On a ship	90-92
Motoring	92-94
The airplane	94-96
The city	96-98
Street signs	98
Sports and amusements	98-100
Agriculture	101-102
Commercial terms	102-105
Professions, trades	105-107
Legal terms	107-108
In the post-office	108-109
Countries and Nations	109-112
Army and Navy	113-116
Government	116-117
CONVERSATION	117-135
A trip to Germany	117-118
Traveling - acquaintances	118
The arrival	118-119
From the station to the hotel	119
At the hotel	119-120
At the restaurant	120-122
In the city	122-123
At the florist	123
At the bank	123-124
At the post-office	124
At the barber-shop	125
At the beauty-parlor	125
A social evening	125-126
At the night-club	126-127
At the theatre	127
In church	127
Between friends	127-128
At the doctor's office	128-129
Shopping	129-130
At the cleaners	130-131
Business calls	131-132
Commercial information	132-133
Business	133-134
At the travel-agency	134-135
FOR THE TOURIST	136-141
ALPHABETICAL GERMAN - ENGLISH VOCABULARY	142-157
ALPHABETICAL ENGLISH - GERMAN VOCABULARY	158-192

INTRODUCTION

This handbook is designed for the English speaking student of German. It provides a simple and efficient method of learning the spoken language. It also furnishes the traveler who wishes to visit German speaking countries with a convenient guide which is easy to handle and in which the works and phrases most frequently used in daily life can be easily found under the appropriate headings. A vocabulary for quick reference is given at the end of the book.

The phonetic spelling used enables anybody who knows English to pronounce every German word contained in this booklet without the aid of a teacher.

German is not a complete stranger to English speaking people. In fact, one is pleasantly surprised to discover that one already knows or can easily guess the meaning of many German words. Since German and English stem from the same teutonic roots, the basic relationship of the two languages is a valuable aid to the student. There are thousands of cognates which show the intimate kinship of English and German. Furthermore, a large number of English and German works are derived from the same Latin roots. Here are some examples of the most common types of cognates:

Words which are spelled differently but whose pronunciation and meaning are identical in German and in English:

Bier	beer	Fisch	fish
Busch	bush	Glas	glass
Eis	ice	Haus	house
fein	fine	Schuh	shoe

Words whose spelling and meaning are identical, but whose pronunciation is different in the two languages:

Butter	(boot-tehr)	butter
Nation	(nah-tsyohn)	nation
Student	(shtoo-dehnt)	student
Hunger	(hoon-gehr)	hunger
international	(in-tehr-nah-tsyoh-nahl)	international
Sack	(Zahk)	sack
warm	(vahrm)	warm

There are other German words whose spelling or pronunciation are only slightly different from those of semantically similar English words. In fact, most cognates belong to this group:

alt	(ahlt)	old
beginnen	(beh-gin-nehn)	to begin
dick	(dick)	thick
Gott	(Goht)	God
grün	(gruen)	green
Grund	(groond)	ground
gut	(goot)	good
kühl	(kuel)	cool
Kuss	(koos)	kiss
Mann	(mahn)	man
Mutter	(moot-tehr)	mother
Vater	(fah-tehr)	father

Finally, German has borrowed words, such as Toast, Sweater, Pullover, Roastbeef, directly from the English, just as English has taken the word Kindergarten from the German.

GERMAN PRONUNCIATION

German pronunciation is relatively simple. Most of the German sounds occur in the English language too, although the spelling is somewhat different. German is far more consistent than English, where words like height, knight, cough, rough, dough, etc., preclude any possibility for drawing up rules, leaving the foreigner learning English no alternative except to memorize the pronunciation of each word individually. In German, as in English, there are long vowels and short vowels. In German, as in English, a vowel is short, if it is followed by a double consonant (double s, double n, etc.). If a vowel is followed by an h, it is long.

PHONETIC REPRESENTATION OF GERMAN SOUNDS

Vowels

Insofar as in German the difference between long vowels and short vowels is not great, we shall simplify the study of the language by employing but one transliteration symbol for each vowel in the alphabet, whether it is long or short.

Long <u>a</u>,	as it occurs in <u>Vater</u> (father), is pronounced as the English <u>a</u> in <u>father</u>.	ah
Short <u>a</u>,	as it occurs in <u>Wasser</u> (water), is pronounced as the British <u>a</u> in <u>staff</u> (a sound similar to the American <u>o</u> in <u>not</u>).	ah
Long <u>e</u>,	as it occurs in <u>Erde</u> (earth), is pronounced almost as the English <u>a</u> in <u>game</u>.	eh
Short <u>e</u>,	as it occurs in <u>Bett</u> (bed, is pronounced as the English <u>e</u> in <u>bet</u>.	eh
<u>ie</u>,	as it occurs in <u>Brief</u> (letter), is pronounced as the English <u>ee</u> in <u>beef</u>.	ee
Short <u>i</u>,	as it occurs in <u>bitte</u> (please), is pronounced as the English <u>i</u> in <u>bit</u>.	i
Long <u>o</u>,	as it occurs in <u>ohne</u> (without), is pronounced as the English <u>o</u> in <u>bore</u>.	oh
Short <u>o</u>,	as it occurs in <u>voll</u> (full), is pronounced as the English <u>o</u> in <u>often</u>.	oh
Long <u>u</u>,	as it occurs in <u>nur</u> (only), is pronounced as the English <u>oo</u> in <u>poor</u>.	oo
Short <u>u</u>,	as it occurs in <u>und</u> (and), is pronounced as the English <u>u</u> in <u>pull</u>.	oo

In addition to the above listed vowels, German also has the so called "Umlaut" (modified) vowels. They are:

<u>ä</u>,	as it occurs in <u>spät</u> (late), which is pronounced almost as the English <u>a</u> in <u>hate</u> (but in a more open manner).	ae
<u>ö</u>,	as it occurs in <u>öffnen</u> (to open), to be pronounced as the French <u>oeu</u> in <u>oeuvre</u>, or almost as <u>eh</u> with rounded lips.	oe
<u>ü</u>,	as it occurs in fühlen (to feel), to be pronounced as the French <u>u</u> in <u>duc</u>, or almost as <u>ee</u> with rounded lips.	ue

äu and eu,	as they occur in Häuser (Houses) and treu (faithful) are pronounced as the English oi in oil.	oi
ei,	as it occurs in fein (fine) is pronounced as the English y in by, or i in dine. It will be represented by ahy.	ahy
ie	(See vowels)	ee
au,	as it occurs in Frau (woman), is pronounced as the English ou in out.	ou

CONSONANTS

While most German consonants are pronounced as their English ccunterparts, the following differences must be noted:

c	occurs seldom in German and it is pronounced as the English k when it precedes a, o, and u and when it is at the end of the word, and as ts when it precedes i and e. Example: Cicero (tsi-tseh-roh), Cato (kah-toh).	k,ts
g	is always hard as in girl, never as in general.	g
h	except at the beginning of a word. is silent.	
j	is always pronounced as the English y in yet.	y
s	Before a vowel at the beginning of a word or between two vowels, this consonant is pronounced as the English z in zebra (sehen--zeh-ehn--to see; Hose--hoh-zeh--pants). Before p and t at the beginning of a word, it is pronounced as the English sh (Spaten--shpaht-ehn--spade; Stein--shtahyn--stone). In German the sound s is most frequently represented by ss.	z,sh,s

v — is pronounced as the English f. For instance: von (fohn) = of. — f

w — is pronounced as the English v. For instance: was (vahs) = what. — v

z — is pronounced as the English ts or tz in quartz. For example: zu (tsoo) = to. — ts

---

ti — is pronounced as ts before a vowel as it occurs in Nation (nah-tsyon) — ts

sch — is always pronounced as the English sh. Example: Schule (shoo-leh) = school. — sh

ch — is pronounced as hard h (or as the Scottish ch in loch) when it is preceded by a, o, or u (Example: Nacht--nahht--night) and as soft h, as in the English name Hugh, when it is preceded by e, i, a, o, u, l, r (Example: nicht--niht--not).

Insofar as German pronunciation is consistent, it is not difficult to learn. Hence, we advise that the phonetic transcription provided in this book be disregarded as soon as the German values have been memorized. By reading German passages aloud and by listening to German being spoken, one can acquire a good pronunciation without great difficulty.

THE GERMAN ALPHABET AND IT'S PRONUNCIATION

The German Alphabet consists of 26 letters:

Character	German Name	Pronunciation	
A a	ah		ah
B b	beh	as in English	b
C c	tseh		k
D d	deh	as in English	d
E e	eh		eh
F f	ehf	as in English	f
G g	geh		g
H h	hah		h
I i	ee		ee
J j	yoht		y
K k	kah	as in English	k
L l	ehl		l

M m	ehm	as in English	m
N n	ehn	as in English	n
O o	oh		oh
P p	peh	as in English	p
Q q	kveh		q
R r	er ehr		r
S s	ehs		z
ss			ss
sch	ehs-tseh-hah		sh
T t	teh		t
U u	oo		oo
V v	fou		f
W w	veh		v
X x	eks		x
Y y	ehpseelohn		y
Z z	tseht		ts

ACCENTUATION

In German the accent usually falls on the first syllable of a word. However, words beginning with one of the following unaccented prefixes do not follow the rule: be, ge, er, ver, zer, emp, and ent. Example: Betrug (beh-troog') = deceit, Erfolg (ehr-fohlg') = success, Verlust (fehr-loost') = loss, zerlegen (tsehr-leh'-gehn) = decompose, empfinden (ehmp-feen'-dehn) feel, entgehen (ehnt-geh'-ehn) = elude.

Foreign words and suffixes usually retain the original foreign accent. However, in most cases, in nouns of foreign origin it is the last syllable that is accented. Example: Offizier (ohf-fee-tseer' = officer, Student (shtoo-dehnt') = student, Nation (nah-tsyohn') = nation, Natur (nah-toor') = nature, Professor (proh-fehs'-sohr) = professor.

The prefixes miss, voll, durch, unter, über, um, and wieder are frequently unaccented. The prefix un, however, is usually accented. Example: unterscheiden (oon-tehr-schahy'-dehn) = distinguish; Unglück (oon-gluek) = unhappiness.

SYLLABICATION

German words are divided into syllables according to pronunciation. The most important rules are: A single consonant between vowels goes with the next syllable: sa-gen, fra-gen, le-sen, re-den, ge-hen, lau-fen, ba-den.

When there are two or more consonants, only the last one goes with the following syllable: Mut-ter, Ret-ter, Don-ner, Hammer, Step-pe, Pfar-rer. However, sk, sch, ch, ph, and st are never separated: Maske, Fi-sche, Ra-che, Stro-phe, Schwe-ster.

The syllabication of words containing the combinations ck and tz is achieved as follows: In Hacke: Hak-ke; in wacker: wakker; in ritzen: rit-zen.

CAPITALIZATION

In German all nouns and all words used as nouns are capitalized:

der Baum (dehr Bahoom) = the tree
das Haus (dahs Hahoos) = the house
die Vier (dee Feer) = the four.

In German, as in most languages, almost any word, (an adjective, an infinitive, a participle) can be used as a noun by placing the article in front of it. In this case, the word following the article and serving as a noun is capitalized just as if it were an actual noun. Example:

Das Singen (dahs zin'-gehn) = the singing
Der Starke (dehr shtahr'-keh) = the strong
Die Tanzende (dee tahn'-tsehn-deh) = the (one) dancing.

PUNCTUATION

In German most punctuation marks are used as in English. The principal differences lie in the use of the comma. In German the comma is used:

1. In Independent sentences:
   a. To separate words which modify or clarify titles or names without being a part of them: (Columbus, der Entdecker Amerikas, (Columbus, the discoverer of America).

b. To separate modifying adjectives which follow the noun (esp. in poetry): der Held, bescheiden und scheu, (the hero, modest and shy).

c. To separate an addressing noun or an interjection from the rest of the sentence: Hörst, Bruder, meine Stimme nicht? (Brother, do you not hear my voice?) Oh, das ist schön. (Oh, this is beautiful!)

d. To separate coordinating parts of a sentence not connected by the conjunctions: und, oder, als, Er fiel, erhob sich und lief davon (He fell, got up and ran away).

2. In compound sentences: To separate the parts of the sentence: Seine Freunde verlassen ihn, und er sinkt tiefer und tiefer. (His friends forsake him, and he sinks deeper and deeper).

The comma also separates the dependent clause from the principal clause in a sentence: (Das ist alles, was ich für dich tun kann. (This is all I can do for you).

Contrary to English, German does not provide for the use of a comma to separate words such as however: Er folgte dem Rufe jedoch gegen seine Überzeugung; (He followed the call, however, against his own conviction).

GRAMMAR

German grammar is considered somewhat difficult for English speaking people, since German has retained the case endings which do not exist in modern English. Furthermore, German nouns can be of any of three genders, and both the definite article and the modifying adjectives must agree with the noun in gender, number, and case. One has a limited basis for guessing the gender of a particular noun. It is, therefore, useful to memorize each word with the respective article which is indicative of the gender:

Der Tisch (dehr tish) = the table, MASCULINE
Das Buch (dahs booh) = the book, NEUTER
Die Blume (dee bloo'-meh)" flower, FEMININE

It is very important to study the grammar section of this book. A good way of becoming proficient in the correct usage of German grammar is to form new sentences based on the construction of any given German sentence or phrase. In German compound sentences are construed similarly to the Latin sentence, where the verb occurs at the end.

In German all names of persons, animals and things (visible or invisible) are nouns. Every noun requires its proper article, which is either masculine, feminine or neuter.

Gender: German has three genders: masculine, feminine, and neuter.

All nouns referring to males (persons or animals) and some nouns ending in tum are masculine. Example:

Der Vater (dehr fah'-tehr) = the father
Der Reichtum (dehr rahyh'-toom) = the wealth

Exception:

Das Eigentum (dahs ahy'-gehn-toom) = the property, which is neuter.

All nouns referring to females (persons or animals), most nouns ending in e, ei, and ung, and all nouns ending in heit, keit, and schaft are feminine.
Example:

Die Mutter (dee moo'-tehr) = the mother
die Rede (dee reh'-deh) = the speech
die Schwindelei (shvin'-deh-lahy) = swindling
die Prüfung (prue'-foong) = examination
die Klugheit = wisdom
die Schlechtigkeit = Badness
die Wissenschaft = science

Exceptions:

das Ende (dahs ehn'-deh) = end, which is neuter
das Geschrei (dahs geh-shrahy') = screaming), which is neuter.
der Ursprung (dehr oor'-shproong) = origin, which is masculine.

By adding the ending in to some masculine nouns referring to persons, we obtain feminine forms: der Held (the hero) die Heldin (the heroine).

Foreign nouns used in German, which end in ie, ik, ion, tat and ur are also feminine: Die Monarchie, die Technik.

Most German rivers are feminine (exception: der Rhein, der Main, der Neckar, der Lech, der Inn).

Abstract nouns such as:die Trauer (sorrow) are feminine.

All infinitives used as nouns: das Lesen (reading). das Schreiben (writing), das Rechnen (arithmetic) and many nouns beginning with Ge and ending in e (das Gehäuse-box) are neuter.

Diminutives ending in -chen or -lein are neuter: das Bäumchen (the little tree), das Blümlein (the little flower).

Most names of countries and towns (exception: die Schweiz, die Türkei) are neuter.

Many nouns ending in -nis, -sal, -sel, -tum are neuter.

All names of metals are neuter: das Gold (the gold).

Compound words acquire, as a rule, the gender of their last component: das Schul-haus: (the schoolhouse).

NUMBER AND CASE

German has two numbers, singular and plural, and four cases: The nominative is the case of the subject or predicate; the genitive corresponds to the English possessive case; the dative is the case of the indirect object and the accusative is the case of the direct object.

THE ARTICLES

In German there is a definite article and an indefinite article. The article must agree with the noun in gender, number and case.

The definite article:

Case	Masc.	Fem.	Neut	Engl.	Plural all Genders
Nom.	der	die	das	the	die
Gen.	des	der	des	of the	der
Dat.	dem	der	dem	to the	den
Acc.	den	die.	das	the	die

Many prepositions form contractions with the dative and accusative of the definite article. Examples:

am - an dem, (at the); im - in dem, (in the); zum - zu dem, (to the); zur - zu der, (to the); ans - an das, (to the); ins-in das, (into the); aufs - auf das, (upon the).

The indefinite article:

Case	Masc.	Fem.	Neut.	Engl.
Nom.	ein	eine	ein	a
Gen.	eines	einer	eines	of a
Dat.	einem	einer	einem	to a
Acc.	einen	eine	einen	a

The indefinite article has no plural.

PRONOUNS

Personal Pronouns:

The German personal pronouns are:

ich (ihh) = I
Du (doo) = you, sing. informal.
er (ehr) = he
sie (zee) = she
es (ehs) = it
wir (veer) = we
Ihr (eer) = you, plural, informal
sie (zee) = they
Sie (zee) = you, sing. & plural formal.

Notice that the English you can be translated into German as:

1. Du, the so called familiar form, which is singular and which is used in addressing the Deity, a member of the family, a close friend, a child, and a pet. It is always written with a capital D. It corresponds to the old English form thou.

2. Ihr, which is the plural of Du and which is used as a familiar form in addressing more than one person. This pronoun is always written with a capital I in order to be distinguished from the possessive pronoun ihr (her and their).

3. Sie, which is the so called polite form, both singular and plural, and which is used in addressing acquaintances and strangers. Since it has the same spelling as the third person plural (sie), we distinguish it from it by writing Sie = you always with a capital S. Please bear in mind that in German one must be on very intimate

terms with a person before switching from Sie to Du. In case of doubt as to which form is more appropriate, use Sie.

Declension of Personal Pronouns:

Singular

	1st person	2nd person
Nominative	ich - I	Du - you
Genitive	meiner - of me	deiner - of you
Dative	mir - to me	dir - to you
Accusative	mich - me	dich - you

3rd person

	Masc.	Fem.	Neuter
Nominative	er - he	sie - she	es - it
Genitive	seiner - of him	ihrer - of her	seiner - of it
Dative	ihm - to him	ihr - to her	ihm - to it
Accusative	ihn - him	sie - her	es - it

Plural

Nominative	wir - we	ihr - you	sie - they
Genitive	unser - of us	euer - of you	ihrer - of them
Dative	uns - to us	euch - to you	ihnen - to them
Accusative	uns - us	euch - you	sie - them

Reflexive Pronouns

In German the reflexive form is used far more frequently and more freely than in English. German employs the personal pronouns as reflexive except in the dative and accusative case of the third person, where sich is used.

Accusative case

mich- myself (Ich sehe mich = I see myself)	uns - ourselves
dich- yourself	euch - yourselves
sich- himself, herself, itself (Er sieht sich - he sees himself)	sich - themselves

Dative case

mir - to myself (Ich sage mir = I tell (to) myself)	uns - to ourselves
dir - to yourself --	euch - to yourselves
sich - to himself, herself, itself (Er sagt sich = He tells himself)	sich - to themselves

The word selbst (zehlbst) added to the reflexive as well as personal pronouns achieves an emphasis: Ich selbst = I myself, mich selbst = me myself; Du selbst = you yourself, dich selbst and dir selbst = you and to you yourself, etc.

Einander (ahyn-ahn'-dehr) means each other: Wir lieben einander (Veer lee'-behn ahyn-ahn'-dehr) = We love each other.

In German there are reflexive verbs, which in English are not reflexive, and they require a reflexive pronoun. Example:
Ich freue mich (I am glad), du freust dich (you are glad), er freut sich (he is glad), wir freuen uns (we are glad), ihr freuet euch (you are glad), sie freuen sich (they are glad).

Possessive Pronouns

They must agree with the noun they qualify in number, gender and case.

mein (my), dein (your), sein (his, its), ihr (her),
unser (our), euer (your), ihr (their).

Declension Of Possessive Pronouns

Singular

Nominative	mein Bruder (my brother)	unser Haus (our house)
Genitive	meines Bruders (of my brother)	unseres Hauses (of our house)
Dative	meinem Bruder (to my brother)	unserem Hause (to our house)
Accusative	meinen Bruder (my brother)	unser Haus (our house)

Plural

Nominative	meine Brüder (my brothers)	unsere Häuser (our houses)
Genitive	meiner Brüder (of my brothers)	unserer Häuser (of our houses)
Dative	meinen Brüdern (to my brothers)	unseren Häusern (to our houses)
Accusative	meine Brüder (my brothers)	unsere Häuser (our houses)

Ich habe deinen Hut und du hast meinen = I have your hat and you have mine. Mein Bruder ist in der Armee, aber ihrer ist noch zu Hause = My brother is in the army, but hers is still at home. Unser Haus ist gross, aber eures ist grösser = Our house is large, but yours is larger. Unser Hund ist schwarz, aber ihrer ist weiss = Our dog is black, but hers is white. Meinetwegen = on my account. Unseretwegen = on our account. Seinetwegen = on his account. Seinethalben = on his behalf. Ihrethalben = on her behalf. um unsretwillen = for our sake. um euretwillen = for your sake.

Demonstrative Pronouns

Masculine	Feminine	Neuter
der = this	die	das
dieser = this	diese	dieses
Jener = that	jene	jener
derjenige = this one	diejenige	dasjenige
derselbe = the same one	dieselbe	dasselbe
solcher, solch = such	solche, solch	solches, solch
(ein solcher....., or	(eine solche Frau, or	(ein solches Kind,
solch ein ....)	solch eine Frau)	solch ein Kind)
Also: so ein	so eine	so ein

Before a noun the pronoun der, die, das, (this) is declined as the definite article. Without a noun it is declined as follows:

	Masc.	Fem.	Neut.	Plural
Nom.	der	die	das	die
Gen.	dessen	deren	dessen	derer
Dat.	dem	der	dem	denen
Acc.	den	die	das	die

This I remember very well = dessen erinnere ich mich sehr gut. Wo is Ihr Bruder? = Where is your brother? Der is weit weg = He is far away. Das ist der, den ich meine = This is the one I mean. Dieses Haus oder das am Berge = This house or the one on the hill. This one, = dieser; points to objects near by or refers to the last one mentioned. That one, or the former one, jener, points to distant objects.

Dieser Mann ist mein Freund, aber jener dort in der Ecke ist mein Feind = This man is my friend but that one in the corner is my enemy. Der jenige, this one; is used with more emphasis instead of der.

Das ist derjenige (diejenige), den(die) ich suche; This is the one I am looking for. Derselbe (dieselbe, dasselbe), = the same, is used to avoid the succession of two pronouns of the same form.

Sie bewundert diese Musik, weil sie dieselbe (instead of another sie) kennt = She admires this music because she knows it.

Solch = such, is usually succeeded by ein: Solch ein Mann = such a man; Solch eine Frau = such a woman; Solch ein Kind = such a baby, while solcher, solche and solches are usually preceded by e in, eine, ein: ein solcher Mann = such a man; eine solche Dame = such a lady. Sometimes instead of solch ein, so ein and ein so are used; So ein guter Knabe = such a good boy. Ein so schöner Baum = such a nice three.

Relative Pronouns

The English who, which, that, are translated into German as either der, die, das, or welcher, welche, welches.

The soldier who = der Soldat, der. The teacher who = die Lehrerin, die. The street which = die Strasse, die. The book which = das Buch, das. This can also be rendered as follows: The soldier who = der Soldat, welcher. The teacher who = die Lehrerin, welche. The book which = Das Buch welches. The plural is either die or welche. The men that = die Männer, welche.

Welcher, welche, welches

	Masculine	Feminine	Neuter
Singular			
Nom.	welcher = who, which	welche	welches
Gen.	dessen = whose	deren	dessen
Dat.	welchem = to whom	deren	welchem
Acc.	welchen = whom	welche	welche
Plural			
Nom.	welche =	welche	welche
Gen.	deren	deren	deren
Dat.	welchen	welchen	welchen
Acc.	welche	welche	welche

Der Hut, welchen er kaufte = The hat which he bought.
Das Kind, welchem ich sagte = The child to whom I said.
Die Frau deren Freunde kamen = The woman whose friends came.

Welcher is also an interrogative pronoun which is declined in the same manner.

The English he who or whoever is translated into German as wer.

Nom.	wer =	he who	Wer lügt, der stiehlt= He who lies, steals.
Gen.	wessen =	of him who (whose)	
Dat.	wem =	to him who	
Acc.	Wen =	he whom	Wer refers to persons

When wer refer to things, we use was.

Wir geben dir das Beste was wir haben =
We give you the best that we have.

Wer and was are also interrogative pronouns which are declined in the same manner.

Interrogative Pronouns

Wer? = Who?; wessen? =whose?; wen? = whom?; wem? = to whom?; was? =what? Who was that? =Wer war das? Whose book is this? = Wessen Buch ist das? Whom do you blame? = Wen tadeln Sie? To whom do you write? =Wem schreiben Sie? What did he say? =Was sagte er? What kind of a tree is that? = Was für ein Baum ist das? What a surprise=Welch ein Wunder.

Indefinite Pronouns

The German "man", translated as one, they, people, is used more frequently than its equivalents in English. It is said = man sagt. Was man will, das glaubt man gern, = What one wishes, one readily believes.

Etwas, means anything, somewhat. Is there anything new? = Gibt es etwas Neues? He is somewhat slow = Er ist etwas langsam.

Nichts, means nothing. He does nothing = Er tut (macht) nichts. Jemand,, is the German word for somebody, anybody. Has anybody seen him? = Hat ihn jemand gesehen? Niemand is nobody. Nobody was there = Niemand war dort. Ein wenig = a little. Give me a little bread = Geben Sie mir ein wenig Brot.

Ein paar = a few. Give me a few apples = Geben Sie mir ein paar Äpfel. (If one pair is meant, "paar" is capitalized.) Wenig = a little. He has a little money = Er hat wenig Geld. Genug = enough. He has enough = Er hat genug. Zuviel = too much. You waste too much time = Sie verschwenden zuviel Zeit. Viel = much. You don't ask for much = Sie verlangen nicht viel. Viel zuviel = far too much. It was far too much = Es war viel zuviel. Wieviel = How much. How much do you want? = Wieviel verlangen Sie? Wieviel(e) = how many. How many brothers does he have? = Wieviele Brüder hat er? Wenige = few. Few (people) understand this = Wenige (Leute) verstehen das. Mehrere = several. I met several friends = Ich traf mehrere Freunde. Viele = many I have seen many of them = Ich habe viele davon gesehen. Beide = both. Will both brothers be there? = Werden beide Brüder dort sein? Einer = one. One of her brothers = Einer ihrer Brüder. Keiner, keine, keines = none. None of his dogs = Keiner seiner Hunde; None of her flowers = Keine ihrer Blumen; None of his toys = Keines seiner Spielzeuge. Irgend eine = anyone.
Anyone of these ladies (men, children); Irgendeine dieser Frauen (irgend einer dieser Männer; Irgend eines dieser Kinder). Jeder = each one. Each one of the sisters = Jede von den Schwestern. Mancher = many a, some. Many a man (woman, child) = Mancher Mann; (manche Frau, manches Kind).

The Plural of Nouns

General rules:

Feminine nouns add "n" or "en" to the singular. (Tante, Tanten; Frau, Frauen).

All other nouns add "e" or "er" to the singular: der Weg, die Wege; das Bild, die Bilder.

Nouns having "a", "o", "u", "au" in the stem change them in the plural into "ä", "ö", "ü", "äu", besides adding "e" or "er": die Hand, die Hände; der Sohn, die Söhne; das Huhn, die Hühner.

Neuter nouns which change the vowel, generally add, "er": das Buch, die Bücher; das Haus, die Häuser.

Masculine and neuter nouns ending in "el", "en", "er", do not change: das Messer, die Messer; der Vogel, die Vögel; der Wagen, die Wagen: der Kasten, die Kästen.

Masculine nouns ending in "e" add "n": der Neffe, die Neffen.

Declension of Nouns

General rules on the declension:

Feminines remain unchanged in the singular. In the plural, the nominative, genitive and accusative are alike. The dative always ends in "-n" or "-en." No plural has less than two syllables. Compounds decline only their last part: das Fahrrad, die Fahrräder.

Strong nouns are those that take "-s," "-es" or remain unchanged in the genitive singular and take "-e" or "-er," or remain unchanged in the nominative plural.

Weak nouns are those that take "-n" or "-en" in all cases of the plural, and, if masculine, in the genitive, dative and accusative singular.

Mixed nouns are those which are strong in singular and weak in the plural.

Strong Declension

Singular

Masculine

Nom.	der Garten	the garden
Gen.	des Gartens	of the garden
Dat.	dem Garten	to the garden
Acc.	den Garten	the Garden

Feminine		Neuter	
die Mutter	the mother	das Bild	the picture
der Mutter	of the mother	des Bildes	of the picture
der Mutter	to the mother	dem Bild(e)	to the picture
die Mutter	the mother	das Bild	the picture

Plural

Masculine

Nom.	die Gärten	the gardens
Gen.	der Gärten	of the gardens
Dat.	den Gärten	to the gardens
Acc.	die Gärten	the gardens

Feminine		Neuter	
die Mütter	the mothers	die Bilder	the pictures
der Mütter	of the mothers	der Bilder	of the pictures
den Müttern	to the mothers	den Bildern	to the pictures
die Mütter	the mothers	die Bilder	the pictures

Singular

Nom.	das Haus	the house
Gen.	des Hauses	of the house
Dat.	dem Haus(e)	to the house
Acc.	das Haus	the house

das Jahr	the year	der Mann	the man
des Jahres	of the year	des Mannes	of the man
dem Jahr(e)	to the year	dem Mann(e)	to the man
das Jahr	the year	den Mann	the man

Plural

Nom.	die Häuser	the houses
Gen.	der Häuser	of the houses
Dat.	den Häusern	to the houses
Acc.	die Häuser	the houses

die Jahre	the years	die Männer	the men
der Jahre	of the years	der Männer	of the men
den Jahren	to the years	den Männer	to the men
die Jahre	the years	die Männer	the men

WEAK DECLENSION

Singular

Nom.	Der Knabe	the boy
Gen.	des Knaben	of the boy
Dat.	dem Knaben	to the boy
Acc.	den Knaben	the boy

der Mensch	the person (human being)
des Menschen	of the person
dem Menschen	to the person
den Menschen	the person

Plural

Nom.	die Knaben	the boys
Gen.	der Knaben	of the boys
Dat.	den Knaben	to the boys
Acc.	die Knaben	the boys

die Menschen	the persons
der Menschen	of the persons
den Menschen	to the persons
die Menschen	the persons

MIXED DECLENSION

Singular

Nom.	das Ohr	the ear
Gen.	des Ohres	of the ear
Dat.	dem Ohr(e)	to the ear
Acc.	das Ohr	the ear

das Bett	the bed	der See	the lake
des Bettes	of the bed	des Sees	of the lake
dem Bett(e)	to the bed	dem See	to the lake
das Bett	the bed	den See	the lake

Plural

Nom.	die Ohren	the ears
Gen.	der Ohren	of the ears
Dat.	den Ohren	to the ears
Acc.	die Ohren	the ears

die Betten	the beds	die Seen	the lakes
der Betten	of the beds	der Seen	of the lakes
den Betten	to the beds	den Seen	to the lakes
die Betten	the beds	die Seen	the lakes

Proper names, i.e. names of persons, are in general uninflected with the exception of the genitive singular. Karl's Testament. Charles' will. This case ends in "s", if not preceded by the article. However, if the article is used: Das Testament des Karl, the will of Charles, the name remains unchanged.

Geographical names, (names of countries) are treated in the same manner as the names of persons, except that feminine names cannot omit the definite article and neuters frequently abandon the genitive for the preposition "von" with the dative; die Berge der Schweiz = mountains of Switzerland; die Flüsse Österreichs = or die Flüsse von Österreich = the rivers of Austria.

ADJECTIVES

Adjectives are attributes of a noun which either follows or is understood. They always give a description of a characterization of a noun: eine schöne Blume, a beautiful flower. Ein grosser Mann = a tall man; eine alte Frau = an old lady; ein grosser Feldherr = a great general. They are declined when they are followed by a noun or used as a noun; ein Alter = an old man. They are not declined when they stand after the noun, or have adverbial meanings: der Apfel ist gut = the apple is good; er singt schön = he sings beautifully; er handelt weise = he acts wisely.

Declension of the Adjectives:
The Weak Declension

The weak declension is used when the adjective is preceded by an article or a pronoun: der grosse Mann = the tall man; das reine Gold = the pure gold; das alte Haus = the old house.

Singular

Nom.	der grosse Mann	the tall man
Gen.	des grossen Mannes	of the tall man
Dat.	dem grossen Mann(e)	to the tall man
Acc.	den grossen Mann	the tall man

das reine Gold	the pure gold
des reinen Goldes	of the pure gold
dem reinen Gold(e)	to the pure gold
das reine Gold	the pure gold

Metals have no plural

Plural

Nom.	die grossen Männer	the tall men
Gen.	der grossen Männer	of the tall men
Dat.	den grossen Männer	to the tall men
Acc.	die grossen Männer	the tall men

The Strong Declension

The strong declension is used where no article or pronoun precedes the adjective.

Singular

(tall tree)	(big sum)	(good child)
Nom. hoher Baum	grosse Summe	gutes Kind
Gen. hohen Baumes	grosser Summe	guten Kindes
Dat. hohem Baum(e)	grosser Summe	gutem Kind(e)
Acc. hohen Baum	grosse Summe	gutes Kind

Plural

(tall trees)	(big sums)	(good children)
Nom. hohe Bäume	grosse Summen	gute Kinder
Gen. hoher Bäume	grosser Summen	guter Kinder
Dat. hohen Bäumen	grossen Summen	guten Kindern
Acc. hohe Bäume	grosse Summen	gute Kinder

Two or more adjectives preceding one noun have the same endings: guter, braver Mann, good, fine man; eine alte, liebe Frau, an old, dear lady; ein grosses, altes Haus, a big, old house.

Adjectives used as nouns, or used without nouns after indefinite (or other) pronouns, are capitalized and have the same endings as attributive adjectives: der Schwache, die Schwachen = the weak; alle Schweden = all Swedes; viele Deutsche = many Germans; etwas Böses = something bad; alles Böse = everything bad; etwas Schönes = something beautiful.

Adjectives denoting languages: Sagen Sie es auf Deutsch = say it in German; Sein Englisch ist nicht sehr gut = his English is not very good; are also capitalized.

The adjective "hoch" = high, drops the "c" before all endings beginning with a vowel: der Berg ist hoch = the mountain is high; der hohe Berg = the high mountain.

Ganz = whole, and halb = half are uninflected unless preceded by an article. These uninflected forms are used only before the names of cities and countries: ganz Deutschland = all of Germany; halb Wien = half of Vienna; but, das ganze Deutschland; - das halbe Wien.

Lauter, when standing for pure, is declined: das lautere Wasser = the pure water; however, it is undeclined when it means nothing but: lauter Wasser = nothing but water.

Adjectives are derived from the names of cities, rarely of countries, by means of the ending "er"; die Wiener Zeitungen = the Vienna newspapers; ein Englischer Graf = An English Count; der Berliner, der Londoner, der New Yorker, der Bostoner, der Washingtoner, etc.

The adjective agrees in number and gender with the noun it qualifies: grosser Mann = tall man; kleine Frau = little woman; liebes Kind = dear child; liebe Kinder = dear children.

Comparison of Adjectives

The comparative is formed by adding "-er", the superlative - by adding "-ste" to the stem of the adjective:

Positive	Comparative	Superlative
reich = rich	reicher = richer	der (die, das) reichste = the richest
klein = small	kleiner = smaller	der (die, das) kleinste = the smallest

In the comparative and superlative a number of very common adjectives change their "a, o, u, " into Umlaut, i.e. into "ä, ö, ü".

Positive	Comparative	Superlative
kalt = cold	kälter	der (die, das) kälteste
stark = strong	stärker	der (die, das) stärkste
schwach = weak	schwächer	der (die, das) schwächste
lang = long	länger	der (die, das) längste
kurz = short	kürzer	der (die, das) kürzeste
klug = clever	klüger	der (die, das) klügste
scharf = sharp	schärfer	der (die, das) schärfste
warm = warm	wärmer	der (die, das) wärmste
jung = young	jünger	der (die, das) jüngste

alt = old	älter	der (die, das) älteste
hoch = high	höher	der (die, das) höchste
arm = poor	ärmer	der (die, das) ärmste
gross = great	grösser	der (die, das) grösste

If the adjective ends in an "s" sound, that is: s, ss, sch, z, tz, x, or in a d or t, the superlative adds "-est" instead of "-st": heiss = hot; der heisseste; kalt = cold; der kälteste; nass = wet; der nasseste.

Adjectives ending in "-el", "-e, "-en", "-er" drop their "e" before the comparative ending, but retain it before the superlative ending:

Positive	Comparative	Superlative
selten = rare	selt(e)ner	der(die, das)seltenste
edel = noble	edler	der (die, das) edelste
tapfer = brave	tapf(e)rer	der(die, das)tapferste

Irregular Adjectives:

Positive	Comparative	Superlative
gut = good	besser	der (die, das) beste
hoch = high	höher	der (die, das) höchste
viel = much	mehr	der (die, das) meiste

Adjectives which have no positive:

Comparative	Superlative
hinter— = hind	der hinterste = hindmost
vorder— = front	der vorderste = foremost
unter— = lower	der unterste = lowest

Comparative	Superlative
inner— = inner	der innerste = innermost
ausser— = outer	der äusserste = outermost
ober— = upper	der oberste = topmost

Comparison are also achieved by means of adverbs, which form the comparative in the same manner as the adjectives: Du singst schöner als sie = you sing more prettily than she. However, in the superlative, "am" is placed in front of the adverb and an "n" is added to the "ste" ending - sten: Er singt am schönsten = He sings most prettily.

The declension of the comparative and superlative is achieved in the same manner as in the positive.

Other forms of comparison: Er ist so gross wie ich = He is as tall as I. Sein Beruf ist so gut wie meiner = His profession is as good as mine. Sein Einkommen ist grösser als meines = His income is greater than mine. Sein Haus ist teurer als deines = His house is more expensive than yours (thine).

There are also superlative forms (adverbial) without case endings. hochst enttäuscht = exceedingly disappointed. äusserst entzückt = extremely delighted. Jüngst erschienen = most recently published. Meist vergessen = mostly forgotten.
Er schreibt allerliebst = he writes most charmingly.

Another superlative is "am meisten" = the most: Ich liebe Dich am meisten = I love you the most.

List of Adjectives

Positive

good	gut	(goot)
bad	schlecht	(shlehht)
clean	rein	(rahyn)
dirty	schmutzig	(shmoot-tsig)
soft	weich	(vahyh)
hard	hart	(hahrt)
fat	fett	(feht)
thin	dünn	(duenn)
wide	breit	(brahyt)
narrow	enge	(ehn-geh)
warm	warm	(vahrm)
cool	kühl	(kuel)
fresh	frisch	(frish)
polite	höflich	(hoef-lih)
impolite	unhöflich	(oon-oef-lih)
sweet	süss	(suess)
bitter	bitter	(bit-tehr)
hungry	hungrig	(hoon-grig)
thirsty	durstig	(door-stig)
wet	nass	(nahss)
dry	trocken	(troh-kehn)
strong	stark	(shtahrk)

weak	schwach	(shvahh)
poor	arm	(ahrm)
rich	reich	(rahyh)
round	rund	(roond)
short	kurz	(koorts)
long	lang	(lahng)
little	klein	(klahyn)
small	klein	(klahyn)
big, large	gross	(grohs)
sharp	scharf	(shahrf)
blunt	stumpf	(shtoompf)
true	treu	(troyu)
false	falsch	(fahlsh)
full	voll	(fohl)
empty	leer	(lehr)
glad	froh	(froh)
sad	traurig	(trou-rig)
deep	tief	(teef)
beautiful	schön	(shoen)
ugly	hässlich	(haess-lih)
heavy	schwer	(shvehr)
light	leicht	(lahyht)
wise	klug	(kloog)
foolish	töricht	(toe-riht)
active	tätig	(tae-tig)
lazy	faul	(foul)
expensive	teuer	(toy-ehr)
cheap	billig	(bil-lig)
brave	tapfer	(tah-pfehr)
coward	feige	(fahy-geh)
proud	stolz	(stohlts)
miserable	elend	(eh-lehnd)
modern	modern	(moh-dehrn)
old-fashioned	altmodisch	(ahlt-moh-dish)
public	öffentlich	(oef-fehnt-lih)
private	privat	(pre-evaht)
quick, rapid	schnell	(shnehll)
slow	langsam	(lahng-sahm)
certain, sure	sicher	(si-hehr)
uncertain	unsicher	(oon-sihehr)
stormy	stürmisch	(stuer-mish)
calm	ruhig	(roo-hig)
busy	beschäftigt	(beh-shaef-tigt)
free	frei.	(frahy)
clear	klar	(klahr)

dark	dunkel	(doon-kehl)
kind	gütig	(gue-tig)
angry	zornig	(tsohr-nig)
blind	blind	(blind)
deaf	taub	(toub)
ill	krank	(krahnk)
healthy	gesund	(geh-soond)
flat	flach	(flahh)
hilly	bergig	(behr-gig)
open	offen	(of-fehn)
closed	verschlossen	(fehr-shlohs-sehn)
loud	laut	(lout)
silent	ruhig	(roo-ig)
quiet	still	(shtil)
ready	bereit	(beh-rahyt)
right	richtig	(rih-tig)
simple	einfach	(ahyn-fahh)
complicated	verwickelt	(fehr-vik-kehlt)
different	verschieden	(fehr-shee-dehn)
just	gerecht	(geh-rehht)
unjust (unfair)	ungerecht	(oon-geh-rehht)
happy	glücklich	(gluek-lih)
unhappy	unglücklich	(oon-gluek-lih)
frequent	häufig	(hoy-fig)
rare	selten	(sehl-tehn)
easy	leicht	(lahyht)
difficult	schwierig	(shvee-rig)

NUMERALS

Cardinal Numbers

0	null	nool
1	eins (m.)	ahyns
1	ein (m. a n.)	ahyn
1	eine (f.)	ahy-neh
2	zwei	tsvahy
3	drei	drahy
4	vier	feer
5	fünf	fuenf
6	sechs	sehhs
7	sieben	zeebehn
8	acht	ahht
9	neun	noyn
10	zehn	tsehn
11	elf	ehlf

12	zwölf	tsvoelf
13	dreizehn	drahy-tsehn
14	vierzehn	feer-tsehn
15	fünfzehn	fuenf-tsehn
16	sechzehn	sehh-tsehn
17	siebzehn	zeeb-tsehn
18	achtzehn	ahht-esehn
19	neunzehn	noyn-tsehn
20	zwanzig	tsvahn-tsig
21	einundzwanzig	ahyn-oond-tsvahn-tsig
22	zweiundzwanzig	tsvahyn-oond-tsvantsig
23	dreiundzwanzig	drahy-oond-tsvahn-tsig
24	vierundzwanzig	feer-oond-tsvahn-tsig
30	dreissig	drahy-seg
31	einunddreissig	in-oond-drahy-sig
40	vierzig	feer-tsig
41	einundvierzig	ahyn-oond-feer-tsig
50	fünfzig	fuenftsig
51	einundfünfzig	ahyn-oond-fuenf-tsig
60.	sechzig	zehh-tsig
70	siebzig	
80	achtzig	ahht-tsig
90	neunzig	noyn-tsig
100.	hundert	hoon-dehrt
101	hunderteins	hoon-dehrt-ahyns
102	hundertzwei	hoon-dehrt-tsvahy
110	hundertzehn	hoon-dehrt-tsehn
120	hundertzwanzig	hoon-dehrt-tsvahn-tsig
200	zweihundert	tsvahy-hoon-dehrt
300.	dreihundert	drahy-hoon-dehrt
400	vierhundert	feer-hoon-dehrt
500	fünfhundert	feenf-hoon-dehrt
600	sechshundert	zehhs-hoon-dehrt
700	siebenhundert	zee-behn-hoon-dehrt
800	achthundert	ahht-hoon-dehrt
900	neunhundert	noyn-hoondehrt
1000	tausend	tou-sehnd
2000	zweitausend	tsvahy-tou-sehnd
10,000	zehntausend	tsehn-tou-sehnd
50,000	fünfzigtausend	fuenf-tsig-tou-sehnd
100,000	hundert-tausend	hoon-dehrt-tou-sehnd
200,000	zweihundert-tausend	tsvahy-hoon-dehrt-tou-sehnd
1,000,000	eine Million	ahy-neh-mil-li-ohn

1,312,211	eine Million dreihundert-zwölf tausend zweihundert-elf	ahy-neh-mil-li-on dri-hoon-dehrt-tsvoelf-tou-sehnd tsvahy-hoon-dehrt ehlf
1,912	ein tausend neunhundert zwölf	ahyn tousehnd noyn-hoon-dehrt-tsvoelf

In German when using tens and units, place the units before the tens: einunddreissig = 31. All tens except dreissig, end in "-zig": sechzig, achtzig. Sechs drops the ending "-s" in sechzehn and sechzig. Sieben drops the syllable "-en" in siebzehn and siebzig. Compounds of tens and units are always written in one word; einundvierzig. Compounds of thousands and of hundreds and their multiples are usually written in one word: vierhundert or vier hundert; fünftausend. Numbers of more than two figures should never be written in one word: dreitausend neunhundert zweiundsiebzig, (3,972) neuntausend einhundert zehn (9,110).

Declension of cardinals: the numeral "eins" is inflected in the same manner as the definite article when it is followed by a noun: ein Knabe = one boy, or a boy; eine Frau = one woman, or a woman; ein Haus = one house, or a house. Das eine Haus = the one house; jenes eine Haus = that one house; die einen und die andern = the ones and the others. In counting, when no other numeral follows, the neuter singular is used: eins, zwei, drei, vier, fünf, ... hundert eins, zweihundert eins. Das Hundert, das Tausend, die Million are nouns. Hundert and Tausend are declined only when not preceded by another cardinal: viele Hunderte von Tieren = many hundreds of animals. Hundert and Tausend are capitalized when used as nouns: mehrere Hunderte = several hundreds; viele Tausende = many thousands. All other numerals are not inflected, but the genitives "zweier", dreier" and the datives "zweien", "dreien" occur when the case is not indicated otherwise: der Bruder zweier Schwestern = the brother of two sisters; die Schwester dreier Brüder = the sister of three brothers.

Ordinal Numbers

	der (m.) die (f.) das (n.)	
First	erste	Ehr-steh
second	zweite	Tsvahy-teh
third	dritte.	Drit-teh

fourth	vierte	Feer-teh
fifth	fünfte	Fuenfteh
sixth	sechste	Sehh-steh
seventh	siebente	Zee-behn-teh
eighth	achte	Ahh-teh
ninth	neunte	Noyn-teh
tenth	zehnte	Tsehnteh
eleventh	elfte	Ehlf-teh
twelfth	zwölfte	Tsvoelf-teh
twentieth	zwanzigste	Tsvahn-tsigs-teh
thirtieth	dreissigste	Drahyis-sigs-teh
fourtieth	vierzigste	Feer-tsigs-teh
fiftieth	fünfzigste	Fuenf-tsigs-teh
sixtieth	sechzigste	Sehh-tsigs-teh
seventieth	siebzigste	Zeeb-tsigs-teh
eightieth	achtzigste	Ahht-tsigsteh
ninetieth	neunzigste	Noyn-tsigs-teh
hundredth	hundertste	Hoon-dehrt-ste
hundred and first	hundert-erste	Hoon-dehrt-ehrsteh
thousandth	tausenste	Tou-sehnds-teh
Millionth	millionste	Milli-ohns-teh

Other Numbers

The half	das Halbe	Dahs hahl-beh
A half	ein halb	Ahyn hahlb
One third	ein Drittel	Ahyn drit-tehl
Two fourths	zwei Viertel	Tsvahy feer tehl
Three fifths	drei Fünftel	Drahy fuenf-tehl
Eight tenths	acht Zehntel	Ahht tsehn-tehl
One hundredth	ein Hundertstel	Ahyn hoon-dehrts-tehl
A part	ein Teil	Ahyn tahyl
Single	einfach	Ahyn-fahh
Double	doppelt	Dohp-pehlt
Triple	dreifach	Drahy-fahh
Tenfold	zehnfach	Tsehn-fahh
Twentyfold	zwanzigfach	Tsvahn-tsig-fahh
A dozen	ein Dutzend	Ahyn doo-tsehnd
half a dozen	ein halbes Dutzend	ahyn hahl-behs Doo-ts-ehnd
A gross	ein Gros	ahyn grohs
A score	zwanzig Stück	Tsvah-tsig stuek
Fortnight	vierzehn Tage	Feer-tsehn tahgeh

The ordinals are adjectives formed by adding the ending "-te" to the respective cardinal from 2 to 19, and the ending "-ste" from 20 upwards. Don't fail to note the irregular forms of 1st, 3rd, 8th. When written in figures, the ending is not written out as in English, but it is replaced by a period: 2nd = 2. 3rd = 3. 5th = 5.

Ordinal adverbs are formed by adding "-ns" to the ordinal numbers: erstens = first(ly); drittens = third(ly); ....

Dates: der zweite Weltkrieg begann im Jahre 1939; World War II started in 1939; heute ist der 18. (read: achtzehnte) August = To-day is the 18th of August; New York, den 1. September 1944 = New York, the 1st of Sept. 1944.

Fractions: 1/2 = die Hälfte (noun), ein halb (adjective). All other fractions are formed by adding "-l" to the ordinal: ein or (das) Viertel = a or (the) fourth; fünf Neuntel = five ninths; ein- or (das) Tausenstel = a- or (the) thousandth; zwei Zwanzigstel = two twentieths.

Hours of the day: Wieviel Uhr ist es? = What time is it? Es ist eins, (ein Uhr) = it is one o'clock. Es ist halb vier = It is half past three. Es ist dreiviertel (drei Viertel auf) sechs = It is a quarter to six. Er kam um zwölf Uhr mittags = he came at twelve noon. Es ist fünfzehn Uhr = It is (15) 3 P:M. Es ist zwanzig Uhr = It is (20) 8 P:M.

Minutes are indicated as in English: Elf Uhr zwanzig = Eleven twenty, or zwanzig nach elf = twenty past eleven.

Note that in German you say "Halb vier" = half of four, instead of half past three.

Multiplications are formed with the syllable "-mal": einmal, fünfmal, zehnmal = once, five times, ten times.

The English ending "-fold" is expressed by the syllable "-fach". Einfach = simple; zweifach = twofold; zehnfach = tenfold.

Measures and weights: fünfzehn Fuss = fifteen feet; zwei Kilogramm = two kilograms; zwanzig Meter = twenty meters.

Other numerals: dreierlei = of three kinds; hunderterlei = of a hundred kinds; vielerlei = of many kinds; je zehn = ten each.

VERB

In German as in English, the verb has two forms; the active and the passive; three (or four) moods: the indicative, the subjunctive, the imperative (and the conditional); Six tenses: present, past (or imperfect), perfect, pluperfect, future and future perfect: three persons; two numbers: singular and plural and two kinds of verbal nouns infinitives and participles.

The English progressive form of the verb "I am going" is unknown in German: ich gehe, stands for both I go and I am going.

In German there is no auxiliary corresponding to the English "do". The German interrogative is formed by placing the verb first; the negative - by adding "nicht": Hörst du ihn? Ich höre ihn nicht = Do you hear him? I don't hear him.

The stem of a verb is found by omitting the ending "-en" or "-n" of the present infinitive: In rufen = call, the stem is "ruf-".

Important Note: Just as every German noun must be learned with its definite article and its declension, every German verb must be memorized at least with its principal parts. Here is an example of the most important forms worthwhile memorizing: gehen, ging, gegangen, geht, ist gegangen = to go, went, gone, goes, has gone. Sagen = to say; sagte = said; gesagt = said (past participle) sagt = says; hat gesagt = has said.

In other words, the forms to be memorized are: the infinitive, the imperfect tense, the past participle, 3rd person sing. of the present indicative, and 3rd person sing. of the perfect tense.

There are weak and strong verbs: A verb is called weak if it adds "-te" to its stem in the first person singular of the past indicative and "-t" in its past participle: glauben = believe; glaubte = believed; geglaubt = believed. Machen = make; machte = made; gemacht = made.

Strong verbs are those which in the first person singular of the past indicative add no ending to the stem, but change the stem vowel, and in the past participle add "-en" to the stem: sehen = see; sah = saw; gesehen = seen. Laufen = run; lief = ran; gelaufen = run.

The present infinitive of most verbs ends in "-en"; those verbs with a stem ending in -el, -er, add the ending "-n": Geben = give; leben = live; nehmen = take; essen = eat; tadeln = blame; wandern = wandern. The infinitive, as in English, is preceded by "zu" = "to": zu gehen = to go; zu lesen = to read; zu laufen = to run. Verbs with separable prefixes insert "zu" between the prefix and the stem: Heimzukommen (from heimkommen) = to return home; aufzustehen = to get up.

All infinitives used as nouns require the neuter article: das Singen = the singing; das Denken = the thinking; das Laufen = the running.

The present participle is formed by adding "-d" to the infinitive: Lesen, lesend = reading; schreiben, schreibend = writing; gehen, gehend = going.

The past participle requires the ending "-t", or "-et" for weak verbs, and "-en" for strong verbs and both, the weak and the strong take the prefix "ge-": geschrieben = written; gelebt = lived; gesagt = said. In verbs ending in "-ieren" (they are of foreign origin), the prefix "ge-" is omitted: reparieren, repariert = repaired. Past participles are declined as adjectives: geliebte Schwester = beloved sister.

Active Form, Indicative Mood

Weak Verbs
Present Tense

Spielen = Play		Fragen = Ask	Kaufen = Buy
ich spiele	I play	ich frage	ich kaufe
du spielst	you play	du fragst	du kaufst
er (sie, es) spielt	he (she, it) plays	er fragt	er kauft
wir spielen	we play	wir fragen	wir kaufen
ihr spielet	you play	ihr fragen	ihr kaufet
sie spielen	they play	sie fragen	sie kaufen
Sie spielen	you play	Sie fragen	Sie kaufen

Past or Imperfect

ich spielte/I played	ich fragte/I asked	ich kaufte/I bought
du spieltest	du fragtest	du kauftest
er spielte	er fragte	er kaufte
wir spielten	wir fragten	wir kauften
ihr spieltet	ihr fragtet	ihr kauftet
sie spielten	sie fragten	sie kauften

Imperative:	spiele!	(sing.)	spielet	(pl.) = play!
	frage!	(sing.)	fraget	(pl.) = ask!
	kaufe!	(sing.)	kaufet	(pl.) = buy!

Strong Verbs
Present Tense

Geben = Give	Singen = Sing	Tragen = Carry
ich gebe/I give	ich singe/I sing	ich trage/I carry
du gibst	du singst	du tragst
er gibt	er singt	er tragt
wir geben	wir singen	wir tragen
ihr gebet	ihr singet	ihr traget

sie geben	sie singen	sie tragen

Past or Imperfect

ich gab/I gave	ich sang/I sang	ich trug/I carried
du gabst	du sangst	du trugst
er gab	er sang	er trug
wir gaben	wir sangen	wir trugen
ihr gabet	ihr sanget	ihr truget
sie gaben	sie sangen	sie trugen

Imperative

gib! gebet! (pl.) give!	singe! singet! (pl.) sing!	trage! traget! carry!
geben Sie! you give!	singen Sie! you sing!	tragen Sie! you carry!

Auxiliary verbs: sein=to be, to exist; haben = to have, to possess; werden = to become.

They function as independent verbs and are also used to form the compound tenses and the passive forms. Sein and haben form the perfect, imperfect, and future perfect tenses; werden forms the future and future perfect and the passive forms.

Conjugation of Auxiliary Verbs
Present Tense

Sein = to be		Haben = to have	
ich bin	I am	ich habe	I have
du bist	you are	du hast	you have
sie, es	she, it	sie, es	she, it
er ist	he is	er hat	he has
wir sind	we are	wir haben	we have
ihr seid	you are	ihr habet	you have
sie sind	they are	sie haben	they have

Werden = to become	
ich werde	you become
du wirst	I become
sie, es	she, it
er wird	he becomes
wir werden	we become
ihr werdet	you become
sie werden	they-become

Past or Imperfect

Sein = I was	Haben = I had	Werden = I became
ich war/I was	ich hatte/I had	ich wurde/I became
du warst	du hattest	du wurdest
er war	er hatte	er wurde
wir waren	wir hatten	wir wurden
ihr waret	ihr hattet	ihr wurdet
sie waren	sie hatten	sie wurden

Simple Future

The future tense of all verbs is formed by using "werden" (appropriately conjugated) before the infinitive of the verb.

Ich werde (werden) = I shall become; du wirst (werden) = You will become; er wird (werden) = he will become; wir werden (werden) = we shall become; ihr werdet (werden) = You will become; sie werden (werden) = they will become.

Future Perfoot

This tense is formed by "werden" succeeded by the past participle and the infinitive of the auxiliary verb.

Ich werde gewesen sein = I shall have been; ich werde gehabt haben = I shall have had; du wirst gewesen sein = you will have been; du wirst gehabt haben = you will have had; etc......

Perfect Tense

This is formed with the auxiliary verbs "haben" and "sein" plus the past participle.

Ich bin geworden = I have become; ich habe gehabt = I have had; du bist gewesen = you have been; du hast gehabt = you have had.

Ich werde sein (I shall be)	Ich werde haben (Ishall have)
Du wirst sein (you will be)	Du wirst haben (you will have)
Er wird sein (He will be)	Er wird haben (He will have)
Wir werden (we shall be)	Wir werden haben (we shall have)
Ihr werdet (you will be)	Ihr werdet haben (you will have)
Sie werden (They will be)	Sie werden haben (they will have)

Pluperfect

This tense is formed as the perfect, however here the auxiliary verb is in the past, instead of present, tense:

Ich war gewesen (geworden) = I had been (become); ich hatte gehabt = I had had; du warst gewesen (geworden) = you had been (become); du hattest gehabt = you had had.

Imperative

sei! = be! (sing.)	habe! = have! (sing.)	werde! = become! (sing.)
seid! (pl.) = be!	habet (pl.) = have	werdet! = become! (pl.)
seien Sie! = be	haben Sie! = have	werden Sie! = become
(politeform)	(politeform)	(politeform)

MODAL AUXILIARY VERBS

The modal auxiliary verbs are irregular verbs.

The six modal auxiliaries are:

dürfen	may, to be permitted
können	can, to be able
mögen	to like
müssen	must, to have to
sollen	should, ought to
wollen	to want (will)

The principal parts of the modal auxiliaries are as follows:

Infinitive	Present	Past	Past Participle
dürfen (may)	ich darf (I may)	ich durfte (I was permitted)	gedurft
können (can)	ich kann (I can)	Ich konnte (I could)	gekonnt
müssen (must)	ich muss (I must)	ich musste (I had to)	gemusst
mögen (to like)	ich mag (I like)	ich mochte (I liked)	gemocht
sollen (ought to)	ich soll (I should)	ich sollte (I should)	gesollt
wollen (to want)	ich will (I want)	Ich wollte (I wanted)	gewollt

All modal auxiliaries are conjugated with haben.

Similar to this conjugation is that of: wissen, wusste, gewusst = know, known...

The Compound Tenses of The Verbs

Perfect

ich habe gegeben,
  I have given
du hast gegeben,
  you have given
er hat gegeben,
  he has given
wir haben gegeben,
  we have given
ihr habt gegeben,
  you have given
sie haben gegeben,
  they have given
ich bin gereist,
  I have traveled
sie ist gereist,
  she has traveled
ihr seid gereist,
  you have traveled

Pluperfect

ich hatte gegeben,
  I had given
du hattest gegeben,
  you have given
er hatte gegeben,
  he had given
wir hatten gegeben,
  we had given
ihr hattet gegeben,
  you had given
sie hatten gegeben,
  they had given
ich war gereist,
  I had traveled
sie war gereist,
  she had traveled
ihr waret gereist,
  you had traveled

Future

du wirst geben,
  you will give
er wird geben,
  he will give
wir werden geben,
  we shall give
ihr werdet geben,
  you will give
sie werden geben,
  they will give

Future Perfect

du wirst gegeben haben,
  you will have given
er wird gegeben haben,
  he will have given
wir werden gegeben haben,
  we shall have given
ihr werdet gegeben haben,
  you will have given
sie werden gegeben haben,
  they will have given

Ich werde ihn bald sehen = I shall soon see him; sie hat mich noch nicht gesehen = she has not yet seen me; ich weiss, dass su sie bald sehen wirst = I know that you will see her soon.

"Können" stands for "can," "could," "be able": ich kann seine Schrift nicht lesen = I cannot read his handwriting; jetzt können Sie gehen = now you can (may) go; er kann sehr gut Englisch = he knows English very well. Darf sie gehen? = May she go? Nein, sie darf nicht gehen = no, she may not go.

Kennen means to know in the sense of being acquainted; wissen = to know facts: sie kennt meinen Bruder = she knows my brother; wir kennen ihre Eltern = we know their parents; er weiss es = he knows that; er weiss nicht = he does not know; ich weiss wer sie ist = I know who she is; wer weiss das? = who knows that?

Müssen and sollen denote different types of obligation: müssen stands for must, have to, be compelled, forced, obliged: alle Menschen müssen sterben = all men must die; er kann es nehmen, muss es aber nicht, he can take it, but he doesn't have to.

Sollen means, should, ought to, be expected to: du sollst nicht stehlen = thou shalt not steal; wir sollen morgen gehen = we are (supposed) to go tomorrow; sie soll sehr reich sein = she is said to be very rich.

Mögen and wollen indicate an impulse to something: sie mag mir nicht schreiben, aber ich will es tun = she doesn't want to write me, - but I will; sie mag ihn nicht sehen = she doesn't like (want) to see him; du magst mich nicht = you don't like me.

Wollen, indicates determination, and stands for wish, be willing, desire, want: wir wollen ihn sehen = we want to see him; wollen Sie gehen? = Are you willing to go? Ich wollte gerade die Tür aufmachen = I was just about to open the door; sie will ihn oft gesehen haben = she claims to have seen him often.

Reflexive Verbs

The reflexive verbs require a reflexive pronoun as an object: ich freue mich, du freutest dich, (I am glad, you were glad); er hat sich gefreut = he has been glad; sie hatte sich gefreut = she had been glad; wir hatten uns gefreut = we had been glad; ihr werdet euch freuen = you will be glad; sie werden sich gefreut haben = they will have been glad. Der Zug bewegt sich = the train moves; er liebt sich = he loves himself. The use of the reflexive verb is much more common in German than in English.

Impersonal Verbs

These are verbs with the subject "es": es regnet = it is raining; es blitzt = it is lightening; es dunkelt = it is getting dark; es donnert = it is thundering; es geht ihm gut = he is well; es tut uns leid = we are sorry; es gibt = there is or there are; es hungert mich I am hungry; es friert uns = we are freezing; es klopft = some one is knocking.

The Passive Form

The passive is formed by combining the past participle of the verb with the auxiliary verb "werden".

Ich werde gewünscht = I am wanted; du wurdest gewünscht =you were wanted; er ist gewünscht worden = he has been wanted; sie war gewüncht worden = she had been wanted; wir werden gewünscht werden = we shall be wanted; sie werden gewünscht worden sein = they will have been wanted.

"By" with the passive is expressed by "von" or "durch": Sie wurde von ihrem Freunde getötet = she was killed by her friend; Er wurde durch Gift getötet = He was killed by poison. "Von" denotes direct action, "durch" indicates means or instrument. Man sagt=it is said; man glaubt=it is believed; das versteht sich = this is understood, Mir wurde von meinen Freunden geholfen = I was helped by my friends.

The Subjunctive Mood

The use of the subjunctive in German differs considerably from that in English. The subjunctive has four tenses, each of which two categories marked (A) and (B) in the examples.

Present

sein (to be)

(A)	(B)
ich sei	wäre
du seist	wärest
er sei	wäre
wir seien	wären
ihr seiet	wäret
sie seien	wären

haben (to have)

(A)	(B)
habe	hätte
habest	hättest
habe	hätte
haben	hätten
habet	hättet
haben	hätten

werden (to become)

(A)	(B)
werde	würde
werdest	würdest
werde	würde
werden	würden
werdet	würdet
werden	würden

Past

(Corresponding to the past, perfect, and pluperfect indicative)

Haben	Sein
(A)	
ich habe gehabt	sei gewesen
du habest gehabt	seist gewesen
er habe gehabt	sei gewesen
wir haben gehabt	seien gewesen
ihr habet gehabt	seiet gewesen
sie haben gehabt	seien gewesen
(B)	
hätte gehabt	wäre gewesen
hättest gehabt	wärest gewesen
hätte gehabt	wäre gewesen
hätten gehabt	wären gewesen
hättet gehabt	wäret gewesen
hätten gehabt	wären gewesen

Future

(A)	(B)
ich werde haben	würde haben
du werdest haben	würdest haben
er werde haben	würde haben
etc.	etc.

Future Perfect

werde gehabt haben	würde gehabt haben
werde gewesen sein	würde gewesen sein
werdest gehabt haben	würdest gehabt haben
werdest gewesen sein	würdest gewesen sein
werde gehabt haben	würde gehabt haben
werde gewesen sein	würde gewesen sein
etc.	etc.

The subjunctive mood is used for indirect statements and questions: Er sagte, er sei zu alt = He said he was too old. Er fragte, wer es wisse = He asked who knew it. Wir fragten, wo sie gewesen sei = We asked where she had been. Man sagte, dass sie hier sei (wäre), they said she was here. Man sagte, dass er hier sein werde (würde) = They said he would have been here. Wenn sie käme, - gingen wir = If she came we would go. Wenn sie noch lebte, - If she were still living. Wir hätten gehen können = We could have gone. Er sollte dort gewesen sein, - He was said to have been there.

The subjunctive expresses unreality, condition contrary to fact, desire, personal impression, concession, comparison, and it is mostly used to report or relate words or thoughts.

Irregular Verbs

Infinitive		Present, 1st and	3rd persons sing.	Imperfect	Past participle
lesen	to read	ich lese	er liest	las	gelesen
sehen	see	ich sehe	er sieht	sah	gesehen
stehlen	steal	ich stehle	er stiehlt	stahl	gestohlen
geben	give	ich gebe	er gibt	gab	gegeben
nehmen	take	ich nehme	er nimmt	nahm	genommen
treten	step	ich trete	er tritt	trat	getreten
bewegen	induce	ich bewege	er bewegt	bewog	bewogen
gehen	go	ich gehe	er geht	ging	gegangen
genesen	recover	ich genese	er genest	genas	genesen
heben	lift	ich hebe	er hebt	hob	gehoben
stehen	stand	ich stehe	er steht	stand	gestanden
treffen	meet	ich treffe	er trifft	traf	getroffen
fallen	fall	ich falle	er fällt	fiel	gefallen
wachsen	grow	ich wachse	er wächst	wuchs	gewachsen
halten	hold	ich halte	er hält	hielt	gehalten
lassen	let	ich lasse	er lässt	liess	gelassen
backen	to bake	ich backe	er bäckt	buk	gebacken
befehlen	command	ich befehle	er befiehlt	befahl	befohlen
betrügen	deceive	ich betrüge	er betrügt	betrog	betrogen
biegen	bend	ich biege	er biegt	bog	gebogen
brechen	break	ich breche	er bricht	brach	gebrochen
denken	think	ich denke	er denkt	dachte	gedacht

Irregular Verbs

Infinitive		Present, 1st and	3rd persons sing.	Imperfect	Past participle
fangen	to catch	ich fange	er fängt	fing	gefangen
finden	find	ich finde	er findet	fand	gefunden
fliegen	fly	ich fliege	er fliegt	flog	geflogen
gewinnen	win	ich gewinne	er gewinnt	gewann	gewonnen
helfen	help	ich helfe	er hilft	half	geholfen
lügen	tell a lie	ich lüge	er lügt	log	gelogen
nennen	name	ich nenne	er nennt	nannte	genannt
rennen	run, race	ich renne	er rennt	rannte	gerannt
schlafen	sleep	ich schlafe	er schläft	schlief	geschlafen
schneiden	cut	ich schneide	er schneidet	schnitt	geschnitten
schwimmen	swim	ich schwimme	er schwimmt	schwamm	geschwommen
sinken	sink	ich sinke	er sinkt	sank	gesunken
trinken	drink	ich trinke	er trinkt	trank	getrunken
verlieren	loose	ich verliere	er verliert	verlor	verloren
weisen	show	ich weise	er weist	wies	gewiesen
wenden	turn	ich wende	er wendet	wandte	gewandt
ziehen	draw, pull	ich ziehe	er zieht	zog	gezogen
zwingen	force	ich zwinge	er zwingt	zwang	gezwungen
weichen	yield	ich weiche	er weicht	wich	gewichen
verderben	spoil	ich verderbe	er verdirbt	verdarb	verdorben
verzeihen	forgive	ich verzeihe	er verzeiht	verzieh	verziehen
treiben	drive	ich treibe	er treibt	trieb	getrieben
schlagen	hit, strike	ich schlage	er schlägt	schlug	geschlagen

List of Regular Verbs

Infinitive		Present, 1st and	3rd persons sing.	Imperfect	Past participle
lieben	to love	ich liebe	er liebt	liebte	geliebt
wünschen	wish	ich wünsche	er wünscht	wünschte	gewünscht
danken	thank	ich danke	er dankt	dankte	gedankt
grüssen	greet	ich grüsse	er grüsst	grüsste	gegrüsst
achten	respect	ich achte	er achtet	achtete	geachtet
hegen	cherish	ich hege	er hegt	hegte	gehegt
pfegen	cherish	ich pflege	er pflegt	pflegte	gepflegt
küssen	kiss	ich küsse	er küsst	küsste	geküsst
umarmen	embrace	ich umarme	er umarmt	umarmte	umarmt
belohnen	reward	ich belohne	er belohnt	belohnte	belohnt
loben	praise	ich lobe	er lobt	lobte	gelobt
hassen	hate	ich hasse	er hasst	hasste	gehasst
anklagen	accuse	ich klage an	er klagt an	klagte an	angeklagt
beschuldigen	blame	ich beschuldige	er beschuldigt	beschuldigte	beschuldigt
tadeln	repremand	ich tadle	er tadelt	tadelte	getadelt
beleidigen	insult	ich beleidige	er beleidigt	beleidigte	beleidigt
drohen	threaten	ich drohe	er droht	drohte	gedroht
bedrohen	threaten	ich bedrohe	er bedroht	bedrohte	bedroht
strafen	punish	ich strafe	er straft	strafte	gestraft
verletzen	hurt	ich verletze	er verletzt	verletzte	verletzt
atmen	breathe	ich atme	er atmet	atmete	geatmet
öffnen	open	ich öffne	er öffnet	öffnete	geöffnet
reden	speak	ich rede.	er redet	redete	geredet

List of Regular Verbs

töten	to kill	ich töte	er tötet	tötete	getötet
schlachten	slaughter	ich schlachte	er schlachtet	schlachtet	geschlachtet
richten	judge	ich richte	er richtet	richtete	gerichtet
verurteilen	sentence	ich verurteile	er verurteilt	verurteilte	verurteilt
ausführen	execute	ich führe aus	er führt aus	er führte aus	ausgeführt

Verbs Relating to Mental Activity

Infinitive		Present, 1st and	3rd persons sing.	Imperfect	Past participle
denken	to think	ich denke	er denkt	dachte	gedacht
begreifen	conceive, comprehend	ich begreife	er begreift	begriff	begriffen
nachdenken	meditate, think over	ich denke nach	er denkt nach	dachte	nachgedacht
wissen	know	ich weiss	er weiss	wusste	gewusst
kennen	know (a p.)	ich kenne	er kennt	kannte	gekannt
studieren	study	ich studiere	er studiert	studierte	studiert
lehren	teach	ich lehre	er lehrt	lehrte	gelehrt
unterrichten	teach	ich unterrichte	er unterrichtet	unterrichtete	unterrichtet
lernen	learn	ich lerne	er lernt	lernte	gelernt
sprechen	speak	ich spreche	er spricht	sprach	gesprochen
erzählen	tell, relate	ich erzähle	er erzählt	erzählte	erzählt
sagen	say	ich sage	er sagt	sagte	gesagt
buchstabieren	spell	ich buchstabiere	er buchstabiert	buchstabierte	buchstabiert
erklären	explain	ich erkläre	er erklärt	erklärte	erklärt
übersetzen.	translate	ich übersetze	er übersetzt	übersetzte	übersetzt
schreiben	write	ich schreibe	er schreibt	schrieb	geschrieben
fragen	ask	ich frage	er fragt	fragte	gefragt
antworten	answer	ich antworte	er antwortet	antwortete	geantwortet
erfinden	invent	ich erfinde	er erfindet	erfand	erfunden

Verbs Relating to Events and Circumstances

To be born	geboren werden, ich bin (wurde) geboren.	Geh-boh-rehn vehr-dehn
to christen	taufen, ich wurde getauft (I was christened)	Tou-fehn
to grow	wachsen, ich wachse (I grow), wuchs, gewachsen	Vahh-sehn
to live	leben, ich lebe (I live), lebte, gelebt.	Leh-behn
to marry	heiraten, ich heirate (I marry), heiratete, verheiratet	Hahy-rah-tehn
to become a widower	ein Witwer werden	Ahyn wit-vehr vehr-dehn
to become old	alt werden, er wurde alt (he became old).	Ahlt vehr-dehn
to become ill	krank werden	Krahnk vehr-dehn
to recover	sich erholen, er erholt sich (he recovers).	Zeih ehr-hoh-lehn
to die	sterben, ich sterbe (I die), starb, gestorben.	Stehr-behn
to bury	beerdigen, sie wurde beerdigt (she was buried).	Beh-ehr-di-gehn
to inherit	erben, ich erbe (I inherit), erbte, geerbt.	Ehrbehn
to smile	lächeln, sie lächelt (she smiles), lächelte, gelächelt.	Lae-hehln
to laugh	lachen, ich lache (I laugh), lachte, gelacht.	Lah-hehn
to cry	weinen, sie weint (she cries), weinte, geweint.	Wahy-nehn

to shout	schreien, wir schreien (we shout), schrie,geschrieen.	Shrahy-ehn
to bathe	baden, er badet (he bathes), badete, gebadet.	Bah-dehn
to wash	sich waschen, ich wasche mich (I wash), wusch, gewaschen.	Zih vah-shehn
to comb	sich kämmen, er kämmt sich (he combs).	Zih kaem-mehn
to dress	sich ankleiden, sie kleidet sich an (she dresses).	Zih ahn-klahy-dehn
to undress	sich auskleiden, sie kleidet sich aus (she undress).	Zeih ous-klahy-dehn
to take the shoes off	die Schuhe ausziehen.	Dee shoo-ehous-tsee-ehn
to change clothing	die Kleider wechseln.	Dee klahy-dehr vehh-sehln
to see	sehen, ich sehe (I see) sah, gesehen.	Zeh-hehn
to look	betrachten, sie betrachtet mich (she looks at me).	Beh-trahh-tehn
to hear	hören, er hört (he hears), hörte, gehört.	Hoe-rehn
to listen	anhören, lauschen, lauschte, gelauscht.	Ahn-hoe-rehn, lou-shehn
to smell	riechen (he smells it, er riecht es), roch, gerochen.	Ree-hehn
to touch	berühren, du berührst (you touch), berührte, berührt.	Beh-rue-rehn
to whistle	pfeifen, er pfeift (he whistles), pfiff, gepfiffen.	Pfahy-fehn
to blow	blasen, ich blase (I blow), bliess, geblasen.	Blah-zehn

to cough	husten, sie hustet (she coughs), hustete, gehustet.	Hoo-stehn
to lay down	niederlegen, ich lege mich nieder (I lay down).	Nee-dehr-leh-gehn
to sleep	schlafen, sie schläft (she sleeps), schlief, geschlafen.	Shiah-fehn
to rest	rasten, wir rasten (we rest), rasteten, gerastet.	Rah-stehn
to dream	träumen, er träumt (he dreams), träumte, geträumt.	Troy-mehn
to snore	schnarchen, er schnarcht (he snores), schnarchte.	Shnahr-hehn
to awaken	aufwachen, er wacht auf (he awakens), wachte auf.	Ouf-vah-hehn
to raise	heben, sich erheben, er erhebt sich (he raises).	Heh-behn
to get up	aufstehen, er steht auf (he gets up), stand auf, aufgestanden.	Ouf-steh-hehn
to invite	einladen, ich lade ein (I invite), lud ein, eingeladen.	Ahyn-lah-dehn
to eat	essen, er isst (he eats), ass gegessen.	Ehs-sehn
to lunch	zu Mittag speisen, wir speisen, wir speisten, zu Mittag, gespeist.	Tsoo mitahg spahysehn
to chew	kauen, er kaut (he chews), kaute, gekaut.	Kou-ehn
to swallow	(ver)schlucken, er verscluckt (he swallows)	Shloo-kehn

to fast	fasten, sie fastet (she fasts), fastete, gefastet.	Fah-stehn
to breakfast	frühstücken, sie frühstückt (she breakfasts).	Fru-stuek-kehn
to eat supper	zu Abend essen.	Tsoo ah-behnd ehs-sehn
to cook	kochen, sie kocht (she cooks).	Ko-hehn
to spice	würzen, er würzt (he spices), würzte, gewürzt.	Wuer-tsehn
to taste	schmecken, (it tastes good), es schmeckt gut.	Shmeh-kehn
to be hungry	hungrig sein, ich bin hungrig (I am hungry).	Hoon-grig zahyn
to be thirsty	durstig sein, sie ist durstig (she is thirsty).	Door-stig zahyn
to be drunk	sich betrinken, er ist betrunken (he is drunk).	Zih beh-trin-kehn
to roast	rösten, er röstet (he roasts), röstete, geröstet.	Roe-stehn
to broil	braten, sie bratet, (she broils), gebraten.	Brah-tehn
to bake	backen, ich backe (I bake) buk, gebacken.	Bahk-kehn
to stew	dämpfen, sie dämpft (she stews), dämpfte.	Dehm-pfehn
to stuff	füllen, er füllt (he stuffs), füllte, gefüllt.	Fuel-lehn

Several Common Expressions

Come on	Komme her, lasset uns gehen.	Kom-meh hehr, lahs-seht oons geh-ehn

Hurry up	Beeilen Sie sich, beeile Dich.	Beh-ahy-lehn zee zih Beh-ahy-leh-dih
So far	so weit, bis hierher.	Zoh vahyt, bis heer-hehr
I don't care	mir liegt nichts d'ran.	Mir leegt nihxts drahn
Be quiet	sei ruhig, stille.	Zahy roo-hig, stilleh
To be fresh	frech sein.	Frehh Zahyn
To get rid of...	etwas (jemand) los werden...	Eht-vahs (yeh-mahnd) lohs vehr-dehn
Poor thing!	armes Ding! armer Kerl!	Ahr-mehs ding! Ahr-mehr kehrl!
At any rate	auf alle Fälle	Ouf ahl-leh fael-leh
In regard to	mit Rücksicht auf...	Mit ruek-siht ouf...
In spite of this	trotzdem...	Trots-dehm...
Sure! (you may be sure)	Sie können sicher sein.	Zee koen-nehn zi-hehr
A chap	ein Bursche, ein Kerl.	Ahyn boor-sheh, ahyn kehrl
Upon my honor	mein Ehrenwort.	Mahyn eh-rehn-vort.
What is your name?	was ist ihr Name, bitte?	Vahs ist eer nah-meh, bitteh?
What is new?	was gibt es Neues?	Vahs gibt ehs noy-ehs?
I have no desire	ich habe kein Verlangen.	Ih hah-beh kahyn fehr-lahn-gehn
To make a fool of..	einen Narren aus sich machen.	Ahy-nehn nahr-rehn ous zeih mah-hehn
Tell it to the marines	Sagen Sie es Ihrer Tante.	Zah-gehn zee ehs ee-rehr tahn-teh
Go away	Geh' weg!	Geh vehg!
Be pleasant, nice	sind Sie freundlich, freundlich sein.	Zind zee froynd-leih, Froynd-lih zahyn

Prepositions

The following prepositions, govern both the dative and the accusative: They govern the accusative when the verb represents motion; and the object answers the German questions "wohin" = where, to what place. If there is no motion they govern the dative and answer the question "wo" = where (static). Hence, we use the accusative with prepositions after verbs of motion and action, such as: gehen (go), kommen (come), stellen (put), setzen (place), etc.; and the dative after verbs of rest: sein (be), stehen (stand), sitzen (sit), liegen (lie), bleiben (remain) etc.

"An" implies close proximity or contact and stands for "at", "on", "near to": Er sitzt am (an dem) Boden = he is sitting on the floor. (no motion) Sie geht ans (an das) Fenster = She is going to the window. (motion) Am Morgen = In the morning. Am 10.September = On the tenth of September.

"Auf" stands for "on", "upon": Er sitzt auf der Bank = He is sitting on the bench. (no motion) Wir steigen auf das Dach = We climb on the roof. (motion) Auf der Universität = at the university; auf der Strasse = in the street; auf dem Markte = at the market place; auf dem Rathaus = in the City Hall.

"Hinter" = behind: Der Baum hinter dem Hause = The tree behind the house.

"In" = in, into, is used for time and place: Er ist im (in dem) Zimmer = He is in the room. Sie geht in das Haus = She goes into the house. Im Jahre 1944 = In the year 1944.

"Neben" = next to, adjoining: Ich gehe neben ihr = I walk at her side, next to her. Stellen Sie sich neben uns = Stand beside us.

"Über" = over, across: Ein Bild hängt über meinen Bett = There is a picture hanging over my bed. Der Ball ging über das Haus = The ball went over the house. Er warf einen Stein über den Fluss = He threw a stone across the river.

"Unter" = under, among: Die Katze ist unter dem Bett = The cat is under the bed. Die Katze lief unter das Bett = The cat ran under the bed. Ich lebte dort unter diesen Menschen = I lived there among these people.

"Vor" = before: referring to time and place: Sie stand vor der Kirche = She was standing before (in front of) the church. Er lief vor die Kirche = He ran in front of the church. Vor fünf Jahren = Five years ago. Vor zwei Monaten = Two months ago.

"Zwischen = between: Zwischen den Bäumen und den Hause = Between the trees and the house.

Prepositions which require the Dative:

"Aus" = out of, from; implies origin, material, or motive: Sie zog aus dem Lande = She went out of the country. Ein Ring aus reinem Gold = A ring of pure gold. Aus Schmerz = From grief.

"Ausser" = outside of, except: Ausser dem Hause = out of the house.

"Bei" = at, near to: Die Schlacht bei Warschau = the battle at Warschau.

"Mit" = with: Sie war mit ihrer Mutter = She was with her mother.

"Nach" = after, to, towards: Nach sechs Wochen = After six weeks. Er reist nach England = He travels (goes) to England.

"Seit" = since: Seit letzten Samstag bin ich krank = I have been sick since last Saturday. Sie hat den Hund seit fünf Jahren = She has had the dog for five years.

"Von" = of, from, by: Sein Ring ist nicht von Gold = His ring is not of gold. Zwei von uns sind Franzosen, zwei sind Deutsche = Two of us are French, two are Germans. Von Wien nach Berlin = From Vienna to Berlin. Werke von Meistern = Works by masters. Die Belagerung von Paris = The siege of Paris. Es ist von mir geschrieben = It is written by me.

"Zu" = to, toward, at: Er kommt zu mir = He comes to me. Sie ging zur (zuder) Stadt = She went to town.

"Zu" means at with names of festivals and cities and with infinitives: Zu Ostern = at Easter; zu Weihnachten = at Christmas; zu seinem Geburtstag = at his birthday. Er wurde zu Heidelberg geboren = He was born at Heidelberg. Du brauchst nicht zu schreiben = You need not write. Brot zum (zu dem) Essen = Bread for eating. Luft zum Atmen = Air for breathing.

Prepositions which require the Accusative:

"Durch" = through, implies transition or means. Er geht durch das Feld = He walks through the field. Er wurde durch Zufall geheilt = He was healed by accident.

"Für" = for, relates to interest or exchange: Wir sterben für unser Vaterland = We die for our country. Sie kaufte einen Hund für hundert Mark = She bought a dog for one hundred Mark.

"Gegen" = against: Er warf es gegen die Wand = He threw it against the wall. Gegen die Dummheit kämpfen selbst die Götter vergebens = Not even the gods can fight against stupidity.

"Ohne" = without: Ohne mich kannst du es nicht tun = Without me you cannot do it. Ohne sie bin ich verloren = Without her I am lost.

"Um" = around, about, at: Geh um das Ecke herum = Go around the corner. Ich treffe sie um fünf Uhr = I meet her at five o'clock. ("o'clock") always requires an ("um").

"Wider" = against: Es ist wider mich = It is against me.

Prepositions which require the Genitive:

"Statt" (anstatt) = instead of: Steine statt Brot = Stones instead of bread. Anstatt dessen = Instead of this.

"Ausserhalb" = outside: Ausserhalb des Dorfes = Outside of the village.

"Innerhalb" = inside: Innerhalb des Hauses = inside of the house.

"Oberhalb und unterhalb" des Dorfes = Above and below the village.

"Dieseits und jenseits" des Meeres = On this and that side of the ocean.

"Längs" des Waldes = Along the forest.

"Unfern" von uns = Not far from us.

Um deines Kindes willen (Um don Willen Deines Kindes) = For the sake of your child.

Seiner Schwestern halber = On behalf of his sister.

Infolge eines Verlustes = As a result of a loss.

ADVERBS

Adverbs are words which modify or clarify the verb. All adjectives can be used as adverbs. Other adverbs are:

"Nicht" = not, is usually placed after the object, but in questions it can be placed before it: Er verkauft sein Pferd nicht = He does not sell his horse. Hat er nicht das Pferd? = Has he not the horse? Siehst du ihn nicht? = Don't you see him? Wir erwarten sie nicht = We do not expect them.

"Nicht" = not, generally stands before the adverb. Wir können nicht hier bleiben = We cannot stay here.

When there are two verbs, the second verb is placed at the end of the sentence, and "nicht" must come before the second verb: Er will es nicht sagen = He does not want to say it.

"Her" = here: Sie kamen her = they came here. Er schrieb ihr = He wrote here.

"Hin" = there: Wir sandten es hin = We sent it there. Hin und her = Back and forth.

"Hin" indicates direction away from the speaker.

"Her" indicates direction toward the speaker.

These words can only be used with verbs indicating direction:

Gehe hin = go there.

"Herauf, hinauf" = up, upstairs: Komme herauf = come up, come upstairs. Bitte, gehen Sie hinauf = Please go up, upstairs.

"Herunter, hinunter" = down, downstairs: Komme herunter = Come down. Gehe hinunter = Go downstairs. (This adverb also indicates direction only).

"Heraus, hinaus" = out: Ich gehe hinaus (from a room, house..) = I go out. Kommen Sie heraus = Come out.

"Herein, hinein" = in: Komme herein = Come in. Gehe hinein = Go in.

"Herüber, hinüber" = over: Kommen Sie herüber = Come over. Wir gehen hinüber zum Nachbar = We are going over to the neighbor.

"Hin and her" can be added to "wo": Wohin geht er? = Where is he going? Woher kommen Sie?= Where do you come from?

Adverbs are derived:

1. From adjectives without any change. Sie tanzt schön = She dances beautifully.

2. From nouns, especially from their genitive forms: mittags = at noon; morgens = in the morning; abends = in the evening; nachts = at night.

3. By the use of the ending "-e" or "lich": Sie schläft lange = She sleeps long. Sie lachte herzlich = She laughed heartily. Ihr Haar ist rötlich = Her hair is reddish. Gelblich, bläulich, weisslich, grünlich = Yellowish, bluish, whitish, greenish.

CONJUNCTIONS

Conjunctions are connecting works.

Coordinating conjunctions are those which connect single words or independent sentences:

Und = and; Frau und Kind = wife and child; sie und ich = She and I.

Oder = or: Wollen Sie erst ruhen oder sofort arbeiten gehen = Do you want to rest first, or go to work immediately?

Entweder...oder = either...or: Entweder er oder ich = Either he or I.

Sowohl...als auch = both...and: Sowohl er als auch sie waren dort = Both, he and she were there.

Aber, jedoch, sondern = but, however: Ich versuche, aber ich kann es nicht machen = I am trying, but I cannot do it. Nicht wir sondern ihr seid verantwortlich = Not we but you are responsible.

Denn = because: Ihr sollt heute nicht arbeiten, denn es ist Sonntag = You must not work today because it is Sunday.

Überdies = besides: Ich konnte nicht kommen, überdies, war es viel zu spät = I could not come, besides it was far too late.

Sogar = even: Sogar mein Bruder kann die Aufgabe nicht lösen = Even my brother cannot solve the problem.

Weder...noch = neither...Nor: Weder sie noch ich = Neither she nor I.

Teils...teils = partly...partly: Teils war es meine Schuld, teils war es ihre = Partly it was my fault but partly it was hers too.

Dagegen = on the other hand: Dagegen, bin ich froh = On the other hand, I am glad.

Trotzdem = nevertheless, despite: Ich warnte ihn, trotzdem ging er hin = I warned him, but he nevertheless went there.

Sonst = otherwise. Beeile Dich, sonst wird es spät = Hurry up, otherwise it will be late. Also = therefore, hence: Es war also traurig = It was, therefore, sad. Folglich = consequently: He commited the crime, consequently the punishment followed.

Daher, deshalb, darum, deswegen = therefore, hence, that is why, because of: Du brauchst es, deswegen gebe ich es Dir = You need it, hence, I am giving it to you.

Subordinating conjunctions are those which introduce dependent sentences.

Dass = that; so dass = so that; auf dass, damit = in order that. Glauben Sie, dass er es getan hat? = Do you believe, that he has done it? Ich sagte ihm, dass Sie hier wohnen = I told him that you live here. Ich kaufte Dir diese Bücher, damit Du sie liest = I bought you these books so that you may read them.

(Als, wenn, wann) = when; (bevor, ehe) = before; (da) = since, because; (indem) = in that; (nachdem) = after; (seit, seitdem) = since; (so-oft-als) = as soon as; (sowie) = as; (während) = while; (ob) = whether; (seit wann) = since when; (bis wann) = until when; (warum) = why; (weshalb, weswegen) = what for; (wo, wohin) = where; (weil) = because; (obwohl, obgleich, obschon) = although; (wenn, auch, wenn schon) = even though; (wenn) = if; (falls, im Falle dass) = in case that; (ohne dass) = without.

Clauses of Comparison: (als, ob, als wenn) = as if.

THE CONSTRUCTION OF THE SENTENCE IN GERMAN

1. Normal Order: The verb stands second, the subject first.

Der Knabe (Subject) geht (Verb) in die Schule = The boy goes to school.

2. Inverted Order: The verb stands second or first, but before the subject:

Geht (Verb) der Knabe (Subj.) in die Schule? = Does the boy go to school?. Gestern war (Verb) der Knabe (Subj.) in der Schule = Yesterday the boy was at school.

3. Dependent Order: (in dependent sent.) the finite verb stands last:

Dies ist der Knabe (Subj.), der gestern in der Schule war (Verb). This is the boy who was at school yesterday.

The normal word order is used: In independent sentences beginning with the subject: Ich (Subj.) gehe in die Schule = I am going to school. In independent questions beginning with the subject: Wer ist das? = Who is that? Du (Subj.) gehst fort? = You are going away? In formal wishes: Dein Geburtstag (Subj.) bringe Dir Glück = May your birthday bring you happiness.

The inverted word order is used: In Independent declaratory sentences; beginning with any part other than the subject: Morgen wird (Verb) sie (Subj.) in die Schule gehen = Tomorrow she will go to school. In independent questions: Wann gehst (Verb) Du (Subj.) in die Stadt? = When are you going to the city?

In imperative sentences: Gehen (Verb) Sie (Subj.) nach Hause! = Go home!

A double infinitive stands last: Meine Mutter war sehr froh, dass sie mich hat sehen (Inf.) können (Inf.) = My mother was very glad, that she could see me.

MEASURES AND WEIGHTS
MASSE UND GEWICHTE

In all European countries the metric system prevails.

Measures of Length

1 Millimeter equals 0.03937 inch.
10 Millimeter are 1 Centimeter or 0.3937 inch.
10 Centimeter are 1 Decimeter or 3.937 inch.
10 Decimeter are 1 Meter or 39.37 inch.
10 Meter are 1 Decameter or 393.7 inch.
10 Decameter are 1 Hectometer or 328 feet 1 inch.
10 Hectometer are 1 Kilometer or 3280 feet 10 inch.
10 Kilometer are 1 Myriameter or 6.214 miles.

Measures of Surface

1 Quadratmeter (square meter) equals 1550 square inches.
1 Ar = 100 Quadratmeter 119.6 square yards.
1 Hektar = 100 Ar or 10,000 Qu.M. 2,471 acres.

Measures of Capacity

1 Kubikcentimeter=0.061 Cu. in.
1 Kubik Decimeter=1000 Kubik Centimeter=6.1022 Cu. in.
1 Kubik Meter=1000 Kubik Dec.=1,000,000 Kubik Cen.=1,308 cu. yds.

Weights

1 Milligram=0.015 grain.
1 Centigram=10 Milligram=0.154 grain.
1 Decigram=100 Milligram=10 Centigram=1.543 grains.
1 Gram=1000 Milligram=100 Centigram=15.432 grains.
1 Dekagram=10 Gram=0.353 oz.
1 Kilogram=100 Dekagram=1000 Gram=2.204 lbs.

Liquid Measures - Flüssigkeitsmasse

1 Milliliter = 1/1000 Liter = 1 Cu. cm. = 0.27 fl. dr.
1 Centiliter=1/100 Liter=10 Cu. cm.=0.338 fl. oz.
1 Deciliter=1/10 Liter=100 Cu. cm.=0.845 gill.
1 Liter=1 Liter=1 Cu. dm.=1.0567 qts.
1 Hektoliter=100 Liter=100 Cu. dm.=26.42 gals.

The Days of the Week

	Die Wochentage	Dee Vohehntahgeh
Sunday	der Sonntag	Dehr sohn-tahg
Monday	Montag	mohn-tahg
Tuesday	Dienstag	deen-stahg
Wednesday	Mittwoch	mit-voh
Thursday	Donnerstag	dohn-nehr-stahg
Friday	Freitag	frahy-tahg
Saturday	Samstag	sahm-stahg
	Sonnabend	sohn-ab-behnd

The Months of the Year

	Die Monate des Jahres	Dee Monahteh Dehs Yahres
January	der Januar	Dehr yah-noo-ahr
February	Februar	feh-broo-ahr
March	März	maerts
April	April	ah-priel
May	Mai	mahy
June	Juni	yoo-ni
July	Juli	yoo-li
August	August	ou-goost
September	September	sehp-tehm-behr

October	der Oktober	Dehr ohk-toh-behr
November	November	noh-vehm-behr
December	Dezember	deh-tsehm-behr

The Seasons of the Year

	Die Jahres-zeiten	Dee Yahreh-stsahytehn
Spring	der Frühling	Dehr frue-ling
Summer	der Sommer	Dehr som-mehr
Autumn, Fall	der Herbst	Dehr hehrbst
Winter	der Winter	Dehr vin-tehr

The Time

	Die Tageszeit	Dee Tahgehstsit
What time is it?	wieviel Uhr ist es?	Vee-feel oor ist ehs?
It is one o'clock	es ist ein Uhr	Ehs ist in oor
It is not yet two	es ist noch nicht zwei	Ehs ist noh niht tsvahy
It is a quarter past two	es ist viertel drei	Ehs ist feer-tehl drahy
It is twenty past two	es ist zwanzig nach zwei	Ehs ist tsvah-tsig nahh tsvahy
It is three o'clock	es ist drei Uhr	Ehs ist drahy oor
It is half past three	es ist halb vier	Ehs ist hahlb feer
Five minutes to five	Fünf Minuten vor fünf	fuenf mi-noo-tehn fohr fuenf
It is early	es ist zeitig (früh)	Ehs ist tsahy-tig (frue)
It is late	es ist spät	Ehs ist spaet
At nine P.M.	neun Uhr abends	Noyn oor ah-behnds
At ten A.M.	um zehn Uhr vormittags	Oom tsehn oor fohr-mit-tahgs
The watch	die Uhr	Dee oor
A pocket watch	eine Taschenuhr	Ahy-neh tah-shehn-oor
A wrist watch	eine Armbanduhr	Ahy-neh ahrmbahnd-oor
An alarm clock	eine Weckuhr	Ahy-neh vehk-oor
A wall clock	eine Wanduhr	Ahy-neh vahnd-oor
The hand (of a watch)	der Zeiger	Dehr tsahy-gehr
dial	das Zifferblatt	Dahs tsif-fehr blaht
(small) hour-hand	der Stunden-zeiger	Dehr stoon-dehn tsahygehr
(big) min.-hand	der Minutenzeiger	Dehr mi-noo-tehn-tsahy-gehr
spring	die Feder	Dee feh-dehr
mechanism	das Uhrwerk	Dahs oor-vehrk

crystal	das Uhrglas	Dahs oor-glahs
To wind (a watch)	aufziehen	Ouf-tsee-hehn
Your watch is slow	Ihre Uhr geht langsam	Ee-reh oor geht lahng-sahm
My watch is fast	meine Uhr geht schnell	Mahy-neh oor geht shnehl
The watch has stopped	die Uhr ist stehen geblieben	Dee oor ist steh-ehn geh-blee-behn
The watchmaker	der Uhrmacher	Dehr oor mah-hehr

Division of Time	Zeiteinteilung	Tsahytahyntahyloong
The calendar, almanac	der Kalender, das Jahrbuch	Dehr kah-lehn-dehr, dahs yahr-booh
century	das Jahrhundert	Dahs yahr-hoon-dehrd
year	das Jahr	Dahs yahr
month	der Monat	Dehr moh naht
week	die Woche	Dee wo-heh
day	der Tag	Dehr tahg
hour	die Stunde	Dee stoon-deh
half an hour	eine halbe Stunde	Ahy-neh hahl-boh stoon-deh
minute	die Minute	Dee mi-noo-teh
second	die Sekunde	Dee seh-koon-deh
sunrise	der Sonnenauf-gang	Dehr soh-nehn-ouf-gahng
sunset	der Sonnenunter-gang	Dehr soh-nehn-oon-tehr-gahng
Morning	Der Morgen	dehr mohr-gehn
Noon	Der Mittag	dehr mit-tahg
Afternoon	Der Nachmittag	dehr nahh-mit-tahg
night	dic Nacht	dee nahht
evening	der Abend	dehr ah-behnd
yesterday	gestern	geh-stehrn
before yesterday	vorgestern	fohr-geh-stehrn
today	heute	hoy-teh
tomorrow	morgen	mohr-gehn
after tomorrow	übermorgen	ueber-mohr-gehn
past	die Vergangen-heit	dee fehr-gahn-gehn hahyt
present	die Gegenwart	dee geh-gehn-vahrt
future	die Zukunft	dee tsoo-koonft

Common Courtesy Expressions

Yes, sir	Yawohl, mein Herr	Yah-vohl mahyn hehr
No, sir	nein, mein Herr	Nahyn, mahyn hehr
Yes, miss	jawohl, mein Fräulein	Yah-vohl, mahyn froy-lahyn
Yes, madam	jawohl, gnädige Frau	Yah-vohl, gnae-di-geh frou
Do you speak German?	sprechen Sie deutsch?	Spreh-hehn zee doych?
Very little	sehr wenig (etwas)	Sehr veh-nahyg (ehtvahs)
But I understand	aber ich verstehe es	Ah-behr ih fehr-steh-eh ehs
Good morning	guten Morgen	Goo-tehn mohr-gehn
Good day (afternoon)	guten Tag	Goo-tehn tahg
Good evening	guten Abend	Goo-tehn ahbehnd
Good night	gute Nacht	Goo-teh nahht
What is your name?	wie heissen Sie, bitte?	Vee hahys-sehn zee, bit-teh
My name is...	mein Name ist...	Mahyn nah-meh ist...
How are you?	wie geht es Ihnen?	Vee geht ehs ee-nehn?
How are you? (fam.)	wie geht es Dir?	Vee geht ehs deer?
Very well, thank you	danke, sehr (recht) gut	Dahn-keh zehr (rehht) goot
And you?	und Ihnen? (Dir, fam.)	Oond ee-nehn? Oond deer?
I am pleased to meet you	es freut mich, Sie kennen zu lernen	Ehs froyt mih zee kehn-nehn tsoo lehr-nehn
The pleasure is mine	es ist mir ein Vergnügen	Ehs ist mir ahyn fehr-gnue-gehn
Do you smoke?	rauchen Sie?	Rou-hehn zee?
No, thanks	danke, nein	Dahn-keh nahyn
Thanks	dankeschön	Dahn-keh shoen
Please	bitte	bit-teh
Sit down, please	bitte, nehmen Sie Platz	bit-teh neh-mehn zee plahts
I must go now	ich muss gehen	ih mooss geh ehn
May I ask?	darf ich fragen?	Dahrf ih frah-gehn?
Of course	gewiss	Geh-viss
I beg your pardon	entschuldigen Sie, bitte	Ehnt-shool-di-gehn zee, bitteh
Do not mention it You are welcome	es ist gerne geschehen	Ehs ist gehr-neh geh-sheh-ehn

You are very kind	Sie sind sehr freundlich	Zee zind sehr froynd-lih
With your permission	Mit Ihrer Erlaubniss	Mit ee-rehr ehr-loub-niss
Good bye (I will see you later)	auf Wiedersehen	Owf vee-dehr-seh nehn

Arithmetical expressions

Once	einmal	Ahyn-mahl
Twice	zweimal	Tsvahy-mahl
Three times (thrice)	dreimal	Drahy-mahl
Fraction	Bruchzahl	Brooh-tsahl
Integer	ganze Zahl	Gahn-tseh tsahl
To add	addieren	Ahd-dee-rehn
To multiply	multiplizieren	Mool-ti pli-tsee-rehn
To subtract	subtrahieren	Soob-trah-hee-rehn
To divide	dividieren	Di-vi-dee-rehn

About the Weather

	Das Wetter	Dahs Veht-tehr
How is the weather?	wie ist das Wetter?	Vee ist dahs veh-tehr
It is warm	es ist warm	Ehs ist vahrm
It is very cold	es ist sehr kalt	Ehs ist zehr kahlt
It is bad weather	es ist schlechtes Wetter	Ehs iste shlehh-tehs veht-tehr
Good weather	schönes (gutes) Wetter	Shoe-nehs (goo-tehs) veht-tehr
The thermometer	das Thermometer	Dahs tehr-moh-meh-tehr
The barometer	das Barometer	Dahs bah-roh-meh-tehr
The atmosphere	die Athmosphäre	Dee aht-mohs-fae-reh
Humidity	die Feuchtigkeit	Dee foyh-tig-kahyt
The cold	die Kälte	Dee kael-teh
The heat	die Hitze	Dee hit-tseh
The rain	der Regen	Dehr reh-gehn
The snow	der Schnee	Dehr shneh
The hail	der Hagel	Dehr hah-gehl
The wind	der Wind	Dehr vind
The dew	der Tau	Dehr tou
It snows	es schneit	Ehs shnahyt
It rains	es regnet	Ehs rehg-neht
It is going to rain	es wird regnen	Ehs vird rehg-nehn
It has frozen	es ist gefroren	Ehs ist geh-fro-rehn
It lightens	es blitzt	Ehs blitst

It thunders	es donnert	Ehs dohn-nehrt
Let us get	lasset uns	Lahs-seht oons
under shelter	Schutz suchen	shoots soo-hehn
The storm	der Sturm	Dehr shtoorm
It is clearing up	es heitert sich auf	Ehs hahy-tehrt sih ouf

The Colors

	Die Farben	Dee Fahr-behn
Red	rot	Roht
Blue	blau	Blou
Yellow	gelb	Gehlb
Green	grün	Gruen
Orange	orangefarben	Oh-rahn-dshehn-fahr-behn
Indigo	indigo	In-di-goh
Violet	veilchenblau	Fahyl-hehn-blou
Gray	grau	grou
Pink	rosa	ro-sah
light	licht, hell	Liht, hehl
Dark	dunkel	Doon-kehl
Black	schwarz	Shvahrts
Darkness	die Dunkelheit	Dee doon-kehl-hahyt
Brightness	der Glanz, die Klarheit	Dehr glahnts, Dee klahr-hahyt
Brown	braun	Broun
Brunette	brünett	Brue-neht
Blonde	blond	Blohnd

Geographical Terms

	Geographische Ausdrücke	Geh-oh-graphi-sheh Ous-drue-keh
The globe	die Erdkugel	Dee ehrd-koo-gehl
earth, land	die Erde, das Land	Dee ehr-deh, dahs lahnd
soil	das Erdreich	Dahs ehrd-rahyh
surface	die Oberfläche	Dee oh-behr flae-heh
continents	die Erdteile	Dee ehrd-tahy-leh
South Pole	der Südpol	Dehr zued-pohl
North Pole	der Nordpol	Dehr nohrd-pohl
East	der Osten	Dehr ohs-tehn
West	der Westen	Dehr vehs-tehn
South	der Süden	Dehr zue-dehn
North	der Norden	Dehr nohr-dehn

Orient, the East	der Orient	Dehr oh-ri-ehnt
Occident	der Westen, das Abendland	Dahs ah-behnd-lahnd
country	das Land,	Dahs lahnd,
native country	das Vaterland	dahs fah-tehr-lahnd
forest	der Wald	Dehr vahld
city	die Stadt	Dee shtaht
village	das Dorf	Dahs dohrf
plain	die Ebene	Dee eh-beh-neh
prairie	die Grasebene	Dee grahs-eh-beh-neh
valley	das Tal	Dahs tahl
mountain	der Berg	Dehr behrg
The slope	der Abhang	Dehr ahb-hahng
cavern	die Höhle, Kaverne	Dee kah-vehr-neh
cave	die Höhle	Dee hoe-leh
summit	die Spitze, Höhe	Dee spit-tseh, hoe-eh
peak	der Gipfel	Dehr gi-pfehl
foot	der Fuss	Dehr fooss
hill	der Hügel	Dehr hue-gehl
landscape	die Landschaft	Dee lahnd-shahft
river	der Fluss, Strom	Dehr flooss, shtrohm
— navigable	schiffbar	Shiff-bahr
Not navigable	nicht schiffbar	Nihxt shiff-bahr
The current	die Strömung, der Lauf	Dee stroe-moong, dehr louf
bank	das Ufer	Dahs oo-fehr
dam	der Damm	Dehr dahm
canal	der Kanal	Dehr kah-nahl
desert	die Wüste	Dee vues-teh
Oasis	die Oase	Dee oh-ah-zeh
volcano	der Vulkan	Dehr vool-kahn
lava	die Lava	Dee lah-vah
fire	das Feuer	Dahs foy-ehr
water	das Wasser	Dahs vahs-sehr
swamp	der Sumpf	Dehr zoompf
pond	der Teich	Dehr tahyh
lake	der See	Dee zeh
waterfall	der Wasserfall	Dehr vahs-sehr-fahll
seashore	der Meeres-strand	Dehr meh-rehs-strahnd
sea	die See, das Meer	dahs mehr
Ocean	der Ozean, das Meer	Dehr oh-tseh-ahn
waves	die Wellen	Dee vehl-lehn
tide	die Gezeiten (Ebbe & Flut)	Dee geh-tsahy-tehn (ehb-beh, floot)

The island	die Insel	Dee in-sehl
peninsula	die Halbinsel	Dee hahlb-in-sehl
beach	der Strand	Dehr strahnd
bay	die Bucht	Dee booht
cape	das Kap	Dahs kahp
cape	das Vorgebirge	Dahs fohr-geh-bir-geh
isthmus	die Landenge	Dee lahnd-ehn-geh
strait	die Meerenge	Dee mehr-ehn-geh
brook	der Bach	Dehr bahh
estuary	der Meeresarm	Dehr meh-rehn-ahrm
flood	die Flut	Dee floot
glacier	der Gletscher	Dehr gleht-shehr
spring	die Quelle	Dee kvehl-leh

Metals and Minerals

	Metalle und Minerale	Meh-tah-leh & Mi-neh-rah-leh
The gold	das Gold	Dahs gohld
platinum	das Platin	Dahs plah-teen
silver	das Silber	Dahs zil-behr
copper	das Kupfer	Dahs koo-pfehr
iron	das Eisen	Dahs ahy-zehn
steel	das Stahl	Dahs shtahl
mercury	das Quecksilber	Dahs kvehk-zil-behr
nickel	das (der) Nickel	Dahs (dehr) ni-kehl
tin	das Zinn	Dahs tsin
tin plate	die Zinnplatte	Dee tsin-plaht-teh
zinc	das Zink	Dahs tsink
lead	das Blei	Dahs blahy
aluminum	das Aluminium	Dahs ah-loo-mi-nee-oom
The bronze	die Bronze	Dee brohn-tseh
brass	das Messing	Dahs mehs-sing
stone	der Stein	Dehr shtahyn
granite	der Granit	Dehr grah-nit
marble	der Marmor	Dehr mahr-mohr
coal	die Kohle	Dee ko-leh
slate	der Schiefer	Dehr shee-fehr
clay	der Lehm	Dehr lehm
lime	der Kalk	Dehr kahlk
plaster	der Gipsmörtel	Dehr moer-tehl
glass	das Glas	Dahs glahs
crystal	der Kristall	Dehr kris-tahl

Precious Stones

	Edelsteine	Eh-dehl-stahy-neh
The brilliant	der Brillant	Dehr bril-lahnt
diamond	der Diamant	Dehr di-ah-mahnt
emerald	der Smaragd	Dehr shmah-rahgd
pearl	die Perle	Dee pehr-leh
amethyst	der Amethyst	Dehr ah-meh-tist
sapphire	der Saphir	Dehr sah-phir
ruby	der Rubin	Dehr roo-bin
turquoise	der Türkis	Dehr tuer-kees

Trees, Vegetables, Fruits, Flowers

	Bäume, Gemüse, Früchte, Blumen	Boyme, geh-mue-seh, fruehte, bloomen
The tree	der Baum	Dehr bonm
plant	die Pflanze	Dee pflahn-tseh
root	die Wurzel	Dee voor-tsehl
trunk	der Stamm	Dehr shtahm
branch	der Ast	Dehr ahst
flower	die Blume, Blüte	Dee bloo-meh, blue-teh
fruit	die Frucht	Dee frooht
ash	die Esche	Dee eh-sheh
oak	die Eiche	Dee ahy-heh
fir	die Kiefer, Föhre	Dee kee-fehr, foe-reh
beech-tree	die Buche	Dee boo-heh
elm	die Ulme	Dee ool-meh
holly	die Stechpalme	Dee stehh-pahl-meh
chestnut-tree	der Kastanien-baum	Dehr kahs-tah-ni-ehn-boum
apple-tree	der Apfelbaum	Dehr ahp-fehl-boum
vine	der Weinstock, die Rebe	Dehr vahyn-shtohk, dee reh-beh
potato	die Kartoffel	Dee kahr-tohf-fehl
	der Erdapfel	Dehr ehrd-ahp-fehl
tomato	die Tomate	Dee to-mah-teh
spinach	der Spinat	Dehr shpi-naht
carrot	die Mohrrübe	Dee mohr-rue-beh
lettuce	der Salat	Dehr sah-laht
beans	die Bohnen (pl)	Dee boh-nehn
string beans	grüne Bohnen	Grue-neh boh-nehn
pea(s)	die Erbse (n)	Dee ehrb-seh
onion	die Zwiebel	Dee tsvi-behl
garlic	der Knoblauch	Dehr knob-louh

cabbage	das Kraut	Dahs krout
The cauliflower	der Blumenkohl	Dehr bloo-mehn-kohl
cucumber	die Gurke	Dee goor-keh
pepper	der Pfeffer	Dehr pfeh-fehr
beet(s)	die rote(n) Rübe(n)	Dee ro-teh(n) rue-beh(n)
eggplant	die Eierfrucht	Dee ahy-ehr-frooht
endive	die Endivie	Dee ehn-dee-vee-eh
celery	der Sellerie	Dehr seh-leh-ree
melon	die Melone	Dee meh-loh-neh
watermelon	die Wassermelone	Dee vahs-sehr-meh-loh-neh
apple	der Apfel	Dehr ahp-fehl
Cherry	die Kirsche	Dee kir-sheh
pear	die Birne	Dee bir-neh
plum	die Pflaume	Dee pflou-meh
apricot	die Aprikose	Dee ah-pri-koh-zeh
fig	die Feige	dee fahy-geh
orange	die Apfelsine	Dee ahp-fehl-zee-neh
lemon	die Zitrone	Dee tsi-troh-neh
grape	die Weintraube	Dee vahyn-trou-beh
grapefruit		
peach	der Pfirsich	Dehr pfir-sih
banana	die Banane	Dee bah-nah-neh
strawberry	die Erdbeere	Dee ehrd-behreh
pineapple	die Ananas	Dee ah-nah-nahs
date	die Dattel	Dee dah-tehl
cocoanut	die Kokosnuss	Dee ko-kos-nooss
currant	die Johannis-beere	Dee yo-hah-nis-beh-reh
raspberry	die Himbeere	Dee him-beh-reh
blackberry	die Brombeere	Dee brohm-beh-reh
mulberry	die Maulbeere	Dee moul-beh-reh
Dried Fruits	Trockenfrüchte	Trol-kehn-frueh-teh
The almond	die Mandel	Dee mahn-dehl
raisin	die Rosine	Dee ro-zee-neh
chestnut	die Kastanie	Dee kahs-tah-nee-eh
filbert	die Haselnuss	Dee hah-zehl-noos
walnut	die Walnuss	Dee vahl-noos
peanut	die Erdnuss	Dee ehrd-noos
Flowers	Blumen	Bloo-mehn
The rose	die Rose	Dee ro-zeh
tulip	die Tulpe	Dee tool-peh
violet	das Veilchen	Dahs fahyl-hehn
carnation	die Nelke	Dee nehl-keh

lily	die Lilie	Dee li-lee-eh
white lily	die weisse Lilie	Dee vahy-seh li-lee-eh
lilac	der Flieder	Dehr flee-dehr
daisy	das Gänseblümchen	Dahs gaen-zeh-bluem-hehn
orchids	die Orchidee	Dee ohr-hi-deh-eh
gardenia	die Gardenia	Dee gahr-deh-neeah
chrysanthemum	die Chrisanteme	Dee kri-sahn-teh-meh
Cereals	das Getreide	Dahs geh-trahy-deh
The wheat	der Weizen	Dehr vahy-tsehn
oats	der Hafer	Dehr hah-fehr
rice	der Reis	Dehr rahys
rye	der Roggen	Dehr roh-gehn
barley	die Gerste	Dee gehrs-teh

Animals, Birds and Fishes

	Tiere, Vögel und Fische	Tee-reh, Foe-gehl, Fisheh
The beast	die Bestie	Dee behsh-tee-eh
The bear	der Bär	Dehr baer
The lion	der Löwe	Dehr loe-veh
The panther	der Panter	Dehr pahn-tehr
The tiger	der Tiger	Dehr ti-gehr
The animal	das Tier	Dahs teer
The bull	der Stier	Dehr shteer
The cow	die Kuh	Dee koo
The calf	das Kalb	Dahs kahlb
The deer	das Rotwild	Dahs roht-vild
The dog	der Hund	Dehr hoond
The donkey	der Esel	Dehr eh-zehl
The elephant	der Elefant	Dehr eh-leh-fahnt
The goat	die Ziege	Dee tsee-geh
The horse	das Pferd	Dahs pfehrd
The lamb	das Lamm	Dahs lahm
The mare	die Stute	Dee shtoo-teh
The monkey	der Affe	Dehr ahf-feh
The mouse	die Maus	Dee mous
The mutton	der Hammel	Dehr hah-mehl
The ox	der Ochse	Dehr ohs
The pig	das Schwein	Dahs shvahyn
The rabbitt	das Kaninchen	Dahs kah-nin-hehn
The rat	die Ratte	Dee rah-teh
The feather	die Feder	Dee feh-dehr
The hoof	der Huf	Dehr hoof

The horn	das Horn	Dahs hohrn
The paw, claw	die Pfote, die Klaue	Dee pfoh-teh, dee klou-eh
The sheep	das Schaf	Dahs shahf
The skunk	das Stinktier	Dahs shtink-teer
The squirrel	das Eichhörnchen	Dahs ahyh-hoern hehn
The wolf	der Wolf	Dehr vohlf
The fox	der Fuchs	Dehr foohs
The cat	die Katze	Dee kah-tseh
The tail	der Schwanz, Schweif	Dehr shvahnts, shvahyf
The cock, rooster	der Hahn	Dehr hahn
The chicken	das Küchlein	Dahs kueh-lahyn
The hen	die Henne	Dee Hehn-neh
The duck	die Ente	Dee ehn-teh
The goose	die Gans	Dee gahns
The pigeon	die Taube	Dee tou-beh
The eagle	der Adler	Dehr ahd-lehr
The owl	die Eule	Dee oy-leh
The gull	die Möve	Dee moe-veh
The parrot	der Papagei	Dehr pah-pah-gahy
The partridge	das Rebhuhn	Dahs reh-hoon
The pelican	der Pelikan	Dehr peh-li-kahn
The pheasant	der Fasan	Dehr fah-zahn
The sparrow	der Sperling	Dehr shpehr-ling
The swan	der Schwan	Dehr shvahn
The turkey	der Truthahn	Dehr troot-hahn
The cuckoo	der Kuckuck	Dehr kook-kook
The thrush	die Drossel	Dee droh-sehl
The finch	der Fink	Dehr fink
The crow	die Krähe	Dee krae-eh
The woodpecker	der Specht	Dehr spehht
The shark	der Hai (fisch)	Dehr hahy (fish)
The whale	der Walfisch	Dehr vahl-fish
The codfish	der Kabeljau	Dehr kah-behl-you
The hake	der Hecht	Dehr hehht
The herring	der Hering	Dehr heh-ring
The mackerel	die Makrele	Dee mah-kreh-leh
The salmon	der Lachs	Dehr lahhs
The sardine	die Sardine	Dee sahr-dee-neh
The sole	die Seezunge	Dee zeh-tsoon-geh
The trout	die Forelle	Dee foh-rehl-leh
The eel	der Aal	Dehr ahl

Invertebrata	Wirbellose Tiere	Vir-behlloseh-teereh
The lobster	der Hummer	Dehr hoo-mehr
The Clam	die Venusmuschel	Dee veh-noos-moo-shehl
The crab	die Krabbe	Dee krah-beh
The shrimp	die Garnele	Dee gahr-neh-leh

Insects and Reptiles	Insekten und Reptilien	In-sehk-ten & Rehp-ti-lee-ehn
The ant	die Ameise	Dee ah-mahy-seh
The bee	die Biene	Dee bee-neh...
The butterfly	der Schmetterling	Dehr shmeh-tehr-ling
The caterpillar	die Raupe	Dee rou-peh
The fly	die Fliege	Dee flee-geh
The mosquito	der Moskito	Dehr mohs-ki-toh
The wasp	die Wespe	Dee Weh-speh
The worm	der Wurm	Dehr voorm
The bumblebee	die Hummel	Dee hoom-mehl
The earthworm	der Regenwurm	Dehr reh-gehn-voorm
The silkworm	die Seidenraupe	Dee zahy-dehn-rou-peh
The beetle	der Käfer	Dehr kae-fehr
The moth	die Motte	Dee moh-teh
The spider	die Spinne	Dee shpin-neh
The flea	der Floh	Dehr floh
The cricket	die Grille	Dee gril-leh
The snail	die Schnecke	Dee shneh-keh
The frog	der Frosch	Dehr frohsh
The toad	die Kröte	Dee kroe-teh
The snake	die Schlange	Dee shlahn-geh
The boa constrictor	die Boa	Dee boh-ah
The rattlesnake	die Klapperschlange	Dee klahp-pehr-shlahn-geh
The cobra	die Kobra	Dee koh-brah
The crocodile	das Krokodil	Dahs kroh-kohdeel

The Human Body

	Der menschliche Körper	Dehr mehnsh-li-heh Koer-pehr
The skeleton	das Skelett	Dahs skeh-leht
The bone	der Knochen	Dehr Kno-hehn
The marrow	das Mark	Dahs mahrk
The muscle	der Muskel	Dehr moos-kehl
The head	der Kopf	Dehr kohpf
The hair	das Haar	Dahs hahr

The forehead	die Stirn	Dee shtirn
The face	das Gesicht	Dahs geh-ziht
The eyebrow	die Augenbraue	Dee ou-gehn-brou-eh
The eyes	die Augen	Dee ou-gehn
The eyelash	die Augenwimper	Dee ou-gehn-vim-pehr
The nose	die Nase	Dee nah-zeh
The mustache	der Schnurrbart	Dehr shnoor-bahrt
The mouth	der Mund	Dehr moond
The lip	die Lippe	Dee lip-peh
The lips	die Lippen	Dee lip-pehn
The tongue	die Zunge	Dee tsoon-geh
The tooth	der Zahn	Dehr tsahn
The teeth	die Zähne	Dee tsae-neh
The gums	die Gaumen	Dee gou-mehn
The cheek(s)	die Wange(n)	Dee vahn-geh(n)
The ear	das Ohr	Dahs ohr
The ears	die Ohren	Dee oh-rehn
The chin(s)	das Kinn, die Kinne	Dahs kin, dee kin-neh
The beard	der Bart	Dehr Bahrt
The throat	die Kehle	Dee keh-leh
The neck	der Hals	Dehr hahls
The shoulder shoulders	die Schulter(n)	Dee shool-tehr(n)
The back	der Rücken	Dehr rue-kehn
The chest	die Brust	Dee broost
The breast, bosom	die Brust, der Busen	Dee broost, dehr boo-zehn
The spine, backbone	das Rückgrat	Dahs ruek-graht
The arm	der Arm	Dehr ahrm
The elbow	der Ellbogen	Dehr ehl-boh-gehn
The wrist	das Handgelenk	Dahs hahnd-geh-lehnk
The hand	die Hand	Dee hahnd
The hands	die Hände	Dee haen-deh
The finger(s)	der Finger, die Finger	Dehr (dee) fin-gehr
The nail(s)	der Nagel, die Nägel	Dehr nah-gehl dee nae-gehl
The visceral	innerlich	In-nehr-lih
The heart(s)	das (die) Herz(en)	Dahs hehrts dee hehr-tsehn
The lungs	die Lungen	Dee loon-gehn
The liver	die Leber	Dee leh-behr
The stomach	der Magen	Dehr mah-gehn
The kidneys	die Nieren	Dee nee-rehn

The bladder	die Blase	Dee blah-zeh
The abdomen	der Unterleib	Dehr oon-tehr-lahyb
The bowels	das Eingeweide	Dahs ahyn-geh-vahy-deh
The pelvis	das Becken	Dahs beh-kehn
The sex	das Geschlecht	Dahs geh-shlehht
The thigh	der Schenkel	Dehr-shehn-kehl
The hip(s)	die Hüfte(n)	Dee huef-teh(n)
The buttocks	die Hinterteile	Dee hin-tehr-tahy-leh
The knee(s)	das (die) Knie(e)	Dahs (dee) knee (eh)
The leg(s)	das Bein, die Beine	Dahs bahyn, dee bahy-neh
The calf of the leg	die Wade	Dee vah-deh
The ankles	die Fussknöchel	Dee foos-knoe hehl
The foot, feet	der Fuss, die Füsse	Dehr foos, dee fue-seh
The toes	die Zehen	Dee tseh-ehn
The heel	die Ferse	Dee fehr-seh
The skin	die Haut	Dee hout
The nerves	die Nerven	Dee nehr-vehn
The veins	die Adern	Dee ah-dehrn
The blood	das Blut	Dahs bloot
The flesh	das Fleisch	Dahs flahysh
The skull, cranium	der Schädel	Dehr shae-dehl
The brain	das Gehirn, Hirn	Dahs geh-hirn, hirn
The nostril	das Nasenloch	Dahs nah-zehn-lohh
The upper arm	der Oberarm	Dehr oh-behr-ahrm
The eyelid	das Augenlid	Dahs ou-gehn-lid
The fingernail	der Fingernagel	Dehr fin-gehr-nah-gehl

The Senses

	Die Sinne	Dee Sen-neh
Sight	die Sehkraft	Dee seh-krahft
To see	zu sehen	Tsoo seh-ehn
Blindness	die Blindheit	Dee blind-hahyt
Blind	Blind	Blind
Hearing	das Gehör	Dahs geh-hoer
To hear	zu hören	Tsoo hoe-rehn
Deafness	die Taubheit	Dee toub-hahyt
Taste	der Geschmack	Dehr geh-shmahck
To taste	zu schmecken	Tsoo shmehk-kehn
Smell	der Geruch	Dehr geh-rooh
To smell	zu riechen	Tsoo ree-hehn
Touch	das Gefühl	Dahs geh-fuel
To touch	zu fühlen	Tsoo fue-lehn

hallucination	Das Truggebilde	Dahs troog-geh-bil-deh
faculty	die Fähigkeit	Dee fae-ig-kahyt
reason	die Vernunft	Dee fehr-noonft
reasoning	urteilen	Oor-tahy-lehn
thought	der Gedanke	Dehr geh-dahn-keh
to think	denken	Dehn-kehn
speech	die Sprache	Dee shprah-heh
to speak	sprechen	shpre-hehn
word	das Wort	Dahs wohrt
voice	die Stimme	Dee shtim-meh
character	der Charakter	Dehr kaah-rahk-tehr
will	der Wille	Dehr vil-leh
determination	der Entschluss	Dehr ehnt-shlooss
morality	die Sittlichkeit	Dee zit-lih-kahyt
vacillation	der Wankelmut	Dehr vahn-kehl moot
courage	der Mut	Dehr moot
coward	der Feigling	Dehr fahyg-ling
cowardice	die Feigheit	Dee fahyg-hahyt
loyalty	die Treue	Dee troy-eh
disloyalty	die Untreue	Dee oon-troy-eh
kindness	die Güte	Dee gue-teh
generosity	der Grossmut	Dehr grohs-moot
altruism	die Nächstenliebe	Dee naehs-tehn lee-beh
abnegation	die Entsagung	Dee ehnt-zah-goong
self-denial	die Selbstverleugnung	Dee zehlbst-fehr-loyg-noong
selfishness	die Selbstsucht	Dee zehlbst-zooht
envy	der Neid	Dehr nahyd
vanity	die Eitelkeit	Dee ahy-tehl-kahyt
bad temper	der Zorn	Dehr tsohrn
wickedness	die Gottlosigkeit	Dee goht-loh-zig-kahyt
affection	die Zuneigung	Dee tsoo-nahy goong
emotion	das Gefühl, die Gefühlserregung	Dahs geh-fuel, Dee geh-fuels ehr-reh-goong
disgust	der Ekel, Widerwille	Dehr eh-kehl, vee-dehr-vil-leh

Circumstances of Life	Lebensereignisse	Leh-behns-ehr-ahyg-nis-seh
The age	das Alter	Dahs ahl-tehr
child	das Kind	Dahs kind
boy	der Knabe	Dehr knah-beh
youth	der Jüngling	Dehr yueng-ling
man	der Mann	Dehr mahn
girl (child)	das Mädchen	Dahs maedhehn
girl (Miss)	das Fräulein	Dahs froy-lahyn
woman	die Frau, das Weib	Dee frou, dahs vahyb
wife	die Ehefrau, Gemahlin	Dee eh-eh-frou, geh-mah-lin
old woman	die Greisin	Dee grahy-zen
old man	der Greis	Dehr grahyz
bachelor	der Junggeselle	Dehr yoong-geh zehl-leh
spinster	die alte Jungfrau	Dee ahl-teh yoong-frou
married man	der Ehemann	Dehr eh-eh-mahn
widower	der Witwer	Dehr vit-vehr
widow	die Witwe	Dee Vit-veh
orphan	die Waise	Dee vahy-zeh
fair sex	das schöne Geschlecht	Dahs shoe-neh geh-shlehht
birth	die Geburt	Dee geh-boort
infancy	die Kindheit	Dee kind-hahyt
youth	die Jugend (m.f.)	Dee yoo-gehnd
old age	das Greisenalter	Dahs grahy-zehn-ahl-tehr
death	der Tod	Dehr tohd
accident	der Unfall	Dehr oon-fahl
agreement	das Überein-kommen	Dahs ue-behr-ahyn-koh-mehn
happiness	die Glückseligkeit	Dee gluek-zeh-lig-kahyt
career	die Laufbahn	Dee louf-bahn
marriage	die Ehe, Heirat	Dee eh-eh, hahy-raht
divorce	die Ehescheidung	Dee eh-eh-shahy-doong
misfortune	das Missgeschick	Dahs mis-geh-shick
expense(s)	die Ausgabe(n) Kosten	Dee ous-gah-beh(n), Kohs-tehn
business	das Gewerbe, Geschäft	Dahs geh-vehr-beh, geh-shaeft
dowry	die Mitgift	Dee mit-gift

bridegroom	der Bräutigam	Dehr broy-ti-gahm
fiance(e)	der (die) Verlobte	Dehr (dee) fehr-lohb-teh
education	die Erziehung	Dee ehr-tsee oong
burial	das Begräbnis	Dahs beh-graeb-nis
custom	die Sitte (der Brauch)	Dee Sit-teh, dehr brouh
heritage	die Erbschaft	Dee ehrb-shahft
heir	der Erbe	Dehr ehr-beh
taxes	die Steuern	Dee shtoy-ehrn
minor	der Unmündige	Dehr oon-muen-di-geh
tutor	der Erzieher	Dehr ehr-tsee ehr
poverty	die Armut	Dee ahr-moot
name	der Name	Dehr nah-meh
fatherhood	die Vaterschaft	Dee fah-tehr-shahft
inheritance	die Erbschaft	dee ehrb-shahft
life pension	die Lebens-pension	Dee leh-behns-pehn-zee-ohn
profession	der Beruf	Dehr beh-roof
work	die Arbeit	Dee ahr-bahyt
present	die Gegenwart	Dee geh-gehn-wahrt
past	die Vergangen-heit	Dee fehr-gahn-gehn-hahyt
future	die Zukunft	Dee tsoo-koonft

The Family

	Die Familie	Dee Fa-me-le-eh
The parents	die Eltern	Dee ehl-tehrn
The father	der Vater	Dehr fah-tehr
mother	die Mutter	Dee Moot-tehr
grandfather	der Grossvater	Dehr grohs-fah-tehr
grandmother	die Grossmutter	Dee grohs-moot-tehr
son	der Sohn	Dehr zohn
daughter	die Tochter	Dee tohh-tehr
grandson	der Enkel	Dehr ehn-kehl
grand daughter	die Enkelin	Dee ehn-keh-lin
greatgrandson	der Urenkel	Dehr oor-ehn-kehl
brother	der Bruder	Dehr Broo-dehr
sister	die Schwester	Dee shvehs- tehr
twins	die Zwillinge	Dee tsvil-lin-geh
uncle	der Onkel	Dehr ohn-kehl
aunt	die Tante	Dee tahn-teh
nephew	der Neffe	Dehr nehf-feh
niece	die Nichte	Dee nih-teh
cousin (f.)	die Base	Dee bah-zeh

The cousin (m.)	der Vetter	Dehr feht-tehr
husband	der Ehemann, Gatte	Dehr eh-eh-mahn, gaht-teh
wife	die Ehefrau, Gattin	Dee eh-eh-frou, gaht-een
father-in-law	der Schwieger-vater	Dehr shvee-gehr-fah-tehr
mother-in-law	die Schwieger-mutter	Dee shvee-gehr moot-tehr
son-in-law	der Schwieger-sohn	Dehr shvee-gehr-zohn
daughter-in-law	die Schwieger-tochter	Dee shvee-gehr tohh-tehr
brother-in-law	der Schwager	Dehr shvah-gehr
sister-in-law	die Schwägerin	Dee shvae-geh rin
stepchild	das Stiefkind	Dahs shteef-kind
stepfather	der Stiefvater	Dehr shteef-fahtehr
stepmother	die Stiefmutter	Dee shteef-moot-tehr

Accidents and Diseases

	Unfälle und Krankheiten	Oon-fael-leh & Krahnk-hahyt-ehn
The headache	das Kopfweh	Dahs kohpf-veh
tootache	das Zahnweh	Dahs tsahn-veh
sore-throat	die Halsent-zündung	Dee hahls-ehnt-tsuen-doong
pain	der Schmerz	dehr shmehrts
sprain	die Verrenkung	Dee fehr-rehn-koong
fracture	der (Knochen-) Bruch	Dehr (knoh-hohn-) Brooh
stroke	der (Schlag-) Anfall	Dehr (shlahg-) ahn-fahl
wound	die Wunde	Dee voon-deh
hemorrhage	der Blutsturz	Dehr bloot-shtoorts
fainting	die Ohnmacht	Dee ohn-mahht
asphyzia	die Erstickung	Dee ehr-shti-koong
poisoning	die Vergiftung	Dee fehr-gif-toong
burns	die Brandwunden	Dee brahnd-voon-dehn
cold	die Erkältung	Dee ehr-kael-toong
vomit	das Erbrechen	Dahs ehr-breh-hehn
pneumonia	die Lungenent-zündung	Dee loon-gehn-ehnt-tsuen-doong
fever	das Fieber	Dahs fee-behr
malaria	die Malaria	Dee mah-lah-ree-ah
typhoid fever	der Typhus	Dehr ti-phoos

The diarrhea	der Durchfall	Dehr doorh-fahl
doctor	der Doktor	Dehr dohk-tohr
physician	der Arzt	Dehr ahrtst
surgeon	der Chirurg	Dehr ki-roorg
dentist	der Zahnarzt	Dehr tsahn-ahrtst
enema	das Klistier	Dahs klis-teer
laxative	das Abführmittel	Dahs ahb-fuer-mit-tehl
hospital	das Spital	Dahs shpi-tahl
nurse	die Kranken-schwester	Dee krahn-kehn-shvehs-tehr
injection	die Injektion	Dee in-yehk-tse-ohn
prescription	das Rezept	Dahs reh-tsehpt
indigestion	die Verdauungs-störung	Dee fehr-dou-oongs-stoe-roong
corn	das Hühnerauge	Dahs Hue-nehr-ou-geh
operation	die Operation	Dee oh-peh-rah-tsee-ohn
influenza	die Influenza	Dee in-flooehn-tsah
appendicitis	die Blinddarm-entzündung	Dee blind-dahrm-ehnt-tsuen-doong
scar	die Narbe	Dee nahr-beh
ulcer	das Geschwür	Dahs geh-shvuer
rheumatism	der Rheumatismus	Dehr reh-oo-mah-tis-moos
diet	die Diat	Dee dee-aet
epidemic (dis.)	die Epidemie, Seuche	Dee eh-pi-deh-mee, soy-h
cancer	der Krebs	Dehr krehbs
scratch	die Schramme	Dee shrahm-meh
eczema	die Hautbläschen	Dee hout-blaes-hehn
constipation	die Verstopfung	Dee fehr-stohpf-oong

First Aid

	die Nothilfe	Dee not-hel-feh
The medicine chest	der Arznei-schrank	Dehr ahr-tsnahy-shrahnk
eyecup	der Augenbecher	Dehr ou-gehn-beh-hehr
alcohol	der Alkohol	Dehr ahl-koh-hohl
iodine	das Jod	Dahs yohd
cotton	die Watte	Dee vah-teh
gauze	die Gaze	Dee gah-zeh
bandage	der Verband	Dehr fehr-bahnd
scissors	die Schere	Dee sheh-reh

The forceps, nippers	die Zange	Dee tsahn-geh
antiseptic	antiseptisch	ahnti-sehp-tish
antidote (counter poison)	das Gegengift	Dahs geh-gehn-gift
ammonia	der Salmiakgeist	Dehr sahl-mi-ahk-gahyst
smelling salts	das Riechsalz	Dahs reeh-zahlts
blood-transfusion	die Blutüber-tragung	Dee blood-ue-behr-trah-goong
needle	die Nadel	Dee nah-dehl
camphor oil	der Kampfer	Dehr kahm-pfehr
ambulance	die Ambulanz	Dee ahm-boo-lahnts

Medicine

	Medikamente	Meh-Di-Kah-Mehn-Teh
The ointment	die Salbe	Dee zahl-beh
plaster	das Pflaster	Dahs pflahs-tehr
vitamins	Die Vitamine	Dee vi-tah-mi-neh
aspirin	das Aspirin	Dahs ahs-pi-reen
pill	die Pille	Dee pil-leh
quinine	das Chinin	Dahs hi-neen
insulin	das Insulin	Dahs in-soo-lin
neosalvarsan	das Salvarsan	Dahs zahl-vahr zahn

In the House

	Im Haus	Im Hous
The blinds	die Jalousie	Dee shah-loo-zee
bedroom	das Schlafzimmer	Dahs shlahf-tsim-mehr
balcony	der Balkon	Dehr bahl-kon
ceiling	die Zimmerdecke	Dee tsim-mehr-deh-keh
cellar	der Keller	Dehr kehl-lehr
chimney	der Schornstein	Dehr shohrn-shtahyn
dining room	das Speisezimmer	shpahy-zeh-tsim-mehr
door	die Tür	Dee tuer
doorbell	die Hausglocke	Dee hous-gloh-keh
drawing room	der Salon	Dehr zah-lohn
fireplace	der Kamin	Dehr kah-meen
floor	der Boden	Dehr bohdehn
floor, story	das Stockwerk	Dahs stohk-vehrk
hall	die Halle, das Vorzimmer	Dee hahl-leh? dahs fohr-tsim-mehr

The key	der Schlüssel	Dehr shlues-sehl
kitchen	die Küche	Dee kue-heh
library	die Bibliothek	Dee bie-bli-oh-tehk
lock	das Schloss (Tür-)	Dahs (tuer-) shlohs
passage	der Durchgang	Dehr doorh gahng
porch	die Veranda	Dee veh-rahn-dah
roof	das Dach	Dahs dahh
room	das Zimmer	Dahs tsim-mehr
stair, step	die Stiege, Stufe, Treppe	Dee shtee-geh, stoo-feh, treh-peh
stairway	das Stiegenhaus	Dahs shtee-gehn-hous
terrace	die Terrasse	Dee teh-rah-seh
flat-roof	das platte Dach	Dahs plah-teh dahh
wall	die Wand	Dee vahnd
wicket	das Pförtchen	Dahs pfoert-hehn
window	das Fenster	Dahs fehn-stehr
bathroom	das Badezimmer	Dahs bah-deh-tsim-mehr
basin	das Waschbecken	Dahs vahsh-behk-kehn
bathtub	die Badewanne	Dee bah-deh-vahn-neh
faucet	der Wasserhahn	Dehr vahs-sehr-hahn
shower	die Dusche	Dee doo-sheh
water-closet	das Klosett	Dahs kloh-zeht
armchair	der Lehnstuhl	Dehr lehn-stool
ashtray	der Aschenbecher	Dee ahshehn-beh-hehr
basket	der Korb	Dehr kohrb
bedspread	die Bettdecke	Dee beht-dehk-keh
box	die Schachtel	Dee shahh-tehl
book	das Buch	Dahs booh
bookcase	der Bücherschrank	Dehr bue-ehr-shrahnk
broom	der Besen	Dehr beh-zehn
lighter	der Anzünder	Dehr ahn-tsuen dehr
candle	die Kerze	Dee kehr-tseh
candlestick	der Kerzenhalter	Dehr kehr-tsehn-hahl-tehr
carpet	der Teppich	Dehr tehp-pih
chair	der Stuhl	Dehr stool
chest	die Kommode	Dee koh-moh-deh
closet	der Schrank	Dehr shrahnk
cupboard	der Speise-schrank	Dehr spahy-zeh-shrahnk
curtain	der Vorhang	Dehr fohr-hahng
cushion	das Kissen	Dahs kis-sehn
drawer	die Lade	Dee lah-deh

The dresser	der (Anrichte) Ankleide-Tisch	Dehr (ahn-ri-hteh) ahn klahy-deh tish
kitchen closet	der Küchenschrank	Dehr kue-hehn-shrahnk
electric light	das elektrische Licht	Dahs eh-lehk-tri-sheh lih
fire	das Feuer	Dahs foy-ehr
hat rack	das Hutgestell	Dahs hoot-geh-stehl
lamp	die Lampe	Dee lahm-peh
ladder	die Leiter	Dee lahy-tehr
mattress	die Matratze	Dee mah-trah-tseh
night-table	der Nachttisch	Dehr nahht-tish
ornament	das Ornament	Dahs ohr-nah-mehnt
painting	das Gemälde	Dahs geh-mael-deh
wall paper	die Tapete	Dee tah-peh-teh
piano	das Klavier	Dahs klah-veer
picture	das Bild	Dahs bield
pillow	das Kopfkissen	Dahs kohpf-kis sehn
pillowcase	der Kissenüberzug	Dehr kis-sehn ue-behr-tsoog
quilt	die Steppdecke	Dee shtehp-dehk-keh
icebox	der Eisschrank	Dehr ahys-shrahnk
refrigerator	der (elect.) Kühlschrank	Dehr kuel-shrahnk
sheet	das Leintuch, Bettuch	Dahs lahyn-tooh, beht-tooh
mirror	der Spiegel	Dehr shpee-gehl
switch	der Umschalter	Dehr oom-shahl-tehr
table	der Tisch	Dehr tish
writing desk	der Schreibtisch	Dehr shrahyb-tish
clothes closet	der Kleiderschrank	Dehr klahy-dehr-shrahnk

<u>In School</u>	<u>In der Schule</u>	<u>In dehr Shooleh</u>
The pupil (m.)	der Schüler	Dehr shue-lehr
pupil (f.)	die Schülerin	Dee shue-leh-rin
teacher (m.)	der Lehrer	Dehr leh-rehr
teacher (f.)	die Lehrerin	Dee leh-reh-rin
classroom	das Klassenzimmer	Dahs klah-sehn-tsim-mehr
lesson	die Aufgabe, Lektion	Dee ouf-gah-beh, lehk-tsee-oh
school book	das Schulbuch	Dahs shool-booh
school desk	der Lehrtisch, das Pult	Dehr lehr-tish, dahs poolt
Inkstand	das Tintenfass	Dahs tin-tehn-fahs
pen	die Schreibfeder	Dee shrahyb-feh-dehr

The pencil	der Bleistift	Dehr blahy-shtift
notebook	das Schreibheft	Dahs shrahyb-hehft
rubber eraser	der Radiergummi	Dehr rah-deer-goom-mee
home work, assignment	die Aufgabe	dee ouf-gah-beh
marks	die Noten	Dee noh-tehn
to teach	lehren (unterrichten)	Leh-rehn, oon-teh-rih-tehn
the course	der Lehrgang	Dehr lehr-gahng
object	der Gegenstand	Dehr geh-gehn-shtahnd
school subject	das Fach	dahs fahh
school subject(s)	die Fächer	dee fae-hehr
The examination	die Prüfung, das Examen	Dee prue-foong, dahs ehkz-ah-mehn
diploma	das Diplom, Zeugnis	Dahs di-plohm, tsoyg-nis
baccalaureate	das Bakkalaureat	Dahs bah-kah-lou-reh-aht
student (m.) (Coll. Univ.)	der Student	Dehr stoo-dehnt
student (f.)	die Studentin	Dee stoo-dehn-tin
pedagogy	die Pädagogik	Dee pae-dah-goh-gik
textbook	das Lehrbuch	Dahs lehr-booh
tutor	der Privat-, Haus-lehrer	Dehr pri-vaht-, hous-leh-rehr
professor	der Professor	dehr pruh-feh-sohr
schoolmate (m.)	der Mitschüler	Dehr mit-shue-lehr
schoolmate (f.)	die Mitschülerin	Dee mit-shue-leh-rin

Tableware	Tischausstattung	Tish-Ous-Staht-Toong
The tablecloth	das Tischtuch	Dash tish-tooh
napkin	die Serviette, das Mundtuch	Dee sehr-vee-eh-teh
plate	der Teller	Dehr teh-lehr
serving dish	die Speiseschüssel	Dee shpahy-zeh shue-sehl
tray	die Serviertasse	Dee sehr-veer-tahs-seh
saucer	die Untertasse	Dee oon-tehr-tahs-seh
cup	die Schale, Tasse	Dee shah-leh, tahs-seh
glass	das Glas	Dahs glahs
wineglass	das Weinglas	Dahs vahyn-glahs
coffee pot	die Kaffeekanne	Dee kah-feh-kahn-neh
tea pot	die Teekanne	Dee teh-kahn-neh

The milk jug	der Milchkrug	Dehr milh-kroog
spoon	der Löffel	Dehr loeffehl
teaspoon	der Teelöffel	Der teh-loeffehl
fork	die Gabel	Dee gah-behl
knife	das Messer	Dahs mehs-sehr
nutcracker	der Nussknacker	Dehr noos-knah-kehr
saltcellar	der Salzstreuer	Dehr sahlts-stroy-ehr
corkscrew	der Korkzieher	Dehr kohrk-tsee-ehr
In the Kitchen	In der Küche	In dehr Kue-heh
The gas stove	der Gasofen	Dehr gahs-oh fehn
gas	das Gas	Dahs gahs
match	das Streichholz	Dahs shtrahyh-holts
matches	die Streichhölzer	Dee Shtrahyhi-hoel-tsehr
closet, cupboard	der Silber-, Speise-schrank	Dehr zil-behr-, shpahy-zeh shrahnk
refrigerator	der elektrische Kühlschrank	Dehr eh-lehk-tri-sheh-kuel-shrahnk
kettle	der Kessel	Dehr kehs-sehl
pantry	die Speisekammer	Dee shpahy-zeh-kah-mehr
pot	der Topf	Dehr tohpf
frying pan	die Bratpfanne	Dee braht-pfahn-neh
ladle	der Schöpflöffel	Dehr shoepf-loef-fehl
In the Restaurant	Im Restaurant	Im rehs-toh-rahnt
To eat	essen	Ehs-sehn
to drink	trinken	Trin-kehn
The breakfast	das Frühstück	Dahs frue-stueck
dinner	das Mittagessen	Dahs mtt-tahg-ehs-sehn
supper	das Abendessen	Dahs ah-behnd-ehs-sehn
bread	das Brot	Dahs broht
white bread	das Weissbrot	Dahs vahys-brot
rye bread	das Roggenbrot	Dahs roh-gehn-brot
roll	die Semmel, das Brötchen	Dee zehmmel, dahs broet-hehn
a slice of bread	eine Schnitte Brot	ahyneh shnitteh broht
the toast	das geröstete Brot	Dahs geh-roes-teh-teh broht
drink(s)	das (die) Getränk(e)	dahs geh-traenk
wine	der Wein	Dehr vahyn
white wine	der Weisswein	Dehr vahys-vahyn

The red wine	der Rotwein	Dehr roht-vahyn
beer	das Bier	Dahs beer
brandy	der Schnaps	Dehr shnahps
cherry-brandy	das Kirschwasser	Dahs Kirsh-vahs-sehr
water	das Wasser	Dahs vahs-sehr
coffee	der Kaffee	Dehr kah-feh
black coffee.	der schwarze Kaffee	Dehr shvahr-tseh-kah-feh
coffee with milk	der Milchkaffee	Dehr milh-kah-feh
chocolate	die Schokolade	Dee shoh-koh-lah-deh
meat	das Fleisch	Dahs flahysch
boiled meat	das gekochte Fleisch	Dahs geh-kohh-teh flahysh
roast meat	der Rostbraten	Dehr rohst-brah-tehn
ham	der Schinken	Dehr shin-kehn
bacon	der Speck	Dehr shpehk
lamb meat	das Lammfleisch	Dahs lahm-flahysh
beefsteak	das Beefsteak	Dahs beef-steak
roast-beef	der Rindsbraten	Dehr rinds-brah-tehn
pork	das Schweinefleisch	Dahs shvahy-neh-flahysh.
sirloin	die Rindslende	Dee rinds-lehh-deh
veal	das Kalbfleisch	Dahs kahlb-flahysh
The egg	das Ei	Dahs ahy
butter	die Butter	dee boo-tehr
milk	die Milch	Dee milh
cheese	der Käse	Dehr kae-zeh
cream	der Rahm, die Sahne	Dehr rahm, dee zah-neh
ice cream	das Gefrorene	Dahs geh-froh-reh-neh
ice cream	das Speise-Eis	Dahs spahyse-ahys
vanilla	die Vanille	Dee vah-nil-leh
cake	der Kuchen	Dehr koo-hehn
pie	die Pastete	Dee pahs-teh-teh
honey	der Honig	Dehr hoh-nig
sugar	der Zucker	Dehr tsoo-kehr
salt	das Salz	Dahs zahltz
oil	das Öl	Dahs oel
vinegar	der Essig	Dehr ehs-sig
sauce	die Sauce, Brühe	Dee brue-eh, zohs
sausage	die Wurst	Dee voorst
flour	das Mehl	Dahs mehl
fat	das Fett	Dahs feht
vegetable	das Gemüse	Dahs geh-mue-zeh
dessert	der Nachtisch, das Dessert	Dehr nahh-tish, dahs deh-sehrt
tobacco	der Tabak	Dehr tah-bahk

The cigar	die Zigarre	Dee tsi-gahr-reh
cigarette	die Zigarette	Dee tsi-gah-reh-teh
pipe	die Tabakspfeife	Dee tah-bahks-pfahy-feh
black coffee	der Mokka (Kaffee)	Dehr moh-kah
jam	die Marmelade	Dee mahr-meh-lah-deh
fruit juice	der Fruchtsaft	Dehr frooht-sahft

Men's Clothing	Männerkleider	Maen-nehr-klahy-dehr
The underwear	die Unterwäsche	Dee oon-tehr-vae-sheh
suit	der Anzug	Dehr ahn-tsoog
undershirt	das Unterhemd	Dahs oon-tehr-hehmd
shorts	die Kniehose die Unterhose	Dee knee-hoh-zeh, oontehr-hoh-zeh
night shirt	das Schlafhemd	Dahs shlahf-hehmd
garter	das Strumpfband	Dahs stroompf-bahnd
socks	die Socken	Dee zohk-kehn
handkerchief	das Taschentuch	Dahs tah-shehn-tooh
shirt	das Hemd	Dahs hehmd
collar	der Kragen	Dehr krah-gehn
tie	Krawatte	Dee krah-vah-teh
suspenders	die Hosenträger	Dee ho-zehn-trae-gehr
slippers	die Hausschuhe	Dee hous-shoo-eh
trousers	die Hosen	Dee ho-zehn
vest	die Weste	Dee ves-teh
coat	der Rock	Dehr rohk
belt	der Riemen	Dehr ree-mehn
raincoat	der Regenmantel	Dehr reh-gehn- mahn-tehl
topcoat	der Überzieher	Dehr ue-behr-tsee-ehr
overcoat	der Winterrock	Dehr vin-tehr-rohk
shoes	die Schuhe	Dee shoo-eh
riding boots	die Reitstiefel	Dee rahyt-shtee-fehl
hat	der Hut	Dehr hoot
cap	die Kappe, Mütze	Dee kahp-peh, mue-tseh
cuff links	die Manschetten- knöpfe	Dee mahn-dsheh- tehn-knoe-pfeh
gloves	die Handschuhe	Dee hahnd-shoo-eh
cane	der Spazierstock	Dehr spah-tseer-shtohk

Ladies' Garments and Accessories	Frauenkleidung	Frou-ehn-klahy-doong
The slip	der Unterrock	dehr oon-tehr-rohk
pajamas	die Pijamas	Dee pid-shah-mahs
brassiere	der Büstenhalter	dehr boo-zehn- hahl-tehr

The panties	die Unterhose	dee oon-tehr-hoh-zeh
belt	der Gürtel	Dehr guer-tehl
blouse	die Bluse	Dee bloo-zeh
dress	das Kleid	Dahs klahyd
skirt	der Rock	Dehr rohk
stockings	die Strümpfe	Dee shtruem-pfeh
girdle	das Mieder	Dahs mee-dehr
coat	der Mantel	Dehr mahn-tehl
furcoat	der Pelzmantel	Dehr pehlts-mahn tehl
pocketbook, purse	die Handtasche, Börse	Dee hahnd-tah sheh, boer-zeh
necklace	das Halsband, die Halskette	Dahs hahls-bahnd, hahls-keh-teh
earrings	die Ohrringe	Dee ohr-ringeh
ring	der Ring	Dehr ring
brooch	die Brosche	Dee broh-sheh
hat	der Hut	Dehr hoot
hairnet	das Haarnetz	Dahs hahr-nehts
handkerchief	das Taschentuch	Dahs tah-shehn-tooh
umbrella	der Regenschirm	Dehr reh-gehn-shirm
shoes	die Schuhe	Dee shoo-heh
suit	das Kostüm	Dahs kohs-tuem
At the Dressmaker	**Bei der Damen-Schneiderin**	**Bahy dehr dah-mehn-shnahy-deh-rin**
The measuring tape	das Messband	Dahs mehs-bahnd
to measure	messen, Mass nehmen	Mehs-sehn, mahs neh-mehn
the material	der Stoff, das Material	Dehr shtohf, dahs mah-teh-ree-ahl
pin	die Stecknadel	Dee shtehk-nah-dehl
safety pin	die Sicherheits-nadel	Dee Zi-hehr-hahyts-nah-dehl
needle	die Nadel	Dee nah-dehl
thread	der Zwirn	Dehr tsvirn
scissors	die Schere	Dee sheh-reh
ribbon	das Band	Dahs bahnd
button	der Knopf	Dehr knohpf
sewing-machine	die Nähmaschine	Dee nae-mah-shee neh
to sew	nähen	Nae-ehn
Toilet Articles	**Die Toiletten-artikel**	**Dee Tohah-lehten-ahr-ti-kehl**
The mirror	der Spiegel	Dehr shpee-gehl
lipstick	der Lippenstift	Dehr li-pehn-shtift

English	German	Pronunciation
The rouge	die Schminke	Dee shmin-keh
(cold) cream	die Hautpomade	Dee hout-poh-mah-deh
tooth brush	die Zahnburste	Dee tsahn-buers-teh
comb	der Kamm	Dehr kahm
nail cleaner	der Nagelrei-niger	Dehr nah-gehl-rahy-ni-gehr
nail polish	die Nagelpolitur der Nagellack	Dee nah-gehl-pohlee-toor, dehr Lahk
remover	der Politurab-nehmer	Dehr poh-lee-toor-ahb-neh-mehr
cuticle	die Oberhaut	Dee o-behr-hout
nail file	die Nagelfeile	Dee nah-gehl-fahy-leh
powder	der Puder	Dehr poo-dehr
powder puff	die Puderquaste	Dee poo-derh-kvahs-teh
face massage	die Gesichts-massage	Dee geh-zihts-mah-sash
permanent wave	die Dauerwelle	Dee dou-ehr-veh-leh
manicure	die Nagelpflege	Dee nah-gehl-pfleh-geh
hairdress	die Frisur	Dee free-zoor
shaving brush	der Rasierpinsel	Dehr rah-zeer-pin-zehl
soap	die Seife	Dee sahy-feh
razor	das Rasiermesser	Dahs rah-zeer-mehs-sehr
razor blade	die Rasier-klinge	Dee rah-zeer-klin-geh
toothpaste	die Zahnpaste	Dee tsahn-pahs-teh
perfume	das Parfüm	Dahs pahr-fuem
cologne	das Kölnisch-wasser	Dahs koel-nish ..-vahs-sehr...
hair pins	die Haarnadeln	Dee hahr-nah-dehln

<u>Traveling</u>	<u>Das Reisen</u>	<u>Dahs rahy-sehn</u>
At the Consulate	im Konsulat	Im kohn-soo-laht
The Consul	der Konsul	Dehr kohn-sool
citizenship, nationality	Staatsangehörigkeit Nationalität	Shtahts-ahn-geh-hoe-rig-kahyt, Nah-tsee-oh-nah-li-tael
Born in	geboren in...	Geh-boh-rehn in...
The age	das Alter	Dahs ahl-tehr
birth certificate	der Geburts-schein	Dehr geh-boorts-shahynn
photograph	die Photographie	Dee phoh-toh-grah-fee
passport	der Reisepass	Dehr rahy-zeh-pahs
visa	das Visum	Dahs vi-zoom

At the Railway Station	auf der Bahnstation	Ouf dehr bahn-shtah-tsee-ohn
The (a) porter	der (ein) Gepäckträger	Dehr (ahyn) geh-paek-trae-gehr
tip	das Trinkgeld	Dahs trink-gehld
newsstand	der Zeitungsstand	Dehr tsahy-toongs-shtahnd
newspaper	die (eine) Zeitung	Dee Tsahy-toong
magazine	die Zeitschrift	Dee tsahyt-shrift
information	die Auskunft	Dee ous-koonft
timetable	der Fahrplan	Dehr fahr-plahn
guidebook	der Reiseführer	Dehr rahy-zeh-fue-rehr
departure	die Abfahrt	Dee ahb-fahrt
ticket office	der Fahrkartenschalter	Dehr fahr-kahr-tehn-shahl -tehr
ticket	die Fahrkarte	Dee fahr-kahr-teh
One way	eine Fahrt	Ahy-neh fahrt
A roundtrip	eine Rundreise	Ahyneh roond-rahy-zeh
a roundtrip	eine Hin-und Rückfahrt	hin-oond ruek-fahrt
The fare	der Fahrpreis	Dehr fahr-prahys
luggage	das Gepäck	Dahs geh-paek
baggage room	der Gepäckraum	Dehr geh-paek-roum
baggage check	der Gepäckschein	Dehr geh-paek-shahyn
bag	die Tasche	Dee tah-sheh
suitcase	die Reisetasche	Dee rahy-zeh-tah-sheh
valise	der Handkoffer	dehr hand-koh-fehr
package	das Paket	Dahs pah-keht
trunk	der Reisekoffer	Dehr rahy-zeh-koh-fehr
label	der Gepäckzettel	Dehr geh-paeck-tseht-tehl
strap	der Riemen	Dehr ree-mehn
signal	das Signal	Dahs sig-nahl
waiting room	der Wartesaal	Dehr vahr-teh-zahl
The men's room	die Herrentoilete	Heh-rehn-toh-ah-leh-teh.
The Ladies room	die Damentoilete	Dah-mehn, - toh-ah-leh-teh.
The station master	der Stationsvorstand	Dehr shtah-tsee-ohns-fohr-stahnd
interpreter	der Dolmetscher	Dehr dohl-meht-chehr
lavatory	der Waschraum	Dehr vash-roum
track	das Geleise	Dahs geh-lahy-zeh
platform	der Bahnsteig	Dehr bahn-stahyg
train	die Eisenbahn, der Zug	Dee ahy-zehn bahn, dehr-tsoog

The engine	die Lokomotive	Dee loh-koh-moh-tee-veh
car	der Eisenbahn-wagen	Dehr ahy-zehn-bahn-vah-gehn
compartment	Abteil	dee ahb-tahyl-oong
seat	der Sitz	Dehr zits
diner	der Speisewagen	Dehr shpay-zeh-vah-gehn
waiter	der Kellner	Dehr kehl-nehr
bill	die Rechnung	Dee rehh-noong
smoking car	für Raucher	Fuer-rou-hehr
No Smoking	Für Nichtraucher	Fuer niht-rou-hehr
The sleeping-car	der Schlafwagen	Dehr shlahf-vah-gehn
menu	die Speisekarte	Dee shpahy-zeh-kahr teh
chambermaid	das Stubenmädchen	Dahs shtoo-behn-maed-hehn
shoe shiner	der Schuhputzer	Dehr shoo-poot-tsehr

The arrival	Die Ankunft	Dee ahn-koonft
The custom house	das Zollamt	Dahs tsohl-ahmt
custom officer	der Zollbeamte	Dehr tsohil-beh-ahm-teh
money exchange	die Wechselstube	Dee vehh-sehl-stoo-beh.
rate of exchange	der Kurs	Dehr koors
taxi	das Taxi	Dehr tah-ksi
driver	der Chauffeur, Fahrer	Dehr shoh-fuer, fah-rehr
subway	die Untergrundbahn	Dee oon-tehr-groond-bahn
hotel	das Hotel	Dahs hoh-tehl
room	das Zimmer	Dahs tsim-mehr
single room	das Einzelzimmer	Dahs in-tsehl-tsim-mehr
double bed	das Doppelbett	Dahs doh-pehl-beht
A single bed	ein Einzelbett	Ahyn ahyn-tsehl-beht
The bed	das Bett	Dahs beht
married couple	das Ehepaar	dahs eh-eh-pahr
One person	eine Person	Ahyme-pehr-so-hn
My wife and myself	meine Frau und ich	Mahy-neh frou oond ih
With food	mit Verpflegung	Mit fehr-pfleh-goong
without food	ohne Verpflegung	O-neh fehr-pfleh goong
the elevator	der Fahrstuhl, Lift	Dehr fahr-stool, lift
bell boy	der Bote, Diener	Dehr boh-teh, dee-nehr
office,	das Bureau,	Dahs bue-roh,
safe	der Geldschrank	Dehr gehld-shrahnk

to deposit	deponieren	Deh-poh-nee-rehn
the receipt	der Empfangs-schein	Dehr ehm-pfahngs-shahyn
manager	der Verwalter, Leiter	Dehr fehr-vahl-tehr, lahy-tehr
landlord	der Hausherr	Dehr hous-hehr
landlady	die Hausfrau	Dee hous-frou
bill	die Rechnung	Dee rehh-noong
one day	ein Tag	Ahyn tahg
two days	zwei Tage	Tsvahy-tah-geh
one week	eine Woche	Ahyneh voh-heh

<u>On a ship</u>	<u>Am Schiff</u>	<u>Ahm shif</u>
To embark	einschiffen, sich einschiffen	(sih) ahyn-shi-fehn
To land	landen	Lahn-dehn
maritime insurance	Schiffsversi-cherung	Shifs-fehr-zi-heh-roong
inspector	Inspektor, Aufseher	In-spehk-tohr, owf-seh-hehr
the wharf	die Werft, der Kai..........	Dee vehrft, dehr keh
pier	der Landungs-platz	Dehr lahn-doongs-plahts
deck	das Deck	Dahs dehk
berth, cabin	die Koje, Kajüte, Kabine	Dee ko-yeh, kah-yue-teh, kah-bee-neh
steward	der Steward,	Dehr ste-ard,
purser	der Zahlmeister	Dehr tsahl-mis-ahy-tehr
the change (silver)	das Kleingeld	Dahs kliahyn-gehld
The Captain	der Kapitän	Dehr kah-pee-taen
chaplain	der Kaplan	Dehr kah-plahn
chapel	die Kapelle	Dee Kah-peh-leh
physician	der Arzt	Dehr ahrtst
nurse	die Kranken-schwester	Dee krahn-kehn-shvehs-tehr
the pilot	der Lotse, Pilot	Dehr lot-seh, pee-lohl
mate	der Maat	Dehr maht
stoker	der Heizer	Dehr hahy-tsehr
passenger	der Reisende	Dehr rahy-zehn-deh
crew	die Mannschaft	Dee mahn-shahft
cook	der Koch	Dehr koh
dining-room	der Speisesaal	Dehr shpahyzeh-dehr zahl
hall	die Halle, der Saal	Dee hah-leh, dehr zahl

the lounge	dor Gesellschafts raum	Dehr geh-zehl-shahfs-roum
deck chair, chaise-longe	der Liegestuhl	Dehr lee-geh-stool
gong	der Gong	Dehr gohng
boat	das Boot	Dahs boht
lifeboat	das Rettungs-boot	Dahs reht-toongs-boht
lifebelt	der Rettungs-gürtel	Dehr reht-toongs-guer-tehl
bow	der Bug	Dehr boog
port	der Hafen,	Dehr Hah-fehn,
mast	der Mast	Dehr mahst
engine room	der Machinen-raum	Dehr mah-shee nehn-roum
engineer	der Ingenieur	Dehr ein-dshehn-noe
pump	die Pumpe	Dee poom-peh
hose	der Schlauch	Dehr shlouh
rope	das Seil	Dahs zahyl
sail	das Segel	Dahs zeh-gehl
sailor	der Seemann, Matrose	Dehr zeh-mahn, mah-troh-zeh
flag	die Flagge, Fahne	Dee flah-geh, fah-neh
The head wind	der Gegenwind	Dehr Geh-gehn-vind
a fair wind	ein günstiger Wind	In guens-ti-gehr vind
the whistle	die Pfeife	Dee pfahy-feh
high sea	das hohe Meer	Dahs ho-eh mehr
swell sea	das schwellende Meer	Dahs shveh-lehn-deh mehr
rough sea	das bewegte Meer	Dahs beh-vehg-teh mehr
breakfast time	die Frühstücks-stunde	Dee frue stueks-shtoon-deh
lunch time	die Mittagszeit	Dee mit-tahgs-tsahyt
supper time	die Abendmahl-Stunde	Dee ah-behnd-mahl-shtoon-deh
seasickness	die Seekrankheit	Dee zeh-krahnk-hahyt
I am seasick	ich bin seekrank	Ih bein zeh-krahnk
the speed	die Schnelligkeit	Dee shnehl-leig-kahyt
log-line	die Loglinie	Dee lohg-li-nee-eh
knot	die Seemcile, der Knoten	Dee zeh-mahy-leh, dehr knoh-tehn
rudder, helm	das Steuerruder	Dahs stoy-chr-roo-dehr
helmsman	der Steuermann	Dehr stoy-ehr-mahn
compass	der Kompass	Dehr kohm-pahs

hold of a ship	der Schiffsraum	Dehr shifs-roum
the freight	die Fracht	Dee frahht
cargo	die Ladung	Dee lah-doong
manifest	das Ladungsver-zeichnis	Dahs lah-doongs fehr-tsahyh-nis
crane	der Krahn	Dehr krahn
warehouse	das Lagerhaus	Dahs lah-gehr-hous
damage	der Schaden	Dehr shah-dehn
insurance policy	die Versiche-rungs-Police	Dee fehr-zi-heh-roongs-poh-lit-tseh
claim	die Forderung	Dee fohr-deh-roong
littoral	das Ufer, Küsten-land	Dahs oo-fehr, kues-tehn-lahnd
latitude	geographische Breite	Geh-oh-grah-phee-shen brahy-teh
The course of a ship	der Schiffskurs	Dehr shifs-koors
distance	die Entfernung	Dee ehnt-fehr-noong
coast	die Küste	Dee kues-teh
to stop at a port	in einem Hafen anlegen	In ahy-nehm hah-fehn ahn-leh-gehn
the towboat	der Schlepper	Dehr shlehp-pehr
to anchor	ankern, anlegen	Ahn-kehrn, ahn-leh-gehn
to unload	ausladen	Ous-lah-dehn
the tonnage	der Tonnen-gehalt	Dehr toh-nehn-geh-hahlt
to reship	wieder einschiffen	Vee-dehr ahyn-shi-fehn
the shipwreck	der Schiffbruch	Dehr shif-brooh
Motoring	Automobilfahren	Ou-toh-moh-bil-fah-rehn
The steering wheel	das Steuerrad	Dahs stoy-ehr-rahd
to drive	zu fahren, lenken	Tsoo fah-rehn, lehn-kehn
to start	anfangen, anfahren	Ahn-fahn-gehn, ahn-fah-rehn
the start	der Anfang, Start	Dehr ahn-fahng, start
the starting gear	der Antrieb	Dehr ahn-treeb
the gear-shift	die Übersetzung	Dee ue-behr-zeht-tsoong
the brakes	die Bremsen	Dee brehm-zehn
starting handle	der Antriebhebel	Dehr ahn-treeb-heh-behl
speedometer	der Meilenzähler	Dehr mahy-lehn-tsae-lehr

a low speed	langsam fahren	Lahng-zsahm fah-rehn
a full speed	schnell fahren	Shnehl fah-rehn
The wheels	die Räder	Dee rae-dehr
rims	die Reifen	Dee rahy-fehn
tires	die Radreifen	Dee rahd-rahy-fehn
pneumatic tires	die Luftreifen Pheumatic	Dee looft-rahy-fehn, Pnoe-mah-tik
to inflate a tire	den Reifen aufblasen	Dehn rahy-fehn ouf-blah-zehn
the air pressure	der Luftdruck	Dehr looft-drook
exhaust pipes	der Auspuff	Dehr ous-poof
mud guard	der Kotfänger	Dehr koht-faen-gehr
windshield	der Windschild	Dehr vind-shild
doors	die Türen	Dee tue-rehn
windows	die Fenster	Dee fehns-tehr
hood	das Autodach	Dahs ou-toh-dahh
seats	die Sitze	Dee zi-tseh
gasoline	das Gasolin	Dahs gah-zoh-lin
garage	die Garage	dee gah-rahd-sheh
lifting jack	die Handwinde	De hahnd-vin-deh
wrenches	die Ramme	Dee rah-meh
screws	die Schrauben	Dee shrou-behn
screwdriver	der Schrauben-zieher	Dehr shrou-behn-tsee-ehr
nut	die Schrauben-mutter	Dee shrou-behn-moot-tehr
battery	die Batterie	Dee bah-teh-ree
to charge	zu laden	tsoo Lah-dehn
the mechanic	der Mechaniker	Dehr meh-xhah-ni-kehr
spark plug	der Zünder	Dehr tzuen-dehr
wires	die Drähte	Dee drae-teh
magnet	der Magnet	Dehr mahg-neht
motor	der Motor	Dehr moh-tohr
accelerator	der Beschleuniger	Dehr beh-shloy-ni-gehr
axle	die Achse	Dee ahh-seh
clutch	die Kuppelung	Dee koo-peh-loong
The clutch	der Griff	Dehr grif
cylinders	die Cylinder	Dee tsi-lin-dehr
dynamo	der Dynamo	Dehr di-nah-moh
ventilator	der Ventilator	Dehr vehn-ti-lah-tohr
oil pump	die Oelpumpe	Dee oel-poom-peh
radiator	der Heiz-apparat	Dehr hahyts-ah-pah-raht
propeller shaft	der Propeller-schaft	Dehr proh-peh-lehr-shahft

the switch	der Umschalter	Dehr oom-shahl-tehr
chassis	das Wagengestell	Dahs vah-gehn-geh-stehl
lamp	die Lampe	Dee lahm-peh
piston	die Pumpenstange	Dee poom-pehn-shtahn-geh
gear	das Getriebe	Dahs geh-tree-beh
valve	das Ventil, die Klappe	Dahs vehn-teel, dee klah-peh
speed gear	die stärkere Triebkraft	Dee staer-keh-reh treeb-krahft
oil tank	der Oelbehälter	Dehr oel-beh-hael-tehr
gas tank	der Gasolinbehälter	Dehr gah-zoh-lin-beh-hael-tehr
plug	der Zapfen	Dehr tsah-pfehn
filling station	die Tankstelle	Dee tahnk-shteh-leh
motor high-way	die Auto-strasse, -bahn	Dee ou-toh-shtrah-seh, -bahn
highway	die Autobahn	Dee ou-to-bahn
country road	die Landstrasse	Dee lahnd-shtrah-seh
"Danger", "Caution"	"Gefahr", Vorsicht"	"Geh-fahr", "Fohr-ziht"
"Slow"	"Langsam"	"Lahng-sahm"
the traffic signals	die Verkehrssignale	Dee fehr-kehrs-sig-nah-leh
curve	die Krümmung	Dee krue-moong
Watch out	"Achtung"	"Ah-toong"
"Keep to the right"	"Rechts halten"	"Rehhts hahl-tehn"
"Keep to the left"	"Links halten"	"Links-hahl-tehn"
Slippery	schlüpfrig	Shlue-pfrig
Steep road	steile Strasse	shtahy-leh shtrah-seh
"Stop"	"Halt"	"Hahlt"
"Go", Forward	"Vorwärts"	"Fohrvaerts"
The map	die Landkarte	Dee lahnd-kahr-teh

<u>The airplane</u>	<u>Das Flugzeug</u>	<u>Dahs Floog-tsoyg</u>
The airfield	das Flugfeld	Dahs floog-fehld
airport	der Flugplatz	Dehr floog-plahts
to take off	aufsteigen	Ohf-stahy-gehn
to land	landen	Lahn-dehn
to fly	fliegen	Flee-gehn
the flight	der Flug	Dehr floog
pilot	der Pilot	Dehr pi-loht
aerial	die Antenne	Dee ahn-tehn-neh
altitude	die Höhe	Dee hoe-eh

	der Höhen-messer	Dehr hoe-hehn-mehs-sehr
the hangar	der Flugzeug-schuppen	Dehr floog-tsoyg-shoop-pehn
to broadcast	fernsprechen	Fehrn-shpreh-hehn
the cockpit	die Piloten-kammer	Dee pi-loh-tehn-kah-mehr
control lever	der Balanzhebel	Dehr bah-lahnts-heh-behl
accelerometer	der Geschwin-digkeits-messer	Dehr geh-shvin-dig-kahyts-mehs-sehr
accelerator	der Beschleu-niger	Dehr beh-shloy-ni-gehr
chart	die Flugtabelle	Dee floog-tah-behl-leh
compass	der Kompass	Dehr kohm-pahs
to dive	tauchen	Tou-hehn
to glide	gleiten	Glahy-tehn
dirigible	lenkbar	Lehnk-bahr
to descend	herabsteigen, sinkon	Hehr-ahb-stahy-gehn, zih-kehn
flatten out	ausgleichen	Ous-glahy-hehn
The drag wire	das Schlepptau	Dahs shlehp-tou
exhaust pipe	das Auspuffrohr	Dahs Ous-poof-rohr
elevator	der Elevator	Dehr eh-leh-vah-tohr
fuselage	der Rahmen	Dehr rah-mehn
gap	die Schlucht, Kluft	Dee shlooht, klooft
landing wire	das Landkabel	Dahs lahnd-kah-behl
landing gear	der Unterbau	Dehr oon-tehr-bou
propeller	der Propeller	Dehr proh-peh-lehr
observer	der Beobachter	Dehr beh-oh-bahh tehr
radio	der Funksender, das Radio	Dehr foonk-sehn-dehr, dahs rah-dio
radiogonio-meter	der Richtungs-weiser	Dehr rih-toongs vahy-zehr
rudder	das Steuer	Dahs stoy-ehr
rudder post	der Steuer-posten	Dehr stoy-ehr-pohs-tehn
to spin	wirbeln, drehen	Vir-behln, dreh-ehn
the spin	der Sturzflug	Dehr shstoorts-floog
starting course	der Anlauf	Dehr ahn-louf
start	der Start	Dehr shtahrt
stabilizer	die Kippsiche-rung	Dee kip-zi-heh-roong
seat	der Sitz	Dehr zits
skid	der Hemmschuh	Dehr hehm-shooh

the tail	das Hinterteil	Dahs hin-tehr-tahy
tail unit	der Endemecha-nismus	Dehr ehnd-meh-hah-neez-moos
wings	die Flügel, Seiten	Dee flue-gehl, zahy-tehn
wing loading	die Seitenladung	Dee-zahy-tehn-lah-doong
wing resistance	der Seitenwider-stand	Dehr zahy-tehn-vi-dehr-shtahnd
radio operator	der Radio-Operateur	Dehr rah-di-o-Opeh-rah-toer

<u>The city</u>	<u>Die Stadt</u>	<u>Dee shtaht</u>
The street	die Strasse, Gasse	Dee shtrah-seh, gah-seh
avenue	die breite Strasse	Dee brahy-teh shtrah-seh
square	der Platz	Dehr plahts
park	der Park, die Anlagen	Dehr pahrk, dee ahn-lah-gehn
traffic	der Verkehr	Dehr fehr-kehr
drive	der Fahrweg	Dehr fahr-vehg
car	das Auto der Wagen	Dahs ou-to, Dehr vah-gehn
bus	der Autobus	Dehr ou-toh-boos
trolley, street car	die Strassen-bahn	Dee shtrah-sehn-bahn
subway	die Untergrund-bahn	Dee oon-tehr-groond-bahn
district, ward	der Bezirk	Dehr beh-tsirk
house, houses	das Haus, die Häuser	Dahs hous, dee hoy-zehr
block	das Häuservier-eck	Dahs hoy-zehr-feer-ehk
policeman	der Polizist	Dehr poh-li-tzist
police head-quarters	das Polizeiamt	Dahs poh-li-tsahy ahmt
sidewalk	das Trottoir	Dahs troh-toh-ahr
street lights	die Strassenbe-leuchtung	Dee shtrah-sehn-beh-loyh-toong
corner	die Strassenecke	Dee shtrah-sehn-eh-keh
building	das Gebäude	Dahs geh-boy-deh
main entrance	der Hauptein-gang	Dehr houpt-ahyn-gahng
skyscrapers	die Wolkenkratzer	Dee vohl-kehn-krah-tsehr

the business section	das Geschäfts-viertel	Dahs geh-shaefts-feer-tehl
store	das Geschäft, der Laden	Dahs geh-shaeft, dehr lah-dehn
grocery	die Spezerei-(Kol-onial)waren-handlung	Dee shpeh-tseh-rahy-(koh-loh-nee-ahl-)vah-rehn-hahnd-loong
drug-store	die Drogerie	Dee droh-geh-ree
pharmacy	die Apotheke	Dee ah-poh-teh-keh
department store	das Warenhaus	Dahs vah-rehn-hous
lamp post	der Laternen-pfahl	Dehr lah-tehr-nehn-pfahl
pavement	das Pflaster	Dahs pflahs-tehr
The hydrant	der Hydrant	Dehr hi-drahnt
school	die Schule	Dee shoo-leh
library	die Bibliothek	Dee bib-li-oh-tehk
market	der Markt	Dehr mahrkt
University	die Universität	Dee oo-ni-vehr-zi-taet
Post Office	das Postamt	Dahs pohst-ahmt
Telephone	das Telephon, der Fern-sprecher	Dahs teh-leh fhohn Dehr fehrn-shpreh-hehr
Telegraph	der Telegraph	Dehr teh-leh-grahf
Church	die Kirche	Dee kir-heh
Convent	das Kloster	Dahs klohs-tehr
Hospital	das Spital	Dahs shpi-tahl
Bank	die Bank	Dee bahnk
Factory	die Fabrik	Dee fah-brik
(work) shop	die Werkstatt	Dee vehrk-shtaht
Museum	das Museum	Dahs moo-zeh-oom
City Hall	das Rathaus	Dahs raht-hous
monument	das Denkmal	Dahs dehnk-mahl
cemetery	der Friedhof	Dehr freed-hof
barracks (mil.)	die Kaserne	Dee kah-zehr-neh
jail	das Gefängnis	Dahs geh-faeng-nis
bar	die Schenke	Dee shehn-keh
night club	das Nachtlokal	Dahs nahht-loh kahl
restaurant	das Restaurant	Dahs rehs-toh-rahnt
theatre	das Theater	Dahs teh-ah-tehr
opera	die Oper, das Opernhaus	Dee oh-pehr, dahs O-pehrn-hous
movies	Kino	Ki-noh

fountain	der Brunnen	Dehr broon-nehn
music hall	das Konzerthaus	Dahs kohn-tsehrt hous
coffee room	das Kaffeehaus	Dahs kah-feh hous
racetrack	der Rennplatz	Dehr rehn-plats
trolley station	die Haltestelle	Dee hahl-teh-shteh-leh
guide	der Fremdenführer	Dehr frehm-dehn-fue-rehr
interpreter	der Dolmetscher	Dehr dohl-meht-shehr
Street Signs	Strassenzeichen	Strahs-sehn-tsahy-hehn
Watch out, wet paint.	Achtung, frisch gestrichen	Ahh-toong, frish geh-shtree-hehn
Dogs not allowed.	Hunde, verboten.	Hoon-deh, fehr-boh-tehn.
Entrance, Exit.	Eingang, Ausgang.	Ahyn-gahng, Ous-gahng.
Danger.	Gefahr.	Geh-fahr.
Silence.	Ruhe.	Roo-eh.
Admission free.	Eintritt frei.	ahyn-tritt frahy
No smoking.	Rauchen verboten.	Roh-hehn fehr boh-tehn.
No spitting.	Spucken verboten.	Shpoo-kehn fehr-boh-tehn.
For smokers.	Für Raucher	Fuer Rou-hehr.
Furnished rooms for rent.	Möblierte Zimmer zu vermieten.	Moe-bleer-teh tsim-mehr tsoo fehr-mee-tehn.
Push, pull	Stossen, Ziehen.	Stoh-sehn, Tsee-ehn.
Prohibited.	Verboten.	Fehr-boh-tehn.
For women.	Für Frauen.	Fuer Frou-ehn.
For men.	Für Männer.	Fuer Mae-nehr.
Fire alarm.	Feuersignal.	Foy-ehr-sig-nahl.
No trepassing.	Durchgang verboten.	Doorh-gahng fehr-boh-tehn.
Warning.	Warnung, Achtung.	Vahr-noong, Ahh-toong.
Waste.	Abfall.	Ahb-fahl.
Keep off the grass	Betreten des Rasens verboten.	Beh-treh-tehn dehs rah-zehns fehr-boh-tehn.
Trolley stop.	Haltestelle.	Hahl-teh-shtehl-leh.
Sports and Amusements	Sport und Vergnügen	Shpohrt oond fehr-gnue-gehn
The theatre...	das Theater	Dahs teh-ah-tehr
box office	die Theaterkasse	Dee teh-ah-ther-kahs-seh
seats	die Sitze	Dee zit-tse
movie	das Kino	Dahs kinoh
film	der Film	Dehr film

The show	die Vorstellung	Dee fohr-stehl-loong
performance	die Aufführung	Dee ouf-fue-roong
play	das Spiel	Dahs shpeel
stage	die Bühne	Dee bue-neh
season	die Saison	Dee seh-zohn
management	die Verwaltung	Dee fehr-vahl-toong
company	die Gesellschaft	Dee geh-zehl-shahft
artist	der Künstler	Dehr kuenst-lehr
actors	die Schauspieler	Dee shou-shpee-lehr
singer(s)	der (die) Sänger	Dehr (dee), zaen gehr
orchestra leader	der Dirigent	Dehr di-ri-gehnt
characterization	die Charakterie-sierung	Dee kah-rahk-teh-ree-zee-roong
soprano	die Sopranistin	Dee soh-prah-nis-tin
tenor	der Tenor	Dehr teh-nohr
baritone	der Bariton	Dehr bah-ri-tohn
contralto	die Altistin	Dee ahl-tis-tin
bass	der Bassist	Dehr bahs-sist
box	die Loge	Dee lohd-sheh
orchestra (seats)	die Orchester-Sitze	Dee ohr-kehs-tehr-zit-tseh
orchestra (mus.)	das Orchester	Dahs ohr-kehs-tehr
gallery	die Gallerie	Dee gah-leh-ree
circus	der Zirkus	Dehr tsir-koos
concert	das Konzert	Dahs kohn-tsehrt
ball room	der Tanzsaal	Dehr tahnts-zahl
dance	der Tanz der Reigen	Dehr tahnts, dehr rahy-gehn
to dance	tanzen	Tahn-tsehn
The dancer (m.)	der Tänzer	Dehr taen-tsehr
dancer (f.)	die Tänzerin	Dee taen-tseh-rin
ballet	das Ballett	Dahs bah-leht
entrance	der Eingang	Dehr ahyn-gahng
exit	der Ausgang	Dehr ous-gahng
ticket	die (Theater)-Karte	Dee (teh-ah-tehr) - kahr-teh
brass instruments	dic Blasinstrumente	Dee blahz-in-shtroo-mehn-teh
string instruments	die Saiteninstru-mente	Dee Zahy-tehn-in-shtroo-mehn-teh
piano	das Klavier	Dahs klah-veer
violin	die Violine, Geige	Dee vee-oh-lee-neh, gahy-geh
tamburine	das Tamburin	Dahs tahm-boo-rin
castanet	die Kastagnette	Dee kahs-tah-nyeh-teh

the band (mus.)	die Musikkapelle	Dee moosik-kahpehleh
game	das Spiel	Dahs shpeel
pastime, entertainment	die Unterhaltung	Dee oon-tehr-hahl-toong
chess	das Schachspiel	Dahs shahh-shpeel
checkers	das Damespiel	Dahs dah-mehn-shpeel
playing cards	die Spielkarten	Dee speel-kahr-tehn
to shuffle	die Karten mischen	Dee kahr-tehn-mi-shehn
to gamble	Für Geld spielen	Fuer gehld shpee lehn
the football	der Fussball	Dehr foos-bahl
team	die Spieler	Dee shpee-lehr
match	der Wettkampf	Dehr veht-kahmpf
ball	der Ball	Dehr bahl
tennis	das Tennis-Spiel	Dahs teh-nis-shpeel
billiards	das Billardspiel	Dahs bi-lahrd-shpeel
golf	das Golfspiel	Dahs golf-shpeel
basketball	basketball	baskesban
baseball	baseball	baseball
horse race	das Pferderennen	Dahs pfehr-deh-rehn-nehn
race - course	der Rennplatz	Dehr rehn-plahts
to bet	wetten	Veh-tehn
The boxing	das Boxen	Dahs boh-ksehn
training	das Trainieren	Dahs treh-nee-rehn
gymnasium	die Turnhalle	Dee toorn-hah-leh
athletics	die Körperübungen	Dee koer-pehr-ue-boon-gehn
swimming	das Schwimmen	Dahs shvi-mehn
mountain climbing	das Bergsteigen	Dahs behrg-shtahy-gehn
hunting	das Jagen, die Jagd	Dahs yah-gehn, dee yahgd
fishing	das Fischen	Dahs fi-shehn
rod	die Angelrute	Dee ahn-gehl-roo-teh
fishhook	die Angel	Dee ahn-gehl
bait	der Köder	Dehr koe-dehr
skating	das Schlittschuhlaufen	Dahs shlit-shoo-lou-fehn
skiing	das Skilaufen	Dahs skee-lou-fehn
to encamp	lagern	lah-gehrn
the encampment	das Lager	Dahs lah-gehr
the outing	der Ausflug	Dehr ous-floog
picnic	das Picknick, die Landpartie	Dahs pik-nik, dee lahnd-pahr-tee

Agriculture	Landwirtschaft	Lahnd-virt-shahft
The farm	das Landgut	Dahs lahnd-goot
farmer	der Landwirt	Dehr lahnd-virt
implements	die Wirtschafts-Geräte	Dee virt-shasfts-geh-rae-teh
plow	der Pflug	Dehr pfloog
tractor	der Traktor	Dehr trahk-tohr
harvester	die Mähmaschine	Dee mae-mah-shee-neh
drill or seeder	die Säemaschine	Dee zae-mah-shee-neh
cultivator	der Kultivator	Dehr kool-tee-vah-tohr
harrow	die Egge	Dee ehg-geh
spade	der Spaten	Dehr Shpah-tehn
thrasher	die Dreschmaschine	Dee drehsh-mah-shee-neh
hoe	die Hacke	Dee hah-keh
pick	die Spitzhacke	Dee shpits-hah-keh
shovel	die Schaufel	Dee shou-fehl
rake	der Rechen	Dehr reh-hehn
cattle raising	die Viehwirtschaft	Dee fee-virt-shahft
cattle	das Vieh	Dahs feeh
flock, herd, drove	die Herde	Dee hehr-deh
a drove of mules	eine Maultierherde	Ahy-neh-moul-teer hehr-deh
a flock of sheep	eine Schafherde	Ahy-neh-shahf-hehr-deh
a herd of swines	eine Schweineherde	Ahy-neh-shvahy-neh-hehr-deh
a pack of hounds	ein Hundekoppel	Ahy-hoon-deh-koh-pehl
the shepherd	der Hirte, Schäfer	Dehr hir-teh-shae-fehr
stable	der Stall	Dehr shtahl
barn	die Scheune	Dee shoy-neh
pigpen	der Schweinestall	Dehr shvahy-neh-stahl
hencoop	das Hühnerhaus	Dahs hue-nehr-hous
yard	der Hof	
drinking trough	der Wassertrog	Dehr vahs-sehr-trohg
a planted field	ein bestelltes Feld	Ahy beh-shtehl-tehs-fehld
untilled land	unbebautes Land	Oon-beh-bou-tehs-lahnd
The kitchen garden	der Gemüse-garten	Dehr geh-mue-zeh-gahr-tehn
irrigated land	künstlich bewässertes land	Kuenst-lih-beh-vaes-sehr-tehs-lahnd
the sugar plantation, planting	die Zuckerpflanzung	Dee tsoo-kehr-pflahn-tsoong
sugar crop	die Zuckerernte	Dee tsook-kehr-ehrn-teh

the coffee plantation, planting	die Kaffeepflanzung	Dee kah-feh-pflahn-tsoong
grove	der Hain	Dehr hahyn
orchard	der Obstgarten	Dehr ohbst-gahr-tehn
windmill	die Windmühle	Dee vind-meu-leh
well	der Brunnen	Dehr broon-nehn
spring, source	die Quelle	Dee kveh-leh
to water, irrigate	künstlich bewässern	Kuenst-lih beh-vaes-sehrn
the water pump	die Wasserpumpe	Dee vahs-sehr-poom-peh
water pipe	die Wasserrohre	Dee vahs-sehr-roe-reh
wheat	der Weizen	Dehr vahy-tsehn
wheat field	das Weizenfeld	Dahs vahy-tsehn-fehld
corn	der Roggen	Dehr roh-gehn
maize	der Mais	Dehr mahys
barley	die Gerste	Dee Gehrs-teh
oats	der Hafer	Dehr hah-fehr
buckwheat	der Buchweizen	Dehr booh-vahy-tsehn
clover	der Klee	Dehr kleh
furrow	die Furche	Dee foor-heh
grain	das Getreide	Dahs geh-trahy-deh
seed	der Same	Dehr zah-meh
straw	das Stroh	Dahs shtroh
hay	das Heu	Dahs hoy
harvester, crop	die Ernte	Dee ehrn-teh
sheaf, (sheaves)	die Garbe, das Bündel	Dee gahr-beh, dahs buen-dehl
sickle	die Sichel	Dee zi-hehl
grass mower	der Grassmäher	Dehr grahs-mae-ehr
an ear of corn	ein Maiskolben	Ahy mahys-kohl-behn
the dairy	die Milchwirtschaft	Dee milh-virt-shahft
beemaster	der Bienenzüchter	Dehr bee-nehn-tsueh-tehr
beehive	der Bienenstock	Dehr bee-nehn-shtohk
bee	die Biene	Dee bee-neh

Commercial Terms	Geschäftsausdrücke	Geh-shaefts-ous-drue-keh
To buy	zu kaufen	Tsoo kou-fehn
to sell	verkaufen	Tsoo fehr-kou-fehn
mortgage	verpfänden	Tsoo fehr-pfaen-dehn
import	einführen	Tsoo ahyn-fueh-rehn
export	ausführen	Tsoo ous-fue-rehn
trade	handeln	Tsoo hahn-dehln
the merchandise	die Ware	Dee vah-reh

the business	das Geschäft	Dahs geh-shaeft
market	der Markt	Dehr mahrkt
customer	der Kunde	Dehr koon-reh
salesman	der Verkäufer	Dehr fehr-koy-fehr
traveling salesman	der Reisende	Dehr rahy-zehn-deh
agent	der Agent	Dehr ah-gehnt
article(s)	der (die) Warenposten	Dehr (dee) vah-rehn-pos-tehn
goods	die Waren	Dee vah-rehn
branch office	die Filiale	Dee fi-lee-ah-leh
consignment	die Übersendung	Dee ue-behr-zehn-doong
cash	die Barzahlung	Dee bahr-tsah-loong
payment	die Zahlung	Dee tsah-loong
demand	die Nachfrage	Dee nahh-frah-geh
competition	die Konkurrenz	Dee kohn-koo-rehnts
steamship line	die Schiffahrts-Gesellschaft	Dee shi-fahrts-geh-zehl-shahft
shipment	die Verladung	Dee fehr-lah-doong
risk	das Risiko	Dahs ree-zee-koh
policy	die Police	Dee poh-lee-tseh
transportation	der Transport	Dehr trahns-pohrt
contract	der Vertrag	Dehr fehr-trahg
order	der Auftrag	Dehr Ouf-trahg
loan	die Anleihe	Dee ahn-lahy-eh
interest	die Zinsen	Dee tsin-zehn
The benefit	der Nutzen	Dehr noot-tsehn
loss	der Verlust, Schaden	Dehr fehr-loost, shah-dehn
quality	Qualität	Kvah-li-taet
price	der Preis	Dehr prahys
rise of price	die Preissteigerung	Dee prahys-shtahy-geh-roong
reduction	die Herabsetzung	Dee heh-rahb-zeht-tsoong
discount	der Rabatt	Dehr rah-baht
estimate	der Voranschlag	Dehr fohr-ahn-shlahg
draft	die Tratte	Dee traht-teh-
duty tariff	der Zoll	Dehr tsohl
balance	die Bilanz, der Saldo	Dee bi-lahnts-dehr sahl-doh
balance sheet	der Rechnungs-abschluss	Dehr rehh-noongs-ahb-shloos
statement	der Rechnungs-auszug	Dehr rehh-noongs-ous-tsoog

the check	der Scheck	Dehr shehk
check-book	das Scheckbuch	Dahs shehk-booh
stock-exchange	die Börse	Dee boer-zeh
stock, securities	die Wertpapiere	Dee vehrt-pah-pee-reh
shares	die Aktien	Dee ahk-tsee-ehn
bonds	die Schuldscheine	Dee shoold-shahy-neh
broker	der Makler	Dehr mahk-lehr
yearbook	das Jahrbuch	dahs yahr-booh
cartage	die Transport-kosten	Dee trahns-port-kohs-tehn
delivery	die Lieferung	Dee lee-feh-roong
on terms to supply	zu versehen, versorgen	tsoo fehr-zeh-ehn, fehr-zoh-gehn
to check	kontrollieren	tsoo kohn-troh-lee-rehhn
to verify	bestätigen	tsoo beh-stae-ti-gehn
to honor a draft	eine Tratte begleichen	ahy-neh traht-teh beh-glahy-hehn
to acknowledge receipt	den Empfang bestätigen	Dehn ehm-pfahng beh-shtae-ti-gehn
to pay in advance	im Voraus be-zahlen	Im fohr-ous beh-tsah-lehn
to settle an account	eine Rechnung begleichen	ahy-neh rehn-noong beh glahy-lh-ehn
to draw on	ziehen auf...	Tsee-ehn ouf
Part payment	Teilzahlung	Tiahyl-tsah-loong
The transfer	die Übertragung	Dee ue-behr-trah goong
rent	die Miete, Pacht	Dee mee-teh, pahht
settlement	die Ausgleichung	Dee ous-glahy-xoong
wholesale	en gros	ahn groh
	der Grosshandel	Dehr grohs-hahn-dehl
retail	der Kleinhandel	Dehr klahyn-hahn-dehl
insurance	die Versicherung	Dee fehr-zi-heh-roong
bankruptcy	der Bankrott	Dehr bahnk-roht
proxy	der Stellver-treter	Dehr stehl-fehr-treh-tehr
attorney	der Anwalt	Dehr ahn-vahlt
to endorse	überweisen	Ue-behr-vahy-zehn
the Board of Directors	der Verwaltungs-rat	Dehr fehr-vahl-toongs-raht
the manager	der Leiter	Dehr layh-tehr
secretary	der Sekretär, die Sekretärin	Dehr seh-kreh-taer, dee seh-kreh-tae-rin

the typist	der (die) Maschinen-schreiber (in)	Dehr (dee) mah-shin-ehn-shrahy-behr
stenographer	der (die) Stenograph (in)	Dehr (dee) steh-noh-grahph (en)
president	der Präsident	Dehr prae-zi-dehnt
bank	die Bank	Dee bahnk
desk	der Schreibtisch	Dehr shrahyb-tish
rate of exchange	der Kurs	Dehr koors
liquidation	die Liquidierung	Dee lik-vi-dee-roong

Professions -, Trades	Berufe-, Gewerbe	Beh-roo-feh-Geh-vehr-beh
The priest	der Priester, Pfarrer	Dehr pree-stehr, pfah-rehr
professor	der Professor	Dehr proh-feh-sohr
teacher	der Lehrer	Dehr leh-rehr
doctor, physician	der Arzt, Doktor	Dehr ahrtst,
surgeon	der Chirurg	Dehr Hi-roorg
dentist	der Zahnarzt	Dehr tsahn-ahrtst
optician	der Optikor	Dehr ohp-ti-kehr
specialist	der Spezialarzt	Dehr speh-tsi-ahl-ahrtst
judge	der Richter	Dehr rih-tehr
magistrate	der Friedens-richter	Dehr free-dehns-rih-tehr
lawyer	der Anwalt	Dehr ahn-vahlt
journalist	der Journalist	Dehr Dshoor-nahl-ist
reporter	der Bericht- -erstatter	Dehr beh-rih ehr-shtaht-tehr
engineer	der Ingenieur	Dehr in-dsheh-nee-oer
architect	der Baumeister der Architekt	Dehr bou-mahy-stehr, ahr-hi-tehkt
aviator	der Flieger	Dehr flee-gehr
chemist	der Chemiker	Dehr heh-mi-kehr
pharmacist	der Apotheker	Dehr ah-poh-teh-kehr
artist	der Künstler	Dehr kuen-stlehr
painter	der Maler	Dehr mah-lehr
sculptor	der Bildhauer	Dehr bild-hou-ehr
author	der Verfasser, Schriftsteller	Dehr fehr-fah-sehr, shrift-stehl-lehr
poet	der Dichter	Dehr dih-tehr
composer	der Komponist	Dehr kohm-poh-nist
publisher	der Verleger	Dehr fehr-leh-gehr
editor	der Redakteur	Dehr reh-dahk-toer
musician	der Musiker	Dehr moo-zi-kehr

the actor	der Schauspieler	Dehr shou-spee-lehr
actress	die Schauspielerin	Dee shou-spee-leh-rin
student	der Studierende, Student	Dehr shtoo-dee-rehn-deh, shtoo-dehnt
The banker(s)	der Bankier, die Bankiers	Dehr bahn-kee-eh, dee bahn-kee-ehs
bookkeeper(s)	der (die) Buch-halter	Dehr (dee) booh hahl-tehr
merchant(s)	der Kaufmann, die Kaufmänner	Dehr kouf-mahn dee kouf-maen-nehr
businessman	der Geschäfts-mann	Dehr geh-shaefts mahn
the businessmen	die Geschäfts-leute	Dee geh-shaefts-loy-teh
cashier (m.,f.)	der (die) Kassierer (in)	Dehr (dee) kahs-see rehr (in)
typist (m.f.)	der (die) Maschinen-schreiber (in)	Dehr (dee) mah-shi-nehn-shrahy-behr (in)
Stenographer (m. f.)	der (die) Stenograph (in)	Dehr shteh-noh-grahf
bookseller (s)	der (die) Buchhändler	Dehr (dee) booh haend-lehr
jeweler	der Juwelier	Dehr yoo-veh-leer
goldsmith	der Goldschmied	Dehr ghold-shmeed
florist	der Blumenhändler	Dehr bloo-mehn-haend-lehr
tailor	der Schneider	Dehr shnahy-dehr
smith	der Schmied	Dehr shmeed
caster (s)	der (die) Giesser	Dehr (dee) gees-sehr
printer (s)	der (die) Drucker	Dehr (dee) droo-kehr
glazier (s)	der (die) Glaser	Dehr (dee) glah-zehr
carpenter	der Zimmermann	Dehr tsi-mehr mahn
mailman	der Briefträger, Postbote	Dehr breef-trae-gehr pohst-boh-teh
decorator	der Dekorateur	Dehr deh-koh-rah-toer
contractor	der (Bau-) Unter-nehmer	Dehr (bou) oon-tehr-neh-mehr
mason (s)	der (die) Maurer	Dehr (dee) mou-rehr
cook (m.f.)	der Koch, die Köchin	Dehr koh. dee koe-heen
welder	der Schweisser	Dehr shvahy-sehr
hair dresser, barber	der Friseur	Dehr fri-zoer
stone cutter	der Steinhauer	Dehr stahyn-hou-ehr
The plumber	der Installateur	Dehr in-shtah-lah-toer

the locksmith	der Schlosser	Dehr shloh-sehr
electrician	der Elektriker	Dehr eh-lehk-tri-kehr
cabinet maker	der Kunst-tischler	Dehr koonst-tish lehr
mechanic	der Mechaniker	Dehr meh-hah-ni-kehr
weaver	der Weber	Dehr veh-behr
baker	der Bäcker	Dehr bae-kehr
milkman	der Milchmann	Dehr milh-mahn
bartender	der Schank-bursche	Dehr shahnk-boor-sheh
butcher	der Metzger	Dehr mehts-gehr
grocer	der Spezerei-(kolonial-) waren-Händler	Dehr shpehtseh-rahy-(koh-loh-nee-ahl-) wah-rehn-haend-lehr
clerk	der Beamte	Dehr beh-ahm-teh
helper	der Gehilfe	Dehr geh-hil-feh
miner	der Bergmann	Dehr behrg-mahn
fireman	der Feuerwehr-mann	Dehr foy-ehr-vehr-mahn
waiter	der Kellner	Dehr kehl-nehr
shoe-shiner	der Schuhputzer	Dehr shoo-poo-tsehr
saddler	der Sattler	Dehr zaht-lehr
miller	der Müller	Dehr mue-lehr
master, expert	der Meister	Dehr mahys-tehr
shoemaker	der Schuhmacher	Dehr shoo-mah-hehr
bookbinder	der Buchbinder	Dehr booh-bin-dehr
watchman	der Nacht-wächter	Dehr nahht-vaeh-tehr
street-cleaner	der Strassen-kehrer	Dehr shtrahs-sehn-keh-rehr
gardener	der Gärtner	Dehr gaert-nehr
roofer	der Dachdecker	Dehr dahh-deh-kehr
glass-blower	der Glasbläser	Dehr glahz-blae zehr

Legal terms	Rechtsaus-drücke	Rehhts-ous-druek-keh
The justice	die Gerechtig-keit	Dee geh-rehh-tig-kahyt
law	das Gesetz, das Recht	Dahs geh- zehts, dahs rehht
judge	der Richter	Dehr rih-tehr
trial	die Untersuchung	Dee oon-tehr-soo-hoong
trial, hearing	das Verhör	Dahs fehr-hoer
attorney	der Anwalt	Dehr ahn-vahlt
defendant	der Verteidiger	Dehr fehr-tahy-di-gehr

court of justice	der Gerichtshof	Dehr geh-rihts-hohf
tribunal	das Gericht	Dahs geh-riht
juvenile court	das Jugendgericht	Dahs yoo-gehnd-geh-rih
defendant	der Angeklagte, Schuldige	Dehr ahn-geh-klahg-teh, dehr shool-di-geh
criminal	der Verbrecher	Dehr fehr-breh-hehr
thief	der Dieb	Dehr deeb
robbery	der Diebstahl	Dehr deeb-stahl
guilt	die Schuld	Dee shoold
plaintiff	der Kläger	Dehr klae-gehr
witness	der Zeuge	Dehr tsoy-geh
claim	der Anspruch	Dehr ahn-shprooh
charge	die Anklage	Dee ahn-klah-geh
oath	der Eid	Dehr ahyd
perjury	der Meineid	Dehr mahyn-ahyd
proof, evidence	der Beweis	Dehr beh-vahys
arrest	die Verhaftung, der Arrest	Dee fehr-hahf-toong, dehr ah-rehst
verdict	der Ausspruch,	Dehr ous-shprooh
sentence	das Urteil	dahs oor-tahyl
bail	die Bürgschaft	Dee buerg-shahft
bondsman	der Bürge	Dehr buer-geh
The penalty, fine	die Strafe	Dee shtrah-feh
appeal	die Berufung	Dee beh-roo-foong
punishment	die Bestrafung	Dee beh-strah-foong
jail	das Gefängnis	Dahs geh-faeng-nis
	der Kerker	Dehr kehr-kehr
imprisonment	die Haft	Dee hahft
juror	der Geschworene	Dehr geh-shvoh-reh-neh
jury	das Geschworen-engericht	Dahs geh-shvoh-reh-nehn-geh-riht..
pardon	die Begnadigung	Dee beh-gnah-di-goong
summons	die gerichtliche Vorladung	Dee geh-riht-li-heh fohr-lah-doong
procedure	das Verfahren	Dahs fehr-fah-rehn
criminal case	der Kriminalfall	Dehr kri-mi-nalh-fahl

In the Post Office	Im Post-amte	Im Pohst-ahmteh
The post-office	das Postamt	Dahs pohst-ahmt
letter(s)...	der Brief, die Briefe	Dehr breef, dee bree-feh
post card(s)..	die Postkarte (n)	Dee pohst-kahr-teh(n)
address	die Addresse,	Dee ahd-drehs-seh
date	das Datum	Dahs dah-toom
writing	das Schreiben	Dahs shrahy-behn

the copy	die Kopie	Dee ko-pee
paper	das Papier	Dahs pah-peer
ink	die Tinte	Dee tin-teh
inkstand	das Tintenfass	Dahs tin-tehn-fahs
pencil	der Bleistift	Dehr blahy-shtift
pen	die Schreibfeder	Dee shrahyb-feh-dehr
fountain pen	die Füllfeder	Dee fuel-feh-dehr
ballpoint pen	der Kugelschreiber	dehr Koo-gehl-shrahy-behr
envelope	der Briefumschlag	Dehr breef-oom-shlahg
stamp	die Marke	Dee mahr-keh
to deliver	liefern	Lee-fehrn
the delivery	die Lieferung	Dee lee-feh-roong
Special delivery	EILPOST	Ahyl-pohst
to register	einschreiben	Ahyn-shrahy-behn
destination	Bestimmungsort	Beh-shti-moongs-ohrt
Reply paid	Rückantwort bezahlt	Rueck-ahnt-vort beh-tsahlt
Parcel post	Paketpost	Pah-keht-pohst
the Postmaster	der Postmeister	Dehr pohst-mahy-stehr
printed matter	Drucksache	Droock-zah-heh
a money order	eine Geldanweisung	ahy-neh gehld-ahn-vahy-zoong
the telegram, cablegram	das Telegramm, die Depesche	Dahs teh-leh-grahm, dee deh-peh-sheh
to telegraph	telegraphieren	Teh-leh-grah-fee-rehn
the telephone	das Telephon, der Fernsprecher	Dahs teh-leh-fohn, dehr fehrn-shpreh-hehr
a telephone call	ein Telephon-anruf	Ahyn teh-leh-fohn-ahn-roof
the telephone number	die Telephon-Nummer	Dee teh-leh-fohn noo-mehr
the line	die Linie	Dee li-nee-eh
busy	besetzt	Beh-zehtst

Countries and Nations	Länder und Volker	Laen-dehr oond Foel-kehr
The country (ies)	das Land, die Länder	Dahs lahnd, dee laen-dehr
the native land	das Vaterland	Dahs fah-tehr-lahnd
the state	der Staat	Dehr shtaht
the empire	das Reich	Dahs rahyh
the republic	die Republik	Dee reh-poo-blik

the kingdom, monarchy	das Königreich, die Monarchie	Dahs koe-nigrahyh, dee moh-nahr-hee
Europe	Europa	eooy-roh-pah
the European (m., f.)	der (die) Europäer (in)	Dehr oy-roh-pae-ehr
Asia	Asien	Ahzee-ehn
the Asiatic (m., f.)	der Asiate, die Asiatin	Dehr ah-zee-ah-teh, dee ah-zee-ah-tin
Asia Minor	Kleinasien	Klahyn-ah-zee-ehn
Africa	Afrika	Ah-fri-kah
the African (m., f.)	der Afrikaner, (die) Afrikane-rin	Dehr ah-fri kah-nehr, dee ah-fri-kah-neh-rin
America	Amerika	Ah-meh-ri-kah
the American (m., f.)	der Amerikaner, die Amerikane-rin	Dehr ah-meh-ri kah-nehr Dee Ah-meh-ri-kah-neh-rin
North America	Nordamerika	Nord-ah-meh-ri-kah
South America	Südamerika	Sued-ah-meh-ri-kah
Central America	Zentral-Amerika	Tsehn-trahl-ah-meh-ri-kah
The United States	die Vereinigten Staaten	Dee fehr-ahy-nig-tehn shtah-tehn
Canada	Kanada	Kah-nah-dah
the Canadian (m., f.)	der(die) Kanadier (in)	Dehr (dee) kah-nah-dee-ehr (in)
the Germany	das Deutschland	Dahs doych-lahnd
the German (m., f.)	der Deutsche, die Deutsche	Dehr (dee) doy cheh
Australia	Australien	ous-trah-lee-ehn
the Australian (m., f.)	der (die) Australier (in)	Dehr (dee) ou-strah-lee-ehr (in)
Austria	Österreich	Oe-steh-rahyh
the Austrian (m., f.)	der (die) Österreicher	Dehr (dee)oe-stehr-rahy hehr (in)
England	das England	Dahs Ehng-lahnd
the Englishman	der Engländer,	Dehr ehng-laen-dehr
the Englishwoman	die Engländer (in)	dee ehng-laeh-deh-rin
Ireland	Irland	Ir-lahd
the Irishman (woman)	der (die) Irländer (in)	Dehr ir-laen-dehr
Scotland	Schottland	Shohtt-lahnd
the Scotsman	der Schotte	Dehr shoh-teh

France	Frankreich	Frahnk-rahy
the Frenchman	der Franzose	Dehr frahn-tsoh-zeh
the French-woman	die Französin	Dee frahn-tsoe-zin
Holland	Holland	Hol-lahnd
the Dutch (m.f.)	der(die) Holländer (in)	Dehr (dee) hoh-laen-dehr (in)
Prussia	Preussen	Proys-sehn
the Prussian (m.f.)	der Preusse, die Preussin	Dehr proys-seh, dee proys-sin
Sweden	Schweden	Shveh-dehn
the Swede (m.f.)	der Schwede, die Schwedin	Dehr shveh-deh, dee shveh-din
Norway	Norwegen	Nohr-veh-gehn
the Norwegian (m.,f.)	der (die) Norweger (in)	Dehr (dee) nohr-veh-gehr (in)
Denmark	Dänemark	Dae-neh-mahrk
the Dane (m.f.)	der Däne, die Dänin	Dehr dae-neh-, dee dae-nin
Finland	Finland	Fin-lahnd
the Fin (m.f.)	der Finne, die Finnin	Dehr fin-noh, dee fin-nin
Switzerland	die Schweiz	Dee shvahyts
the Swiss (m.f.)	der (die) Schweizer (in)	Dehr (dee) shvahy-tsehr (in)
Italy	Italien	I-tah-lee-ehn
the Italian (m.f.)	der Italiener, die Italierin	Dehr i-tah-lee-eh nehr
Spain	Spanien	Shpah-nee-ehn
the Spaniard (m.f.)	der (die) Spanier(in)	dehr (dee) spah-nee-ehr, (in)
Portugal	Portugal	Pohr-too-gahl
the Portuguese (m.f.)	der (die) Portugiese (in)	dehr pohr-too-gee-zeh
Russia	Russland	Roos-lahnd
a Russian (m.f.)	ein Russe, eine Russin	Ahyn roos-seh, ahy-neh roos-sin
Greece	Griechenland	Gree-hehn-lahnd
a Greek (m.f.)	ein Grieche, eine Griechin	Ahyn gree-heh, neh gree-hin
Turkey	die Türkei	Dee tuer-kahy
the Turk (m.f.)	der Türke, die Türkin	dehr tuer-keh, dee-tuer-kin
a Jew, a Jewess	ein Jude, eine Jüdin	Ahyn yoo-deh, ahyneh yue-din

Army and Navy	Armee und Marine	Ahrmeh oond mah-ree-neh
The Army	die Armee, das Heer	Dee ahr-meh, dahs hehr
the Navy	die Marine, Seemacht, die Kriegsflotte	Dee mah-ree-neh, zeh-mahht, dee kreegs-floh-teh
the Infantry	die Infantrie	Dee in-fahn-tree
the Riflemen	die Jäger	Dee yae-gehr
the Field Artillery	die Feldartillerie	De fehld-ahr-ti-leh-ree
Mountain Artillery	Gebirgsartillerie	Geh-birgs-ahr-ti-leh-ree
Coast Artillery	Küstenartillerie	Kue-stehn-ahr-tileh-ree
the Air-Force	die Luftwaffe	Dee looft-vahf-feh
the Engineers	die Technische Truppe	Dee tehh-ni-sheh troop-peh
the Medical Corps	die Sanitätsabteilung	Dee sah-ni-taets ahb-tahy-loong
the Signal Corps	das Signalkorps	Dahs sig-nahl-kohr
the Supply Corps	die Verpflegungsgruppe	Dee fehr-pflehgs groo-peh
Military Service	Militärdienst	Mi-li-taer-deesnt
the Volunteer	der Freiwillige	Dehr frahy-vi-li-geh
the Recruit	der Rekrut	Dehr reh-kroot
the Enlistment	die Anwerbung	Dee ahn-vehr-boong
the Flag	die Flagge	Dee flah-geh
the Oath	der Eid	Dehr Ahyd
the Barracks	die Kasernen	Dee Kah-zehr nehn
the Training	die Übung	Dee ue-boong
the Discipline	die Zucht, Ordnung	Dee tsooht-, ohrd-noong
the Garrison	die Garnison	Dee gahr-nee-zohn
the Parade	die Parade	Dee pah-rah-deh
the Band	die Militärkapelle	Dee mi-li-taer-kah-pehl-leh
the Troops	die Truppen	Dee troo-pehn
the Intelligence Service	der Geheimdienst	Dehr geh-hahym-deenst
the Deserter	der Fahnenflüchtige	Dehr fah-nehn-flueh-ti-geh
the Spy	der Spion	Dehr Shpi-ohn
.the escort	die Eskorte, das Geleit	Dee ehs-kor-teh, dahs geh-lahyt
The Section	die Sektion	Dee sehk-tsee-ohn
Patrol	die Patrouille	Dee pah-troo-leh
Detachment	die Abteilung	Dee ahb-tahy-loong
Company	die Kompanie	Dee kohm-pah-nee

Battalion	das Bataillon	Dahs bah-tah-yohn
Regiment	das Regiment	Dahs reh-gi-mehnt
Brigade	die Brigade	Dee bri-gah-deh
Division	die Division	Dee di-vi-zi-ohn
Army Corps	das Armeekorps	Dahs ahr-meh-kohr
Column	die Kolonne	Dee koh-loh-neh
Maneuver	das Manöver	Dahs mah-noe-vehr
Tactic	die Taktik, Kriegskunst	Dee tahk-tik, kreegs-koonst
Strategy	die Strategie, List	Dee strah-teh-gee, list
Staffs	der General-Stab	Dehr geh-neh-rahl-stahb
Vanguard	die Vorhut	Dee fohr-hoot
Rearguard	die Nachhut	Dee nahh-hoot
Battle	die Schlacht	Dee shlahht
Engagement	das Treffen	Dahs trehf-fehn
Struggle	der Kampf	Dehr kahmpf
Fight	das Gefecht	Dahs geh-fehht
Combatant(s)	der (die) Kämpfer	Dehr (dee) kaem-pfehr
Uniform	die Uniform	Dee oo-ni-fohrm
Equipment	die Ausrüstung	Dee ous-rues-toong
Rifle	die Büchse, das Gewehr	Dee bueh-seh, dahs geh-vehr
Bayonet	das Bajonett	Dahs bah-yoh-neht
Helmet	der Helm	Dehr Hehlm
Gas mask	die Gasmaske	Dee gahz-mahs-keh
Cartridge	die Patrone	Dee pah-trohneh
Bullet	die Kugel,	Dee koo-gehl
Cannon	die Kanone	Dee kah-noh-neh
Mortar	der Mörser	Dehr moer-sehr
The Machine gun	das Maschinen-gewehr	Dahs mah-shee nehn-geh-vehr
Battery	die Batterie	Dee bah-teh-ree
Gunner	der Kanonier	Dehr kah-noh-ner
Fortification	die Festung	Dee feh-stoong
Sentry	die Schildwache	Dee shild-vah-heh
Trenches	die Schützen-graben	Dee shue-tsehn-grae-behn
Mine	die Mine	Dee mahy-neh
Field hospital	das Feldspital	Dahs fehld-shpi-tahl
Field glasses	die Feldgläser	Dee fehld-glae-zehr
Right flank	die rechte Flanke	Dee rehh-teh flahn-keh
Left flank	die linke Flanke	Dee lin-keh flahn-keh

an Indian (am.)	ein Indianer	Ahyn in-dee-ah-nehr
an Indian (India)	ein Inder	Ahyn in-dehr
Poland	Polen	Poh-lehn
a Pole (m.f.)	ein Pole, eine Polin	Ahyn poh-leh, ahy-neh poh-lin
Czecho Slovakia	Tschecho-Slowakei	Tsheh-hoh-sloh-vah-kahy
a Czech.	ein Tscheche	Ahyn tsheh-heh
Hungary	Ungarn	Oon-gahrn
the Hungarian (m.f.)	der (die) Ungar (in)	Dehr (dee) oongahr (in)
Roumania	Rumänien	Roomae-nee-ehn
a Roumanian (m.f.)	ein Rumäne, eine Rumänin	Ahyn roo-mae-neh; ahy-neh roo-mae-nin
Bulgaria	Bulgarien	Bool-gah-ree-ehn
a Bulgarian (m.f.)	ein Bulgare, eine Bulgarin	Ahyn bool-gah-reh, ahy-neh bool-gah rin
Belgium	Belgien	Behl-gee-ehn
a Belgian (m.f.)	ein Belgier, eine Belgierin	Ahyn behl-gee-ehr ahy-neh behl-gee-eh-rin
China	China	Hi-nah
a Chinese	ein Chinese	Ahyn hi-neh-zeh
Japan	Japan	Yahpahn
a Japanese (m.f.)	ein (eine) Japaner (in)	Ahy (ahyneh) yah-pah-nehr (in)
Mexico	Mexiko	Meh-kse-koh
a Mexican (m.f.)	ein (eine) Mexikaner (in)	Ahyn (ahyneh) meh-ksee-kah-nehr (in)
Argentina	Argentinien	Ahr-gehn-ti nee-ehn
an Argentinian (m.f.)	ein (eine) Argentiner (in)	Ahyn (ahyneh) ahr-gehn-ti-nehr, (in)
Brazil	Brasilien	Brah-zi-lee-ehn
a Brazilian (m.f.)	ein (eine) Brasilianer (in)	Ahyn brah-zi-lee-ah-nehr
the native	der Eingeborene	Dehr ahyn-geh-boh-reh-neh
the citizen	der Bürger	Dehr buer-gehr
the emigrant	der Auswanderer	Dehr ous-vahn-deh-rehr
the immigrant	der Einwanderer	Dehr ahyn-vahn-deh-rehr
a foreigner	ein Ausländer, Fremder	Ahyn ous-laen-dehr, frehm-dehr

Line of battle	die Feuerlinie	Dee foy-ehr-li-ni-eh
Wounded	der Verwundete	Dehr fehr-voon-deh-teh
Hero	der Held	Dehr hehld
Expedition	der Feldzug	Dehr fehld-tsoog
Enemy	der Feind	Dehr Fahynd
Gun shell	die Geschoss-hülse	De geh-shohs-huel-zeh
Shot	der Schuss	Dehr shoos
Battleship	das Kriegsschiff	Dahs kreegs-shiff
heavy cruiser	der Kreuzer	Dehr kroy-tsehr
Destroyer	der Zerstörer	Dehr tsehr-shtoe-rehr
Torpedo	das Torpedoboot	Dahs tohr-peh-doh-boht
Invasion	der Angriff, Einbruch	Dehr ahn-grif, ahyn-brooh
Victory	der Sieg	Dehr zeeg
Defeat	die Niederlage	Dee nee-dehr-lah-geh
Submarine	das Unterseeboot	Dahs oon-tehr-zeh-boht
Offensive	die Offensive	Dee of-fehn-zi-veh
Defensive	die Defensive	Dee deh-fehn-zi-veh
War prisoner	der Kriegsgefangene	Dehr kreegs-geh fahn-geh-neh
Reserve	die Reserve	Dee reh-zehr-veh

Military and Naval Ranks	Rangstufen in Heer und Marine	Rahng-stoo-fehn en hehr & mah-re-neh
The soldier	der Soldat	Dehr sol-daht
private	der Infantrist, etc.	Dehr in-fahn-trist, etc.
private first class	der Gefreite	Dehr geh-frahy-teh
private first class	der Patrouille-Führer	Dehr pah-troul-fue-rehr
corporal	der Korporal	Dehr kohr-poh-rahl
sergeant	der Zugsführer	Dehr tsoogs-fue-rehr
top sergeant	der Feldwebel	Dehr fehld-veh-behl
drummer	der Trommler	Dehr trohm-lehr
trumpeter	der Hornist	Dehr hohr-nist
officer	der Offizier	Dehr ohfi-tseer
second lieutenant	der Fähnrich	Dehr faen-rih
lieutenant	der Leutnant	Dehr loyt-nahnt
first lieutenant	der Oberleutnant	Dehr ohbehr-loyt-nahnt
captain	der Hauptmann	Dehr houpt-mahn
major	der Major	Dehr mah-yohr
lieutenant colonel	der Oberstleutnant	Dehr oh-behrst-loyt-nahnt
colonel	der Oberst	Dehr ohbehrst

The general	der General	Dehr geh-neh-rahl
chaplain	der Feldkurat	Dehr fehld-koo-raht
doctor	der Militararzt	Dehr mi-li-taer-ahrtst
marshal	der Marshall	Dehr mahr-shahl
Field marshal	der Feldmar-schall	Dehr fehld-mahr-shahl
Officer of the Staff	Generalstabs-Offizier	Geh-neh-rahl-shtahbs-oh-fi-tseer
Commander in Chief	Oberbefehlsha-ber	Oh-behr-beh-fehls-hah-behr
The sailor	der Matrose	Dehr mah-troh-zeh
apprentice seaman	der Schiffsjunge	Dehr shifs-yoon geh
2nd class seaman	der Matrose zweiter Klasse	Dehr mah-troh-zeh tsvahy-tehr klahs-seh
1st class seaman	Matrose erster Klasse	Mah-troh-zeh-ehr-stehr klahs-seh
3rd class petty off.	Unteroffizier dritter Klasse	Oon-tehr-oh-fi tseer 3. klahs-seh
2nd class petty officer	Unteroffizier 2. Klasse	Oon-tehr-oh-fi tseer 2. klahs-seh
1st cl. petty off.	Unteroffizier 1. Klasse	Oon-tehr-oh-fi tsee 1. klahs-seh
Act. chief petty off.	Stabsunterof-fizier	Shtahbs-oon-tehr-oh-fi tseer
ensign	Seekadett	zeh-kah-deht
lieutenant jr. grade	Unterleutnant	Oon-tehr-loyt-nahnt
lieutenant	Leutnant zur See	Loyt-nahnt tsoor zeh
lieutenant commander	kommandieren-der Leutnant	Koh-mahn-dee rehn-dehr loyt-nahnt
captain	Kapitän	Kah-pi-taen
Rear-admiral	Konteradmiral	Kohn-tehr-ahd-mi-rahl
Vice-Admiral	Vizeadmiral	Vi-tseh-ahd-mi-rahl
Admiral	Admiral	Ahd-mi-rahl
the mate	der Maat	Dehr maht
the boatswain	der Bootsmann	Dehr bohts-mahn
the crew	die Mannschaft	Dee mahn-shahft

Government	Regierung	Reh-gee-roong
The governmental house	das Regierungs-haus	Dahs reh-gee-roongs-hah-oos
the Chancellor	der Kanzler	Dehr kahn-tslehr
the President	der Präsident	Dehr prae-zi dehnt
the Ministry	das Ministerium	Dahs mi-ni-steh ree-oom

the Prime Minister	Der Minister-präsident	Dehr mi-ni stehr-prae-zi dehnt
the Cabinet Council	der Ministerrat	Dehr mi-ni stehr-raht
the Ministry of:	das Ministerium des (für)	Dahs mi-ni-steh ree-oom dehs, fuer
the Interior	des Innern	dehs in-nehrn
Foreigh Affairs	des Aeusseren	dehs oys-seh-rehn
for Defense	für Verteidi-gung	fuer fehr-tahy-dee-goong
Finance	für Finanzen.	fuer fi-nahn-tsehn
Labor	Arbeitsminis-terium	dahs ahr-bahyts-mi-ni-steh-ree-oom
for Learning and Education	für Erziehung und Unterricht	fuer ehrtsee-oong oond-oon-tehr-riht
Agriculture	für Landwirtschaft	fuer lahnd-virt-shahft
the Parliament	der Reichstag	Dehr rahyhs-tahg
the Supreme Court	Der oberste Gerichtshof,	Dehr oh-behr-steh geh-rihts hohf,
the Constitution	die Verfassung	Doo fehr-fah-soong

Conversation

A trip to Germany
Eine Reise nach Deutschland

How much is the round trip to Berlin?	Wieviel kostet die Rundreise nach Berlin?
It costs 500 Marks	Sie kostet 500 Mark
At what time does the train leave?	Wann fährt der Zug ab?
At 9 A. M.	Um 9 Uhr vormittags
To the station, please	Zum Bahnhof, bitte!
We want a porter	Wir wollen einen Gepäcktrager
Which are your bags?	Welche Koffer gehören Ihnen?
I have five suitcases	Ich habe fünf Handkoffer
I wish to check a trunk	Ich möchte einen Reisekoffer einstellen
Where is the baggage room?	Wo ist der Gepäckraum?
Have you bought your ticket?	Haben Sie Ihre Fahrkarte gekauft?
I haven't bought it yet	Ich habe sie noch nicht gekauft
Your baggage exceeds the maximum weight	Ihr Gepäck übersteigt das erlaubte Gewicht
Where is the waiting room?	Wo ist der Wartesaal?
Where is the men's room?	Wo ist die Herrentoilete?
Where is the ladies' room?	Wo ist die Damentoilete?

Where is the restaurant?	Wo ist das Restaurant?
Where is the ticket office?	Wo ist der Schalter?
Where is the information office?	Wo ist das Auskunftsbureau?
From which track does the train for Berlin leave?	Von welchem Bahnsteig fährt der Zug nach Berlin?
Do you have a time table?	Haben Sie einen Fahrplan?
Do I have to change trains?	Muss ich umsteigen?
This is a direct train	Das ist ein direkter Zug
How long is the ticket valid?	Wie lange ist die Karte gültig?
Two second class one way tickets	Zwei Fahrkarten zweiter Klasse
One round trip third class ticket	Eine Rundreisekarte dritter Klasse
We want a Pullman reservation	Wir möchten einen Schlafwagenplatz reservieren
Where is the dining car?	Wo ist der Speisewagen?
It is at the end of the train	Er ist am Ende des Zuges
I have missed my train	Ich habe den Zug versäumt
At what time does the next train leave?	Wann fahrt der nächste Zug?
The next train leaves tomorrow	Der nächste Zug fährt morgen
The emergency signal	Die Notleine

Traveling Acquaintances	Reisebekanntschaften
I am very glad to meet you	Es freut mich, Sie kennen zu lernen
The pleasure is mine	Es ist mir ein besonderes Vergnügen
Are you an American?	Sind Sie Amerikaner?
Yes sir, and you?	Jawohl mein Herr, und Sie?
I am Swiss	Ich bin Schweizer
Where are you going?	Wohin fahren Sie?
I am going to Vienna	Ich fahre nach Wien
I intend to do some business in Vienna	Ich beabsichtige, in Wien einige Geschäfte zu machen
Do you know Vienna?	Kennen Sie Wien?
No, it is my first visit to the city	Nein, ich besuche die Stadt das erste Mal
And you Miss, what is your destination?	Und Sie, Fräulein, Wohin reisen Sie?
I am going to Berlin	Ich fahre nach Berlin

The Arrival	Die Ankunft
Next stop, Innsbruck	Die nächste Station ist Innsbruck
The customs officers	Die Zollbeamten

Your passport, please	Ihren Pass, bitte
How long do you expect to stay in this country?	Wie lange beabsichtigen Sie im Lande zu bleiben?
Only six weeks	Nur sechs Wochen
Do you have the keys to this trunk?	Haben Sie die Schlüssel zu diesem Koffer?
Open your bag	Öffnen Sie Ihre Reisetasche
Have you anything to declare?	Haben Sie etwas zu verzollen?
Perfume, tobacco, jewelry, etc.?	Parfüm, Tabak, Juwelen, etc.?
I have only clothing	Ich habe nur Kleidungsstücke
I have nothing to declare	Ich habe nichts zu verzollen
Do I have to declare a few cigarettes?	Müssen einige Zigaretten verzollt werden?
No, they are free of duty	Nein, die sind zollfrei
Your luggage has been examined	Ihr Gepäck ist überprüft
All right	Alles in Ordnung
Mr. X arrives in Innsbruck	Herr X kommt in Innsbruck an
Look for my luggage	Sehen Sie nach meinem Gepäck

From the Station to the Hotel	Vom Bahnhof zum Hotel
To what hotel do you wish to go?	In welchem Hotel wollen Sie absteigen?
Which is the best hotel?	Welches ist das beste Hotel?
There are several very good ones	Es gibt mehrere sehr gute hier
The hotel Kaiserhof is very comfortable	Das Hotel Kaiserhof ist sehr behaglich
Let us go there	Gut, lasset uns hinfahren
Drive quickly, please	Bitte, fahren Sie schnell
Drive slowly, please	Bitte, fahren Sie langsam
Stop here	Halten Sie, bitte
I wish to get off	Ich will absteigen
Wait a few minutes	Warten Sie einige Minuten
Straight ahead	Gerade aus
Turn right	Gehen Sie nach rechts
Turn left	Gehen Sie nach links
We have arrived, sir	Wir sind angekommen
How much is it?	Was kostet es?
Two Marks and fifty Pfennige	Zwei Mark und fünfzig Pfennige

At the Hotel	Im Hotel
Any rooms available?	Haben Sie einige Zimmer frei?
I would like a room with bath	Ich möchte ein Zimmer mit Bad
Single or double beds?	Einzelbett oder Doppelbett?
May I see the rooms?	Kann ich die Zimmer sehen
What is the price of this room?	Was kostet dieses Zimmer?

With breakfast ten marks	Mit Frühstück zehn Mark
With three meals twenty marks	Mit drei Mahlzeiten zwanzig Mark
I would like a room facing the street	Ich möchte ein Zimmer mit Strassenaussicht
I want a quiet room	Ich will ein ruhiges Zimmer
I want a room at a moderate price	Ich möchte ein Zimmer zu mässigem Preise
It is too expensive	Es ist zu teuer
Don't you have a less expensive room?	Haben Sie kein billigeres Zimmer?
Not at the present time	Nicht gegenwärtig
How long do you intend to stay at the hotel?	Wie lange beabsichtigen Sie im Hotel zu wohnen
I shall stay about a month	Ich bleibe ungefähr einen Monat
Don't you have special monthly rates?	Haben Sie nicht Monatsraten?
I shall consult the manager	Ich werde den Hotel-Direktor darum befragen
I will take this room	Ich nehme dieses Zimmer
What is my room number?	Welches ist meine Zimmernummer?
The room number is one hundred one	Die Zimmernummer ist ein-hundert-eins
To the first floor, please	Am ersten Stock, bitte
Where is the telephone?	Wo ist das Telephon?
May I have the key to my room please?	Bitte, kann ich meinen Zimmer-schlüssel haben?
Please, call a taxi	Bitte, bestellen Sie ein Taxi
We wish you a nice trip	Wir wünschen Ihnen eine gute Reise
We hope you will come again	Wir hoffen, dass Sie wieder-kommen
So do I	Ich auch
See you again	Auf Wiedersehen

<u>At the Restaurant</u>	<u>Im Restaurant</u>
Could you recommend a good restaurant?	Können Sie mir ein gutes Restaurant empfehlen?
What kind of food do you prefer?	Was für eine Küche ziehen Sie vor?
Do you like German, Austrian or French cooking?	Wünschen Sie deutsche, österreichische oder französische Küche?
I prefer Viennese cooking	Ich ziehe die Wiener Küche vor.
At what time do you serve lunch?	Wann speisen Sie zu Mittag?

At one o'clock	Um ein Uhr
Let us go to lunch	Gehen wir zum Mittagessen
How many are you?	Wie viele Personen?
We are three, but we expect a friend	Wir sind drei, aber erwarten noch einen Freund
Do you want to sit here?	Wollen Sie hier sitzen?
This table is too small	Dieser Tisch ist zu klein
Don't you have a larger table?	Haben Sie keinen grösseren Tisch?
I like this table	Mir gefällt dieser Tisch
I am sorry, but it is reserved	Ich bedaure, dieser Tisch ist reserviert
Please reserve a table for a party of four	Bitte, reservieren Sie einen Tisch für vier Personen
Would the gentlemen like a drink before lunch?	Wollen die Herren etwas trinken vor dem Essen?
Bring me a cognac	Bringen Sie mir einen Kognak
Are you going to eat a la carte or the regular meal?	Wollen Sie a la carte essen oder unser gewöhnliches Mittagsessen nehmen?
What is the price of the regular meal?	Was kostet das gewöhnliche Mittagsessen?
Are the drinks included?	Sind die Getränke mitgerechnet?
Take my coat	Bitte, nehmen Sie meinen Mantel
We are in a hurry	Wir haben es eilig
Let me see the menu	Bitte, geben Sie mir die Speisekarte
Lunch is served	Das Mittagessen ist serviert
I could use another spoon and knife	Ich möchte noch einen Löffel und ein Messer
What do you wish to drink?	Was wünschen Sie zu trinken?
Cold water for me	Kaltes Wasser für mich
Bring me the wine list	Bringen Sie mir die Weinkarte
Let me have a glass of white wine	Bitte, bringen Sie mir ein Glas Weisswein
Imported or domestic?	Importierten oder heimischen?
Rheinwine, if you please	Rheinwein, bitte
The wine is good	Der Wein ist gut
I'll take a glass of beer	Mir, ein Glas Bier, bitte
Light or dark?	Hell oder dunkel?
Dark, please	Dunkel, bitte
I want a bottle of Bavarian beer	Ich möchte eine Flasche bayrisches Bier
It is refreshing	Es ist erfrischend

You forgot to bring the butter	Sie haben vergessen, die Butter zu bringen
We don't serve butter with meals, but if you wish you may have some	Wir servieren keine Butter mit Mahlzeiten, aber wenn Sie wünschen, können Sie welche haben
Bring half a bottle of red wine	Bringen Sie eine kleine Flasche Rotwein
This wine is very sweet	Dieser Wein ist sehr süss
What do you wish for dessert?	Was wünschen Sie zum Nachtisch?
One apple strudel, coffee cake, one cream puff and one ice cream	Eine Portion Apfelstrudel, Kaffeetorte, einen Cremekrapfen und ein Gefrorenes
What kind of ice cream would you like?	Was für Gefrorenes wünschen Sie?
Strawberry, raspberry, vanilla, coffee or chocolate?	Erdbeeren, Himbeeren, Vanille Kaffee oder Schokolade?
Do you want coffee?	Wünschen Sie Kaffee?

In the City	In der Stadt
Where is the National Bank?	Wo ist die National-Bank?
How can I find it?	Wie kann ich sie finden?
Which street car should I take?	Welche Strassenbahn soll ich nehmen?
Take the "G" line	Nehmen Sie die "G" Linie
Where do I get it?	Wo kann ich einsteigen?
At the corner of this block	Am Ende dieses Häuserviertels
Let me off at the National Bank	Ich möchte bei der Nationalbank absteigen
Walk two blocks and turn to your right	Gehen Sie zwei Häuserviertel und biegen Sie rechts ein
Is the main street far away?	Ist die Hauptstrasse weit von hier?
Last stop	Letzte Haltestelle
We will take a bus	Wir wollen einen Auto nehmen
Where are you going?	Wohin gehen (fahren) Sie?
Where does this street lead to?	Wohin führt diese Strasse?
Keep to the left	Halten Sie sich links
Cross the street	Kreuzen Sie die Strasse
One way	Eine Fahrtrichtung
What kind of a street is this?	Was ist das für eine Strasse?
A fine street	Eine schöne (gute) Strasse
Good (bad) pavement	Gutes (schlechtes) Pflaster
How far is the next village from here?	Wie weit ist das nächste Dorf von hier?

About ten miles	Ungefähr zehn Meilen
I am a stranger here	Ich bin fremd hier
I didn't understand you, sir	Ich habe Sie nicht verstanden, mein Herr
Superintendent	Portier
Could you tell me whether Mr. X lives in this house?	Können Sie mir sagen, ob Herr X in diesem Hause wohnt?
Yes sir, he does	Gewiss, er wohnt hier
What a pleasant surprise	Welch eine angenehme Überraschung
Where can we meet?	Wo können wir uns treffen?
In your hotel at three o'clock	In ihrem Hotel um drei

At the Florist	Im Blumenladen
I wish to buy some flowers	Ich möchte einige Blumen kaufen
We have: roses, carnations, violets, orchids, lilies of the valley, forget-me-nots and asters.	Wir haben: Rosen, Nelken, Veilchen, Orchideen, Maiglöckchen,Vergissmeinnicht und Astern
Give me some roses	Geben Sie mir einige Rosen
How many?	Wie viele?
Two dozens, please	Zwei Dutzend, bitte
Prepare a nice bouquet of mixed flowers	Bitte, machen Sie einen schönen Strauss gemischter Blumen
Do you wish to take the flowers with you or should we deliver them?	Wollen Sie die Blumen mitnehmen, oder sollen wir sie schicken?
Please send them to the following address	Bitte, senden Sie sie an folgende Addresse
Mrs. F. M. .....,	Frau F. M. .....,
XVIII, Schulgasse 25 Second floor Vienna	XVIII, Schulgasse 25,zweiter Stock,Wien
Will she receive them this morning?	Wird sie sie noch diesen Morgen erhalten?
At once, sir	Sofort, mein Herr

At the Bank	In der Bank
Please, drive me to the National Bank	Bitte, bringen Sie mich zur National-Bank
Could you tell me where I can exchange some money?	Können Sie mir sagen, wo ich fremdes Geld einwechseln kann?
At window number ten	Am Schalter zehn

How many dollars do you wish to exchange?	Wie viel Dollar wollen Sie einwechseln?
What is the rate of exchange today?	Was ist der heutige Kurswert?
Could you cash this check for me?	Wollen Sie mir diesen Scheck einlösen?
The check has to be endorsed	Der Scheck muss indossiert sein
Do you want the money in large or small bills?	Wünschen Sie grosse oder kleine Banknoten?
Half of each, please	Halb und halb, bitte
Your identification, please	Ihre Identifizierung, bitte
Here it is	Hier ist sie
I would like to open an account	Ich möchte ein Bankkonto eröffnen

At the Post Office	Am Postamt
Where is the post office?	Wo ist das Postamt?
It is at the next corner	An der nächsten Strassenecke
I would like to mail this letter	Ich möchte diesen Brief abschicken
The postage is 25 pfennige	Das Porto beträgt fünf-und-zwanzig Pfennige
I would like to air-mail this letter to England	Ich möchte diesen Brief per Luftpost nach England senden
The postage will be 50 Pfennige	Das Porto ist fünfzig Pfennige
I wish to have it registered	Ich möchte den Brief einschreiben lassen
This will cost another twenty Pfennige	Das kostet weitere zwanzig Pfennige
Does it contain anything of value?	Ist der Inhalt von besonderem Wert?
Yes, it contains a money order for fifty Marks	Ja, er enthält eine fünfzig-Mark-Geldanweisung
Please, let me have twenty two Pfennig and ten one-Pfennig stamps	Bitte geben Sie mir zwanzig zwei-Pfennig und zehn ein-Pfennig Marken.
At the next window	Am nächsten Schalter
At what time does the Post Office close?	Um wie viel Uhr wird das Postamt geschlossen?
The office hours are eight o'clock in the morning till seven in the evening	Die Amtsstunden sind von acht Uhr morgens bis sieben Uhr abends

At the Barber Shop	Im Barbier-Laden
Do you wish a shave?	Rasieren gefällig?
Yes, but shave me carefully	Ja, aber bitte sind Sie vorsichtig
Do you wish to have a hair cut?	Wollen Sie das Haar geschnitten haben?
Only a trim, please	Nur stutzen, bitte
How do you like your hair long or short?	Wollen Sie Ihr Haar lang oder kurz?
I don't like it too short	Ich will es nicht zu kurz
Do you want your hair parted?	Wollen Sie Ihr Haar gescheitelt?
Many people comb their hair back	Viele Leute kämmen Ihr Haar zurück
I would like some hair tonic	Ich möchte irgend ein Haarwasser
How much do I owe you?	Wieviel bin ich schuldig?
Two marks	Zwei Mark

At the Beauty Parlor	Im Frisierladen
I wish to have a permanent	Ich möchte eine Dauerwelle
What kind of a permanent?	Was für eine Dauerwelle?
Could you show me some of your Styles?	Können Sie mir einige Ihrer Modelle zeigen?
I don't like a narrow curl, I prefer wide waves.	Ich mag keine kleinen Locken, ich ziehe grössere Wellen vor
How about this hairdo?	Möchten Sie so eine Frisur haben?
Yes, high and straight in the front and one wave in the back	Ja, hoch und gerade vorne und eine Welle hinten
This is the style I had in mind	Das ist die Frisur die ich im Sinne hatte
When could I have an appointment?	Wann kann ich kommen?
Thursday at nine o'clock in the morning	Donnerstag um neun Uhr morgens
Good morning, here I am	Guten Morgen, hier bin ich
Take this seat and in about three hours your hair will be done	Setzen Sie sich hier und in ungefähr drei Stunden wird Ihr Haar gerichtet sein

A Social Evening	Eine Abendunterhaltung
Friends invited me to a party	Freunde von mir haben mich zu einem geselligen Abend eingeladen
Formal dress required?	Abendkleidung verlangt?
No, attend in street dress	Nein, kommen sie im Strassenanzug
Please excuse my late arrival	Bitte, entschuldigen Sie die Verspätung

Why hasn't your wife, come?	Warum ist Ihre Frau Gemahlin nicht gekommen?
She feels indisposed and requests you to accept her apologies	Sie ist nicht ganz wohl und bittet freundlichst sie zu entschuldigen
I want to introduce you to several of our friends	Ich möchte Sie einigen unserer Freunde vorstellen
What a lovely party!	Welch ein vergnügter Abend!
The most interesting group of people	Eine überaus interessante Gesellschaft
Would you like to have some liqueur?	Möchten Sie irgendeinen Likör?
Thank you very much, I had plenty of everything	Danke schön, ich habe von allem genug gehabt
May I have the pleasure of the next dance?	Darf ich Sie um den nächsten Tanz bitten?
You dance very well, Miss B...	Sie tanzen sehr gut, Fräulein B...
Thank you, but not as well as you dance	Ich danke schön, aber Sie tanzen viel besser
Would you care, to sit down for a little while?	Wollen Sie sich ein Wenig ausruhen?
Gladly, I am rather tired	Gerne, ich bin wirklich müde
Kindly introduce me to that blond lady	Bitte, möchten Sie mich dieser blonden Dame vorstellen?
Do you prefer blondes to brunettes?	Gefallen Ihnen Blondinen besser als Brünette?
I prefer blondes	Mir gefallen Blondinen
You are very nice	Sie sind sehr liebenswürdig
Let us all go to a night club	Gehen wir alle in ein Kabarett!
Will you please bring me my coat	Bitte, bringen Sie mir meinen Mantel

At the Night Club — Im Kabarett

What kind of seats would you like for your company?	Was für Sitze möchten Sie für Ihre Gesellschaft haben?
We have orchestra and balcony seats	Wir haben Orchester und Balkon-Sitze
Tables for two, four, six and eight persons	Tische für zwei, vier, sechs und acht Personen
We would prefer the orchestra with a table for eight persons	Wir möchten im Orchester einen Tisch für acht Personen
Yes, I have a table for eight right in the middle	Ich habe einen Tisch für acht in der Mitte des Orchesters
What is the price of these seats?	Wieviel kosten diese Sitze?
Two marks each	Zwei Mark per Sitz

How much are similar seats on the balcony	Wieviel kosten ähnliche Sitze am Balkon?
One mark	Eine Mark
Please, give me the eight orchestra seats	Bitte geben Sie mir die acht Orchester Sitze
Here are the tickets, Sixteen marks please	Hier sind die Karten, sechzehn Mark bitte
At the Theatre	**Im Theater**
Do you like to go to the theatre?	Gehen Sie gerne ins Theater?
Yes, I do	Ja, ich gehe sehr gerne
I enjoy drama particularly	Besonders gut gefällt mir ein gutes Drama
Do you go to the opera?	Gehen Sie in die Oper?
I would enjoy to see a good opera	Ich möchte sehr gerne eine gute Oper sehen
Then let us see "Die Meister-singer" this evening	Dann sehen wir uns "Die Mei-stersinger" heute abend an
At what time does the per-formance begin?	Um wieviel Uhr fängt die Vorstellung an?
At eight o'clock sharp	Punkt acht Uhr
In Church	**In der Kirche**
What is your religion?	Was ist Ihre Religion?
I am a Lutheran	Ich bin Lutheraner
In Germany there are two main denominations	In Deutschland gibt es zwei führende Kirchengruppen
They are the Lutherans and Catholics	Sie sind Lutheraner und Katholiken
Between Friends	**Unter Freunden**
Good morning, John	Guten Morgen, Johann
Where have you been for the past two weeks?	Wo warst du während der zwei letzten Wochen?
I was on a very important business trip	Ich war auf einer sehr wichtigen Geschäfts-reise
How is your business?	Wie geht Dein Geschäft?
Business is not so good these days	Das Geschäft geht nicht so gut heutzutage
Competition is too keen	Die Konkurrenz ist zu gross
We suffer from over-production	Wir leiden an Über-produktion
I would rather think it is the uncertainty of the world situation	Ich möchte eher sagen, es ist die Unsicherheit der Weltlage

And yet there are still many countries which need plenty of goods	Und doch gibt es noch viele Länder die viele Waren benötigen
Unfortunately these countries lack the funds	Leider fehlt diesen Ländern das Geld
Countries which have the funds are producers themselves	Länder, welche die Mittel haben sind auch zugleich die Erzeuger

At the Doctor's Office	Beim Arzte
How does the climate agree with you?	Wie sagt Ihnen das Klima zu?
It really does not take very long to become aclimatized	Es dauert wirklich nicht lange um sich dem Klima anzupassen
But I think I suffer from indigestion	Aber ich glaube ich leide an Verdauungs-störungen
In that case I should like to recommend to you my doctor	In diesem Falle möchte ich Ihnen meinen Arzt empfehlen
When will he be able to see me?	Wann kann ich ihn sehen?
His hours are from 3 to 5 every afternoon	Seine Sprech-stunden sind täglich von drei bis fünf
The doctor will be able to see you in about ten minutes	Der Herr Doktor wird Sie in ungefähr zehn Minuten empfangen
Good day, sir	Guten Tag, mein Herr
What is bothering you?	Was fehlt Ihnen?
I feel somewhat tired and have no appetite	Ich bin etwas müde und habe keinen Appetit
You are a foreigher?	Sie sind fremd hier?
Yes, I am an American	Ja, ich bin Amerikaner
Of course, the climate, the food, the water and many other little things will disturb you for a little while	Gewiss, das Klima, die Nahrung, das Wasser und viele andere kleine Dinge werden Sie für eine Weile stören
I would advise you to be moderate in eating, to keep away from spicy food and to eat more fruit preferably	Ich möchte Ihnen raten im Essen bescheiden zu sein, gewürzte Kost zu vermeiden und eher mehr Obst zu essen
Are you going to prescribe some medicine?	Wollen Sie mir irgendwelche Medizin verschreiben?
No medicine whatsoever	Keinerlei Medizin
I would advise you rather not to attempt to do too much in one day	Ich möchte Ihnen eher raten.. nicht zu viel in einem Tage erledigen zu wollen

Avoid overtiring	Vermeiden Sie Übermüdung
You can rest and at the same time enjoy our objects of interest in museums and parks	Sie können sich ausruhen und zugleich unsere Sehenswürdigkeiten in Museen und Parkanlagen geniessen
Don't worry, there is nothing wrong with you	Sorgen Sie sich nicht, Sie sind nicht krank
Shopping	Einkaufen
I would like to do some shopping	Ich möchte gerne einige Einkäufe besorgen
That can be done	Das kann geschehen
We have a few very nice department stores here	Wir haben hier einige sehr schöne Warenhäuser
Do you want me to go with you?	Wollen Sie, dass ich Sie begleite?
I would appreciate it very much	Ich würde Ihnen sehr dankbar sein
Let us first visit the ATLAS Store	Dann besuchen wir zuerst das Atlas Waren-haus
They carry domestic and imported goods	Sie führen heimische und importierte Waren
Where is the dress shop, please?	Wo ist die Frauenkleider-Abteilung, bitte?
In the center of the second floor	In der Mitte des zweiten Stockwerks
I would like to see some evening dresses	Ich möchte gerne einige Abendkleider sehen
Here we have a large selection madam	Hier haben wir eine reiche Auswahl, gnädige Frau
Your size, madam?	Ihre Grösse, gnädige Frau?
Forty, I believe	Vierzig glaube ich
I wear size 10 in America	Ich trage Nummer zehn in Amerika
You may choose one of these, they are all your size	Hier ist Ihre Wahl, sie sind alle in Ihrer Grösse
Let me see the pale blue one please	Bitte, lassen Sie mich das Hell-blaue sehen
There is the dressing room	Dort ist das Probierzimmer
The seamstress is there	Die Näherin ist dort
A few alterations have to be made, our sizes are different here	Kleine Änderungen müssen gemacht werden, unsere Grössen hier sind anders als bei Ihnen
When can delivery be made?	Wann kann die Lieferung gemacht werden?
Within 48 hours	Binnen achtundvierzig Stunden

I assume that the price is the one marked on the tag	Ich nehme an, dass der Preis der ist, welcher auf dem Zettel vermerkt ist
Certainly, the price of all of our goods is clearly marked	Gewiss, der Preis aller unserer Waren ist deutlich vermerkt
I would like to buy a few more things	Ich möchte noch einige Sachen einkaufen
As you walk along on this floor you will find everything to complete your wardrobe	Wenn Sie auf diesem Stockwerk weiter gehen, finden Sie alles um Ihre Garderobe zu vervollständigen
There is the glove counter	Dort ist die Handschuhabteilung
What size and what kind of gloves do you wish?	Welche Grösse und was für Handschuhe wünschen Sie?
We carry leather and nylon gloves in many colors and all sizes	Wir führen Leder-und Nylon-Handschuhe in vielen Farben und allen Grössen
Here are pretty street-dresses and blouses	Hier sind schöne Strassenkleider und Blusen
I need shoes and stockings too	Schuhe und Strümpfe brauche ich auch
I notice there, raincoats, umbrellas and rubbers	Dort bemerke ich Regenmäntel, Schirme und Gummischuhe
And I always need lingerie and handkerchiefs	Ich kann immer Unterwäsche und Taschentücher gebrauchen

At the Cleaners — In der Reinigung (Putzerei)

I would like to have these suits pressed	Ich möchte diese Anzüge gebügelt haben
Do you want to have them dry cleaned too?	Wollen Sie sie auch gereinigt haben?
I would appreciate it if you think you could do a quick and nice job	Ich möchte es gerne getan haben, wenn es schnell und gut gemacht werden kann
They will be ready next Tuesday	Sie werden nächsten Dienstag fertig sein
Do you also clean ladies' dresses?	Reinigen Sie auch Damenkleider?
Yes, sir we do	Gewiss, mein Herr
Do you have anybody to call for our laundry?	Haben Sie jemand,der unsere Wäsche abholen könnte?
Yes, we call for the laundry and deliver it	Ja, wir holen die Wasche ab und liefern sie auch
What is your address, please	Ihre Addresse, bitte

The Park Hotel, room 52	Park Hotel, Zimmer-Nummer zwei-und-fünfzig
When will you call for the laundry?	Wann kann die Wäsche abgeholt werden?
<u>Business Calls</u>	<u>Geschäfts-Besuche</u>
Good morning, sir, what can I do for you?	Guten Morgen, mein Herr, was kann ich für Sie tun?
I would like to see Mr. X...	Ich möchte gerne Herrn X... sehen
I am sorry, Mr. X is very busy	Es tut mir sehr leid, Herr X. ist sehr beschäftigt
Then, would you be good enough to hand him my card?	Dann, möchten Sie so gut sein und ihm meine Karte einhändigen?
Oh, Mr. B., no doubt Mr. X. will wish to see you immediately	Oh, Herr B., sicherlich wird Herr X. Sie sofort sehen wollen
Just a moment, please	Nur einen Augenblick, bitte
Just step in, please	Bitte, treten Sie ein
Good morning, Mr. X., I am Mr. B., the announced representative of the Y and Z Co. of New York	Guten Morgen, Herr X., ich bin Herr B. der angekündigte Vertreter der Firma X und Z in New York
I am pleased to know you, Mr. B.	Es freut mich, Sie kennen zu lernen, Herr B.
Mr. X., here are my credentials	Herr X, hier sind meine Beglaubigungspapiere
Here are cigars or cigarettes, please help yourself	Hier sind Zigarren oder Zigaretten, bitte, bedienen Sie sich
I studied your Company's offer very thoroughly	Ich habe das Angebot Ihrer Gesellschaft gründlich studiert
I think, Mr. B. that we will have to discuss the offer together, in order to avoid any misunderstandings	Ich glaube, Herr B., dass wir das Angebot zusammen besprechen müssen, um etwaige Missverständnisse zu vermeiden
Well Mr. B. with your valuable assitance we have reached perfect agreement in every respect	Nun Herr B... mit Ihrer wertvollen Hilfe haben wir eine in jeder Beziehung volle Übereinstimmung erreicht
You, in the name of your Company agree, that for the duration of the next five years, I am to remain your sole representative in Central Europe	Im Namen Ihrer Firma stimmen Sie zu, dass ich für die Dauer der nächsten fünf Jahre Ihr alleiniger Vertreter in Zentral-Europa sein werde

Yes Mr. X., my Company empowered me to give you this assurance	Gewiss Herr X., meine Firma hat mich ermächtigt, Ihnen diese Zusicherung zu geben
Tomorrow at ten o'clock we meet our attorney in order to sign the contracts	Morgen um zehn Uhr treffen wir unsern Rechtsanwalt um die Verträge zu unterschreiben
Mr. B., it will be a pleasure to work with you and your Company	Herr B., es wird ein Vergnügen sein mit Ihnen und Ihrer Gesellschaft zu arbeiten
After such hard work I think we owe ourselves a little pleasure	Nach so schwerer Arbeit denke ich, sind wir uns ein kleines Vergnügen schuldig
Mr. B., I invite you to be my guest to-night	Herr B., ich lade Sie ein, heute Abend mein Gast zu sein
Good morning Gentlemen, you are as punctual as good business men can be	Guten Morgen, meine Herren, Sie sind pünktlich wie es sich für güte Geschaftsmänner geziemt
The contract has been photographed and will be photographed again after you have signed it	Der Vertrag wurde photographiert und er wird noch einmal photographiert nachdem Sie ihn unterschrieben haben
One copy of each will remain with me for the duration of the contract	Je eine Kopie, wird für die Dauer des Vertrages bei mir bleiben
Congratulations and success in every way!	Glückwünsche und guten Erfolg in jeder Hinsicht!
What is your next destination, Mr. B?	Welches ist Ihr nächster Bestimmungsort, Herr B?

Commercial Information	Geschäfts-auskunft
Could you give me some information about Mr. A.?	Können Sie mir über Herrn A. einige Auskunft geben?
I am sorry, I don't know him very well	Es tut mir leid, ich kenne ihn nicht sehr gut
But I think he is an honest man	Aber ich denke dass er ein ehrlicher Mensch ist
He enjoys the friendship of the leaders of our community	Er geniesst die Freundschaft der Führer unserer Gemeinde
He is a member of the Elders in this church	In seiner Kirche ist er Mitglied des Kirchenrates
Two of his four sons are students at Heidelberg, a rather expensive university	Zwei seiner vier Söhne studieren in Heidelberg, eine ziemlich kostspielige Universität

This information is perfectly satisfactory	Diese Auskunft ist vollkommen befriedigend
What could you tell me about Mr. B.?	Was konnen Sie mir über Herrn B. sagen?
He is very reliable and keeps his promises	Er ist zuverlässig und hält seine Versprechen
<u>Business</u>	<u>Geschäft</u>
What is your occupation?	Was ist Ihre Beschäftigung?
We export and import from and to Germany	Wir exportieren und importieren von und nach Deutschland
Do you sell on credit?	Verkaufen Sie auf Kredit?
Yes, we sell on terms of three and six months	Ja, wir verkaufen mit Zahlungsfristen von drei und sechs Monaten
We are licensed brokers	Wir sind konzessionierte Geschäftsvermittler
What brokerage fee- do you charge for your services?	Was sind die Maklergebühren für Ihre Dienste?
The brokerago dopcnds on the quantity and quality of goods, which you have on hand	Die Makiergebühr hängt von der Quantität und Qualität der Waren ab, über welche Sie verfügen
I represent the largest radio factory	Ich vertrete die grösste Radiofabrik
Do you think there would be a market in Europe for our radios?	Glauben Sie, dass wir in Europa für unsere Radios einen Markt finden konnten?
Yes, if your prices and qualities can compete with those of our native products	Ja, wenn Ihre Preise und die. Qualität Ihrer Waren mit jenen unserer heimischen Produkte konkurrieren können
Do you think that we could sell a few thousand sets?	Glauben Sie, dass wir einige Tausend Apparate verkaufen könnten?
Have you a few sets for demonstration?	Haben Sie einige Apparate als Muster?
Yes, I have three sets	Ja, ich habe drei Apparate
I shall invite our radio expert to test them and to give us his opinion	Ich werde unsern Radio-Fachmann ersuchen, sie zu prüfen und uns sein Urteil zu geben
What is the opinion of your expert?	Was ist das Gutachten Ihres Fachmannes?

In his opinion the three sets work excellently	Nach seiner Meinung arbeiten die drei Muster ausgezeichnet
Well, then it should not be hard to place a big order	Nun, dann sollte es nicht schwer sein, eine grosse Bestellung zu machen
The high priced set is out of consideration	Das teuerste Muster kommt nicht in Betracht
Is there anything wrong with this set?	Was gefällt Ihnen nicht an diesem Muster?
It is the high price	Der hohe Preis
But for the two lower priced sets, I think, I can place with you a rather substantial order	Aber für die zwei billigeren Apparate, glaube ich, dass ich Ihnen einen ziemlich grossen Auftrag geben kann
When do you think we could close the contract?	Wann glauben Sie, dass wir den Vertrag abschliessen könnten?
In about eight days	In ungefähr acht Tagen
I should like to buy some goods, which I could import to the United States	Ich möchte gerne einige Artikel einkaufen, die ich nach den Vereinigten Staaten einführen könnte
What could you recommend?	Was könnten Sie mir empfehlen?
The Leipzig Fair opens next Monday	Die Leipziger Messe beginnt nächsten Montag
One of our representatives is going there, and I would advise you to join him	Einer unserer Vertreter fährt hin, und ich möchte Ihnen raten, sich ihm anzuschliessen

At the Travel Agency / Im Reisebüro

I wish to take a trip to New York	Ich möchte eine Reise nach New York machen
When do you wish to go?	Wann wünschen Sie abzureisen?
Next week	Nächste Woche
How do you wish to travel by airplane or by steamer?	Wie wollen Sie reisen, mit dem Flugzeug oder mit dem Schiff?
I would prefer the airplane	Ich würde das Flugzeug vorziehen
There is a flight Monday afternoon at five o'clock	Ein Flugzeug fliegt am Montag nachmittag um fünf Uhr ab
There is another one via Madrid on Wednesday morning at ten o'clock	Ein anderes fliegt über Madrid am Mittwoch vormittag um zehn Uhr ab
There are no more tickets to be had for the Monday plane	Für das Montag-Flugzeug sind keine Karten mehr zu haben

There is just one ticket left for Wednesday	Für Mittwoch ist noch eine Karte zu haben
May I have it?	Kann ich sie haben?
Here it is; your name and address, please	Hier ist sie; bitte, kann ich Ihren Namen und Addresse haben?
Will you accept an American check?	Nehmen Sie einen amerikanischen Scheck an?
Who is the issuer of the check?	Wer ist der Aussteller des Schecks?
The American Express Company	Die American Expressgesellschaft
Accepted; this check is as good as cash	Angenommen; dieser Scheck ist so gut wie Bargeld
Would you cash an additional check for me?	Möchten Sie mir noch einen Scheck in Bargeld einlösen?
Gladly, but not over five hundred dollars	Gerne, aber nicht über fünfhundert Dollar
What is the official exchange value of the dollar to-day?	Was ist der offiziele Kurswert des Dollars heute?
It is four marks for 1 $.	Er ist vier Mark für einen Dollar.

The following sentences must be read carefully for practice in conversation and pronunciation. They will also give you an idea about a few German cities. Try to understand both the vocabulary and the grammar of each sentence before proceeding to the next one. The English translation provided after each sentence will be helpful.

Arrival in Hamburg

Wir sind gerade heute aus Amerika in Hamburg angekommen. Da wir nur wenige Tage hier verbringen können, möchten wir gerne eine Rundfahrt durch die Stadt machen.

(We have just arrived in Hamburg from America today. Since we can only spend a few days here, we would like to make a tour through the city.)

Es wird mir ein Vergnügen sein, Ihnen einige der Sehenswürdigkeiten zu zeigen. Dort drüben steht mein Auto. Wenn es Ihnen recht ist, können wir gleich abfahren.

(It will be a great pleasure (for me) to show you some of the sights. My car is over there. If it is all right with you, we can leave right now.)

Ich bin ganz überraschet, dass Hamburg so modern ist. Dabei ist es doch eine alte Stadt, nicht wahr?

(I am quite surprised that Hamburg is so modern. And yet it is an old city, isn't it?)

Sie haben recht, Hamburg ist über tausend Jahre alt. Aber die Bomben-angriffe des zweiten Weltkrieges haben das alte Hamburg fast zerstört, und die Stadt musste neu aufgebaut werden; nun ist Hamburg eine der modernsten Städte Europas.

(You are right, Hamburg is more than a thousand years old. However, the bombing during World War II almost completely destroyed the old city, and it had to be rebuilt. Now Hamburg is one of the most modern cities in Europe.)

Vielleicht können Sie uns das Geschäftsviertel zeigen. Meine Frau möchte morgen einige Einkäufe machen.

(Perhaps you could show us the business section. My wife would like to do some shopping tomorrow.)

Dies ist die Binnenalster, and deren Ufer die Geschäfte, Banken und Hotels liegen. Hinter der Brücke liegt die Aussenalster mit ihrem blauen Wasser und ihren weissen Segelbooten, mit ihren grünen Ufern, Gärten und Parks, in denen die reichen Geschäftsleute ihre Villen haben..

(This is the Binnenalste (Inner Alster Lake), on whose shores the stores, banks and hotels are situated. Behind the bridge lies the Aussenalster (Outer Alster Lake) with its blue water, white sailboats and green shores, gardens and parks, where the rich businessmen have their villas.)

Hamburg ist wirklich eine schône Stadt. Ich finde den Hafen auch sehr interessant.

(Hamburg is indeed a beautiful city. I also find the harbor very interesting.)

Ja, Hamburg ist vor allem eine Handels-und Hafenstadt, die als Durchgangshafen für die Ausfuhr und Einfuhr von Waren nach und von vielen Ländern wichtig ist.

(Yes, Hamburg is above all a commercial city and a port. It is important as a gateway for the export and import of goods to and from many countries.)

Mein Sohn würde gerne den berühmten Hamburger Zoo besuchen.

(My son would like to visit the famous Hamburg zoo.)

Dann fahren wir jetzt zum Tierpark. Er liegt etwas ausserhalb der Stadt. Er wurde von dem weltberühmten Hagenbeck gegründet, und der Name "Tierpark" besagt, dass er kein gewöhnlicher Zoo ist.

(Then we shall now drive to the Tierpark (animal park). It is situated somewhat outside the city. It was founded by the famous Hagenbeck, and the name "animal park" indicates that this is no ordinary zoo.)

Sie haben recht. Die wilden Tiere scheinen hier wirklich wie in einem Park zu leben. Sehen Sie dort die Tiger! Sie laufen frei herum!

(You are right. The wild animals indeed seem to live here as in a park. Just look at the tigers over there! They run about free!)

Sie brauchen keine Angst haben. Ein Graben trennt die Tiere von den Menschen.

(Don't be afraid! A moat separates the animals from the people.)

Das war ein schöner aber anstrengender Tag. Am besten wäre es, wenn wir uns ein wenig im Hotel ausruhen könnten.

(That was a beautiful but strenuous day. It would be best if we could rest a little at the hotel.)

Dürfte ich Sie heute zum Abendessen einladen?

(May I invite you for dinner tonight?)

Ich nehme Ihre Einladung gerne an. Nach dem Essen können wir dann zusammen in die Oper gehen. Um sechs Uhr treffen wir uns wieder im Hotel. Auf Wiedersehen!

(I gladly accept your invitation. After dinner we can go to the opera together. At six o'clock we'll meet again at the hotel. So long!)

Berlin, a City of Contrasts

Jetzt sind wir also in Berlin! Das Leben und Treiben hier erinnert mich an New York.

(So we are now in Berlin! The hustle and bustle here reminds me of New York.)

Ja, Berlin ist noch immer eine europäische Hauptstadt. Weder der Krieg noch die Russen haben das ändern konnen.

(Yes, Berlin is still one of the capitals of Europe. Neither the war nor the Russians have been able to change this.)

Es ist erstaunlich, dass Berlin als geteilte Stadt existieren kann. Hier auf dem schönen, breiten Kurfürstendamm mit seinen eleganten Geschäften, grossen Restaurants und modernen Kinos vergesse ich, dass es auch ein Ostberlin gibt.

(It is amazing that Berlin can exist as a divided city. Here, on the beautiful, wide Kurfürstendamm with its elegant stores, large restaurants and modern motion picture theatres I forget that there is an East Berlin too.)

Sie müssen sich auch die Stalinallee anschauen. Das ist die Hauptstrasse Ostberlins. Sie besteht aus riesigen Mietshausern, und von Leben und Glanz ist dort keine Spur. Bei Nacht ist der Kurfürstendamm hell erleuchtet und lärmend. Die Stalinalle dagegen ist dunkel und still.

(You must also see the Stalinalle. That is the main street of East-Berlin. It consists of huge apartment houses, and one sees no sign of life or brilliance there. At night the Kurfürstendamm is brightly illuminated and noisy. The Stalinalle, on the other hand, is dark and silent.)

Das Brandenburger Tor gehört zu den Sehenswürdigkeiten Berlins, die der Krieg beschädigt aber nicht zerstört hat. Dieses majestätische Tor soll einmal das Symbol des Glanzes und des Ruhmes der Stadt Berlin gewesen sein.

(The Brandenburg Gate belongs to the important sights of Berlin which were damaged but not destroyed by the war. This majestic gate is said to have symbolized once the splendor and fame of the city of Berlin.)

Jetzt aber hat das Tor eine andere Bedeutung. Hinter ihm beginnt der politische Osten, der bis Peking reicht. Und vor dem Tor beginnt der politische Westen, der bis Washington reicht. Hier wird man sich erst richtig bewusst, dass Berlin eine geteilte Stadt ist.

(Now, however, the gate has a different significance. Behind it begins the political East, which reaches as far as Peking. And here, on this side of the gate begins the political West, which extends all the way to Washington. Only here does one actually realize that Berlin is a divided city.

Nürnberg, a Medieval City

Wie man bei Bayreuth sofort an Richard Wagner denkt und die Stadt Frankfurt mit Deutschlands Dichter Goethe verbindet, so erinnert einen Nürnberg an Albrecht Dürer, den grössten deutschen Künstler des 15. and 16. Jahrhunderts.

(Just as Bayreuth makes one think immediately of Richard Wagner and Frankfurt evokes the memory of Germany's poet Goethe, Nürnberg reminds one of Albrecht Dürer, the greatest German artist of the 15th and 16th century.)

Ich erinnere mich gut an das Goethehaus in Frankfurt, in dem der grosse Dichter geboren wurde und seine Kindheit verbracht hat. Gibt es hier wohl auch ein Dürerhaus?

I remember very well the Goethe-house in Frankfurt, in which the great poet was born and lived there during his childhood. Is here such a Dürer-house?

Gewiss, und wir werden es jetzt besuchen. Sehen Sie, wir verlassen den modernen, industriellen Teil Nürnbergs und kommen bereits zur Altstadt. Diese Burg existierte schon im elften Jahrhundert.

(Certainly, and we shall visit it now. You see, we are leaving the modern, industrial part of Nürnberg and we are coming to the old part of town. This fortress already existed in the eleventh century.)

Darüber habe ich schon im Reiseführer gelesen. Wie alle Städte des Mittelalters, war Nürnberg von einer durch Brücken, Türmen und Toren unterbrochenen Mauer umgeben. Diese Befestigungen haben sich bis heute erhalten. Innerhalb der Mauer befindet sich die Altstadt mit den schönsten alten Bauwerken.

(I have already read about it in the travel guide. Like all medieval towns, Nürnberg was surrounded by a wall interrupted by bridges, towers and gates. These fortifications have been preserved until today. Within the wall lies the old town with the most beautiful old building.)

Plötzlich sieht man sich in die Romantik des Mittelalters versetzt! Diese alten Fachwerkhäuser mit ihren Giebeln sind bezaubernd!

(Suddenly one is transported into the romanticism of the Middle Ages! These old timber-frame houses with their gables are enchanting!)

Hier ist das Dürerhaus, in dem der grosse Maler und Kupferstecher bis zum Ende gelebt hat. Das Haus wurde während des Krieges zerstört, ist aber inzwischen wieder aufgebaut worden.

(Here is the Dürer House, in which the great painter and engraver lived and died. It was destroyed during the war but has since been rebuilt.)

Gehen wir gleich hinein, denn hier befinden sich viele Original-werke Dürers.

(Let us go in now, for there are many of Dürer's original works inside.)

In Nürnberg gibt es viele Denkmäler der späten Gothik. Dort drüben steht die St. Lorenzkirche mit ihren vielen zum Himmel strebenden Türmen. Und dies ist der "Schöne Brunnen", ein Meisterwerk filigranfeiner Steinmetzarbeit.

(In Nürnberg there are many monuments of the late Gothic period. Over there is the Church of St. Lawrence with its many towers that reach toward the heavens. And this is the "Beautiful Fountain", a masterpiece of Filigree stone masonry.)

Mir scheint es, dass hier fast jedes Haus ein Kunstwerk ist!

(It seems to me that almost every house here is a work of art!)

Observe the letters "m", "f", and "n" after each noun, indicating the gender. This will facilitate the usage of the article. All masculine nouns ("m") require the masculine article "der"; all feminine nouns ("f") require the feminine article "die"; and all neuter nouns ("n") require the neuter article "das".

a

abbiegen - to turn off (a road)
Abend, m. - evening
Abendessen, n. - dinner, supper
aber - but
Abfahrt, f. - departure
Abflug, m. - departure of a plane
Abführmittel, n. - laxative
Absatz, m. - heel (of a shoe)
Absender, m. - sender (of letter)
Abteil, n. - compartment
Abteilung, f. - department
acht - eight
acht geben - to pay attention
Achtung! - Look out!
achtzehn - eighteen
achtzig - eighty
adressieren - to address
ähnlich - similar
alkoholfrei - nonalcoholic
all, alle, - all
allein - alone
alles - everything
als - than, when
Amt, n. -bureau, government office
Ananas, f. - pineapple
Andenken, n. - souvenir
ander/er, -e. -es - other
Anfang, m. - beginning
Anfrage, f. - inquiry
angeben - declare (at customs)
ankommen - to arrive
Ankunft, f. - arrival
annehmen - to accept, assume
Anruf, m. - telephone call
anrufen - to call (to telephone)
Ansichtskarte, f.-souvenir postcard
Antwort, f. - answer
Anzeige, f. - ad (in newspaper)
Anzug, m. - suit
anzünden-to light (cigarette, etc.)
Apfel, m. - apple
Apfelsine, f. - orange
Apotheke, f. - pharmacy
Apotheker, m. - pharmacist
Apparat, m. apparatus, telephone
Arbeit, f. - work
Arm, m. - arm
arm - poor
Armband, n. - bracelet
Armbanduhr, f. - wristwatch
Ärmel, ., m. - sleeve
Art, f.-kind, type, sort, manner
Arznei, f. - medicine, drugs
Arzt, m. - physician
atmen - to breathe
auch - also, too
auf - on, upon
Aufenthalt, m.-stay, sojourn
aufgeben-to give up, to mail
aufhängen - to hang up
aufheben - to lift
aufhören - to stop
Auf Wiedersehen-good-bye, so long
Aufzug, m. - elevator
Auge, n. - eye
Augenblick, m. - moment
aus - out of, from
Ausflug, m. -excursion, trip
ausfüllen-to fill out, (a form)
Ausgang, m. - exit

Auskunft, f. - information
Auslage, f. -display, window display
Ausländer, -m. -foreigner
ausmachen-arrange, extinguish, matter
Ausrede, f. - excuse, pretext
ausruhen - to rest
aussen - outside
ausser, ausserdem-besides, except
ausserhalb - outside
Aussicht, f. - view, prospect
ausspucken - to spit, expectorate
ausstellen - to issue, to exhibit
Ausweis, m. -certificate, document
Auto, n. - automobile, car
Autobahn, f. - highway
Autobus, m. - bus

b

Bach, m. - brook
Backe, f.- cheek (same as Wange)
Bäckerei, f. -bakery, pastry shop
Bad, n. - bath
Bahn, f. - way, railroad
Bahnsteig, m. - platform
bald - soon
Ball, m. - ball
Band, n. - ribbon
bar, Bargeld - cash
Bart, m. - beard
Baum, m. - tree
Baumwolle, f. - cotton
Beamter, m. (government) official, employee
bedeckt - covered
Bedeutung, f. - meaning, importance
Bedienung, f. - service
befehlen - to order, command
befinden (sich) to be located, found
begegnen - to meet
beginnen - to begin
Begriff, m. - concept, idea
behandeln - to treat
behalten - to keep
bei - at, near
Bein, n. - leg
beinah(e) - almost
beissen - to bite
Bekanntschaft, f. -acquaintance
beklagen (sich) - to complain
bekommen - to receive
belästigen- to annoy, bother
belegtes, Brot - sandwich
benachrichtigen -to notify, inform
beobachten - to watch, observe
bequem - comfortable
bereit - ready, prepared
Berg, m. - mountain
beruhigen - to calm
berühren - to touch
beschäftigt - busy
beschränkt - limited
beschweren (sich) to complain
besetzt - occupied, filled up
besitzen - to own
besonders - special, especially
besser - better
Besteck - cutlery, table silver
bestehen -to considt of, exist
bestellen - to order
Besuch, m. - visit
Betrag, m. - amount, sum
betreten - to walk on, step on
Bett, n. -bed
Bettler, m. - beggar
bevor - before
bewegen - to move
bezahlen - to pay
Bezirk, m.- district
biegen - to bend
Bierstube, f. - beer tavern
Bild, n. - picture
billig - cheap
bis, bisher, - until, up to
Bissen, m. - bite
bitte - please
bitten - to request
blau - blue

bleiben - to remain
Bleistift, m. - pencil
Blitz, m. - lightning
Blume, f. -flower
Bluse, f. - blouse
Blut, n. - blood
Boden, m. - floor, soil
Boot - boat
borgen - to borrow
Börse, f. - stock exchange, change purse
Botschaft, f. - message, embassy
Branntwein, m. - brandy
brauchen - to need
Brause, f. - shower
brechen - to break
Brei, m.-puree, hot cereal
breit - broad, wide
Bremse, f. - brake
Brief, m. - letter
Briefkasten, m. - mailbox
Briefmarke, f. - postage stamp
Brille, f. - eyeglasses
Brot, n. - bread
Bub, m. - boy
Buch, n. - book
Buchhandlung, f. - bookshop
Büchse, f. - can, container
Bügeleisen, n.-iron(for pressing)
bügeln - to iron, press
Bürgersteig, m. -sidewalk
Büro (Bureau), n. - office
Bürste, f. - brush
Butter, f. - butter

c

Cafe, n. - coffeehouse
Chirurg, m. - surgeon

d

da - here, because
danke - thank you
danken - to thank
dann - then
daran, darin - in it
darauf - on it
Datum, n. - date
Daumen, m. - thumb
Decke, f. - blanket
denken - to think
Denkmal, n - monument
Depesche, f. - telegram
deutsch, Deutscher - German
dicht - dense
dick - thick, fat
dienen - to serve
Dienstag, m. - Tuesday
Dienstbote, m. - servant
Dienstmädchen, n. -servant-girl, maid
dieser - this
Ding, n. - thing
Dom, m. -cathedral
Donner, m. -thunder
Donnerstag, m. - Thursday
Dorf, n. - village
dort - there
Draht, f. - wire
drehen - to turn
drei - three
dreissig - thirty
dreizehn - thirteen
dritte - third
Drogerie, f. - drugstore
drucken - to push, press
Drucksache, f. - printed matter
du - you
dunkel - dark
durch - through, by
Durchgang, m. - passage
Durst, f. - thirst
Dutzend, f - dozen

e

eben - just
Ecke, f. - corner
Ei, n. - egg

Eilbrief, m. -special delivery letter
Eile, f. - haste, hurry
ein - a, one
einbegriffen - included
einfach - simple
Eingang, m. - entrance
einige - some
einkaufen - to shop, buy
einschreiben - to register (a letter)
Eintritt, m. - entrance
einverstanden - agreed
einzig - only, unique
Eis, n. - ice
Eisen, n. - iron
Eisenbahn, f. - railroad
elf - eleven
empfangen - to receive
Empfänger, m. - receiver
empfehlen - to recommend
Empfehlung, f. - recommendation
Ende, n. - end
Endstation, f. - terminal
Enge, f. - narrowness, narrow passage
Entfernung, f. - distance
entlang - along
Entschuldigung, f. - excuse, apology
entweder...oder - either...or
er - he
Erdapfel, m. - potato
Erde, f. - ground, earth
erhalten - to receive; to preserve
erinnern - to remind, remember
erklären - to state, to explain
erlauben - to permit
ernst - serious, earnest
erreichen - to reach, to attain
Ersatz, m. - replacement, substitute
erschrecken - to be frightened
erst - first; only
erwarten - to expect, to wait for
es - it
essen - to eat
Esszimmer, n. - dining room
Etage, f. - floor, story
etwas - something

f

fahren - to drive, to travel
Fahrer, m. - driver, motorman
Fahrrad, n. - Bicycle
Fahrt, f. - trip
Fall, m. - case
fallen - to fall
falsch - false, wrong
Familie, f. - family
Familienname, m. - family name
Farbe, f. -color
fast - almost
Feder, f. - pen, feather
fehlen - to be missing
Feiertag, m. - holiday
Fenster, n. - window
Ferne, f. - distance
Fernsehapparat, m. -television set
Fernsprecher, m.-telephone
fertig - ready
Fest, n. - festival, celebration
feucht - damp, humid
Feuer, f. - fire
Feuerwehr, f.-fire department
Feuerzeug, n.- lighter (for cigarettes)
Fieber, n. - fever
finden - to find
Flamme, f. -flame
Flasche, f. - bottle
Fleckenwasser, n. -cleaning fluid
Fleisch, n. - meat
fliegen - to fly
Flucht, f. - escape, flight
Flug, m. -flight (plane)
Flügel, m. -wing; grand piano
Flughafen, m. -airport
Flugplatz, m.- airfield

Flugzeug, n.- airplane
Fluss, m. - river
folgen - to follow;obey
Formular, n.- printed form, blank
fragen - to ask
Franzose, m. -Frenchman
Frau, f. -woman, wife, Mrs.
Fräulein, n. -young lady, Miss
frei - free
Freitag, m. -Friday
Freund, m. -friend (masc.)
frisch - fresh
Friseur, m. -hairdresser
froh - happy, glad
Frucht, f. -fruit
früh - early
Frühling, m. - spring
Frühstück, n. - breakfast
fühlen - to feel
Führer, m. -leader, guide, driver
füllen - to fill
Füllfeder, f. -fountain pen
Fundamt, n.- Fundbüro, n.-
lost-and-found office
fünf - five
fünfzehn - fifteen
fünfzig - fifty
Fuss, m. - foot
Fussball, m. - soccer
Fussgänger, m. - pedestrian

g

Gabel, f. - fork
Gallerie, f. - gallery
Galoschen, pl. - overshoes
Gang, m. - course(meal);
passageway
gear - (automobile)
ganz - completely, whole,
entire
garnicht - not, not at all
Garten, m. - garden
Gasse, f. - narrow street, alley
Gasthaus, n. - inn
Gatte, m. - husband
Gattin, f. - wife
Gebäck, n. - pastry
geben - to give
geboren - born
gebraucht -used, second hand
Gefahr, f. - danger
gefährlich - dangerous
Gefrorene(s), n. -sherbet, ice-
cream
gegen - against
Gegensatz, m. -contrast,
opposition
Gegenstand, m. - object
gegenüber - opposite
gehen - to walk, to go
gelb - yellow
Geld, n. - money
Geldanweisung, f. -money order
Gelegenheit, f. -occasion,
opportunity
Gelegenheitskauf, m. - bargain
Gemahl, m. - husband
Gemahlin, f. - wife
Gemälde, n. - painting
Gemüse, n. - vegetable
genug - enough
Gepäck, n. - baggage
Gepäckaufbewahrung, f. -baggage
room, check room
Gepäckschein, m. - baggage check
Gepäckträger, m. -railroad porter,
redcap
gerade - straight;just now;exactly
gern - gladly
Gesandschaft, f. -embassy
Geschäft, n. - shop, business
Geschäftsführer, m. -manager
Geschenk, n. - gift, present
geschickt (adj.) - handy, clever
skilful
geschlossen - closed
Geschmack, m. - taste
geschwind - fast
Geschwindigkeit, f. -speed

geschwollen - swollen
Gesellschaft, f. - company, society
Gesicht, n. - face
gestatten - to allow, permit
gestern - yesterday
Gesundheit, f. -health
gewiss - certain, certainly
gewöhnlich -ordinary, customary
Gift, n. -poison
Glas, n. -glass
glauben - to believe
gleich - same, immediately
Glocke, f. -bell
Glück, n. -luck, happiness
Gott, m. - God
gratis - free of charge
grau - gray
Griff, m. -grip, handle
gross - large, big, tall
Grösse, f. - size, measure, greatness
grün - green
Gruss, m. - greeting
grüssen - to greet
gültig - valid
Gürtel, m. -belt
gut - good, well
Güte, f. - kindness
Gummi, n. -rubber, eraser
Gummischuhe, pl. -rubbers

h

Haar, n. -hair
Haarnadel, f. -hair pin
Hafen, m. - harbor
Hagel, m. - hail
Hahn, m-rooster; faucet
halb - half
Hälfte, f. half(noun)
Halle, f. -hall
Hals, m. -neck, throat
halten - to stop, to hold
Haltestelle, f. -stop, station
Hand, f. - hand
handeln - to bargain
Handschuhe, pl. - gloves
Handtasche, f. - handbag
Handtuch, n. - towel
hart - hard
haupt - principal, chief, main
Haus, n. - house
Hausschuhe, pl. -slippers
Haut, f. -skin
heben - to lift
heiss - hot
heizen - to heat
Heizung, f. -heating, radiator
helfen -to help
Hemd, n. - shirt
Herberge, f. -hostel
Herbst, m. - autumn
hereinkommen - to enter
Herr - sir, Mr., master
herrlich - wonderful
herrschen - to rule
Herz, n. -heart
heute - today
hier - here
Hilfe, f. - help
Himmel, m. -sky, heaven
hinauf - up
hinaus - out
hineinkommen - to enter
hinten - behind, back
hinter - behind
hinüber - across
hinunter - downward
hinuntergehen - to go down, descend
Hitze, f. - heat
hoch - high, tall
Höchstgeschwindigkeit, f. - maximum speed, speed limit
Hof, m. - court, courtyard
Höflichkeit, f. -politeness
Höhepunkt, m. -climax, higest point
Holz, n. - wood

hören - hear
hübsch - pretty, nice
Huhn, n. - chicken
hungrig - hungry
husten - to cough
Hut, m. - hat

i

ich - I
ihm - to him
ihn - him
ihnen, Ihnen, -to them, to you
ihr - you (plural, familiar); her (poss.) to her; their
immer - always
Impfung, f. -vaccination, inoculation
irgendein - some, any
irgendwo - somewhere, anywhere
irren (sich) - to make a mistake
Irrtum, n. -mistake

j

ja - yes
Jacke, f. - jacket, sweater
Jahr, n. -year
jeder - each, each one, everyone
jemand - someone
jetzt - now
Jod, n. - iodine
Jugend, f. - youth
Jugendherberge, f. - youth hostel
Juli - July
jung - young
Junge, m. - boy
Juni - June
Juwelier, m. -jeweler

k

Kabel, n. - cable, telegram
Kabine, f. - cabin, stateroom
Kaffee, m. - coffee
Kalbfleisch, n.- veal
kalt - cold
Kappe, f. - cap
Karte, f. - map, ticket, card
Kartoffel, f. - potato
Käse, m. -cheese
Kasse, f. - cashier's desk or window, box office
Kassierer, m. -cashier, teller (bank)
Kasten, m. - box
kaufen - to buy
kaum - hardly
Kellner, m. - waiter
kennen - to know(a person or place)
kennen lernen - to make the acquaintance of, to get to know
Kerze, f. - candle
Kette, f. - chain
Kind, n. - child
Kino, n. -movie house, movie show
Kirche, f. - church
Kirsche, f. - cherry
Kissen, n. - pillow
klar - clear
Klasse, f. - class
Kleid, n. - dress
klein - small, little
Kleingeld, n.- small change
klopfen - to knock
Klosett, n. - toilet, W. C.
Klosettpapier, n. - toilet paper
Knabe, m. - boy
Knie, n. - knee
Knochen, m. - bone
Knopf, m. - button
kochen - to cook
Koffer, m. - trunk
Kölnischwasser, n. - cologne
Kolonialwarenhandlung, f. - delicatessen, grocery
kommen - to come
Konditorei, f. -pastry shop, coffee house

König, m. - king
können - to be able, can
Kopf, m. - head
Kopfschmerzen, pl. -headache
kopieren - to copy
Korb, m. - basket
Körper, m. - body
kosten - to cost
Kraft, f. - strength, force
krank - sick, ill
Krankenhaus, n. - hospital
Krankheit, f. -sickness
Kravatte, f. -necktie
Kreuzung, f. -crossing,crossroad
Krieg, m. -war
Krug, m. -pitcher
Küche, f. -kitchen
kühl -cool
Kühlanlage, f. -cooling system, air conditioner
Kunst, f. art
Kurs, m. -exchange rate
Kürschner, m. - furrier
kurz - short
Kuss, m. - kiss
Kutsche, f. - horse carriage
Kuvert, n. -envelope

l

lachen - to laugh
Laden, m. -store
laden - to load
Landkarte, f. -map
lang - long
Länge, f. - length
langsam - slowly
Larm, m. - noise
lassen - to let, to leave
Lastwagen, m. - truck
Laterne, f. - lantern,street light
laufen - to run
laut - loud
Leben, n. -life, to live
Lebensgefahr, f. -danger of death
Lebensmittelgeschäft, n. -grocery-store
Leber, f. - liver
Leder, n. - leather
leer - empty
Lehnsessel, m. -armchair
lehren - to teach
Lehrer, m. -teacher
leicht - easy, light
Leid, n. -sorrow
leider - unfortunately
Leintuch, n. -bedsheet
leise -softly (not loud)
Leiter, f. - ladder
Leitung, f. -leadership, connection line; management
lenken - to steer
lernen - to learn
lesen - to read
letzt - last
Leute - people
Licht, n. - light
Liebe, f. -love
Lied, n. - song
Lieferung, f. - delivery, shipment
liegen - to lie
Liegestuhl, m. -deck chair, chaise lunge
Likör - liqueur, cordial
links - left
Lippe, f. - lip
Lippenstift, m. -lipstick
Liste, f. - list
Loch, n. -hole
Löffel, m. -spoon
Lohn, m. -reward
Luft, f. -air
Luftpost, f. -air mail
Lüge, f. -falsehood, lie
lustig -gay, jolly

m

machen - to make, do
Mädchen, n. -girl

Magen, m. - stomach
Mahlzeit, f. -meal
Mai - May
Mal, n. - time, once
malen - to paint
Maler, m. - painter
Mann, m. -man, husband
Marke, f. - stamp, brand
Markt, m. -market
März - march
Mass, n. - measurement
Matratze, f. -mattress
Mauer, f. -wall(outdoors)
Meer, n. -ocean, sea
Mehlspeise, f. -pudding, dessert, pastry
mehr - more
meinen - to mean, my(acc.)
Mensch, m. -human being, man
Messe, f. -Mass, fair
messen - to measure
Messer, n. - knife
Metzger, m. -butcher
mich - me
mieten - to rent, hire
Milch, f. -milk
Milliarde - milliard
mir - to me
mit - with
Mittag, m. -noon
Mittagessen, n. -luncheon
Mitte, f. -middle
Mitteilung, f. -communication
Mitternacht, f. -midnight
Mittwoch, m. -Wednesday
Möbel, pl. -furniture
Mode, f. -fashion, style
Modistin, f. - milliner
mögen -to wish, to like
möglich - possible
Möglichkeit, f. -possibility
Monat, m. -month
Mond, m. -moon
Montag, m. -Monday
Morgen, m. -morning, tomorrow
morgen früh - tomorrow morning
Motorrad, n. - motorcycle
Mücke, f. -fly, mosquito, gnat
müde - tired
Mühe, f. - trouble
Mund, m. - mouth
Museum, n. - museum
müssen, - to have to, must
Mutter, f. - mother
Mütze, f. - cap

n

nach, nachher- after, afterwards
nachahmen - to imitate
Nachbar, m. - neighbor
nachfragen - to inquire
Nachmittag, m. - afternoon
Nachricht, f. - message, news
nachsehen - to check, to look after
nächst - next
Nacht, f. - night
Nachtisch, m. -dessert
Nadel, f. - needle
Nagel, m. -nail
Nagellack, m. -nailpolish
nah - near
Name, m.- name
Nase, f. - nose
nass - wet
natürlich -natural, naturally
Nebel, m. -fog, mist, haze
neblig -foggy, hazy
neben -next to, near
nehmen - to take
Neid, m. -envy
Neigung, f. -slope, inclination
nein - no
nennen -to name, to call
Netz, n. - net
neu - new
neun - nine
neunzehn - nineteen
neunzig - ninety
nicht - not

nichts - nothing
nie - never
niedrig - low
niemand - nobody
noch - still, yet
Norden, m. - north
nördlich - northern
nun - now
nur -only
nützen - to be useful

o

ob - if, whether
Ober - headwaiter
Obst, n. -fruit
oder - or
Ofen, m. - oven
offen - open
öffnen - to open
oft - often
ohne - without
Ohr, n. - ear
Öl - oil
Onkel, m. -uncle
Oper, f. - opera
Optiker, m. - optician
Osten, m. -east
östlich - eastern

p

Paar - pair, couple
Pantoffel, m. - slipper
Papier, n. - paper
Papierhandlung, f. -stationery store
Parfüm, n. - perfume
Park, m. - park
parken - to park
Parterre, n. -ground floor
Pass, m. - passport
Passagier, m. - passenger
Pelz, m. -fur
Pension, f. - boardinghouse, pension
Pfeife, f. - pipe(smoking), whistle
Pferd, n. - horse
Pfirsich, m. - peach
Pflaume, f. - plum
Pforte, f. - gate
Pille, f. - pill
Plakat, n. - poster
Platz, m. - place, public square, theater seat
Plombe, f. - filling (tooth)
Polizei, f. - police
Portier, m. -doorman
Porto, n. - postage
Postamt, n. - post office
Postanweisung, f. -postal money order
postlagernd - by general delivery
Preis, m. - price
Priester, m. - priest
Prosit! - to your health! (toast)
Puder, m. - powder
Punkt, m. - point
putzen -to clean, shine(shoes)

r

Rabatt, m. - discount
Rabbiner, m. -rabbi
Rad, n. -wheel, bicycle
radieren - to erase
Rahm, m. - cream
Rasen, m. - lawn, verb-rage, rave
rasieren (sich) - to shave
Rasierklinge, f. - razor blade
Rasierpinsel, m.-shaving brush
Rat, m. - advice, counsel
Rathaus, n. - city hall
rauchen - to smoke
rechnen - calculate, figure out
Rechnung, f. - bill
Recht, n.-law, right, justice
recht haben -to be right
rechts -to the right(direction)

reden - to talk
Regen, m.- rain
Regenmantel, m. - raincoat
Regenschirm, m. - umbrella
regieren - to rule
Regierung, f. - government
reich - rich
Reifen, m. -tire
reinigen - to clean
Reis, m. - rice
Reise, f. - trip
Reisender, traveler.
Reisepass, m. - passport
Reissverschluss, m. - zipper
rennen - to run
Rennplatz, m. - race track
Reparatur, f. - repair
Rettungsgürtel, m. -life preserver
Rezept, n. -prescription, recipe
Richter, m. -judge
Richtung. f. - direction
Rind, fleisch, n. -beef
Rolle, f. - roll, role
Roman, novel
rosa - pink
Rostbraten, pl. - roast beef
rot - red
Rücken, m. -back
Rückreise, f. - return trip
rückwarts - backwards
Ruf, m. -call
rufen - to call
Ruhe, f. -quiet, calm
ruhig -quiet, quietly
Rühreier, pl. -scrambled eggs
rund - round

S

Saal, m. -hall, large room
Sache, f. -thing, matter
sagen - to say
Sahne, f. -cream
Salbe, f. -ointment
Salz, m. -salt
sammeln -to collect, gather
Samstag, m. -Saturday
Samt, n. -velvet
Sand, m. -sand
sauer - sour
Säure, f. -acid
Schachtel, f. -box
Schaf, n. -sheep
Schaffner, m. -conductor (train)
Schallplatte, f. -phonograph record
Schalter, m. -light switch, ticket window
Scheck, m. -check
scheinbar -apparently, seemingly
scheinen -to shine, to seem, appear
schenken-to give a present
Schere, f. -scissors
schicken - to send
schieben - to push
Schiff, n. -ship
Schild, n. - sign
Schinken, m.-ham
Schlaf, m. -sleep
schlafen - to sleep
Schlafwagen, m. -sleeping car, Pullman
schlagen - to beat
Schlagsahne, f. -whipped cream
schlecht - bad
schliessen - to close
Schloss, n. -castle, lock
Schlüssel, m. - key
schmecken - to taste
Schmerz, m. -pain
Schmuck, m. -jewelry
Schmutz, m. -dirt
schmutzig - dirty
Schnee, m. - snow
schneien - to snow
Schneider, m. - tailor
schneiden - to cut
schnell - fast, quickly
Schnurrbart, m. -mustache
Schokolade, f. - chocolate
schön - beautiful

schon - already
Schönheit, f. - beauty
Schrank, m. -closet
schreiben - to write
Schreibmaschine, f. -typewriter
Schritt, m. -step
Schublade, f. -drawer
Schuh, m. -shoe
Schuhmacher, Schuster, m.-
shoemaker
Schutzmann, m. -policeman
schwach - weak
schwarz - black
Schwein, n. -pig, pork
schwer - heavy, difficult
Schwester, f. -sister, nurse
schwimmen - to swim
Schwimmanzug, m. -bathing suit
schwindeln -to cheat, to lie,
to swindle
schwindlig - dizzy
schwitzen - to sweat, perspire
sechs - six
sechzehn - sisteen
sechzig - sixty
See, m. -lake;f. -sea
seekrank - seasick
segeln -to sail
sehen - to see
sehr - very
Seide, f. -silk
Seife, f. -soap
Seil, n. -rope
sein - to be
seit- since
Seite, f. - page
selbe, derselbe - same
selbst - self, even
selbstverständlich - of course
selten - seldom, rare, rarely
Serviette, f. -napkin
Sessel, m. -armchair
sicher - sure, certain
Sicherheit, f. -security, certainty
Sicherheitsnadel, f. -safety pin
Sie - you;she;they
sieben - seven
siebzehn - seventeen
siebzig - seventy
singen - to sing
Sinn, m. - meaning, mind, sense
sitzen - to sit
Socken, pl. -socks
sofort -immediately
Sohn, m. -son
sonder - special
Sonnabend, m. - Saturday
Sonne, f. - sun
Sonntag, m. -Sunday
sonst - otherwise
sorgfältig - careful
spät - late
spazieren (gehen) to take a walk
Spaziergang, m. -walk
Speisekarte, f. - menu
Speisewagen, m.-dining car
(railroad)
Spiel, n. -game, play
spielen - to play
Spielzeug, n. - toy
Spitze, f. -peak; lace
Sprache, f. - language
sprechen - to speak
spucken - to spit
Staat, m. -state, nation
Staatsangehörigkeit, f. -nationality
Stadt, f. -city, town
Stahl, m. -steel
stark - strong
Stärke, f. -strength, starch
Staub, m. - dust
Steckkontakt, m. - electrical outlet
Stecknadel, f. -pin
stehen - to stand
stehlen - to steal
steigen - to climb
Stelle, f. -place
stellen - to put
Stellung, f. - position, job
Stellvertreter, m. -representative

sterben - to die
Stern, m. -star
Steuer, f. -tax
steuern - to steer
Steuerrad, n. -steering wheel
Stil, m. -style
Stille, f. -silence
Stirn , f. - forehead
Stockwerk, n. -story, floor
stören - to disturb, bother
Störung, f. -disturbance, bother
Strafe, f. -punishment, fine, penalty
Strand, m. -beach
Strasse, f. - street
Strassenbahn, f. -streetcar
Strassenkreuzung, f. -crossroad
Streichholz, n. -match
Stroh, n. - straw
Strom, m. -stream, large river, electric current
Strumpf, m. -stocking
Stück, n. - piece
Stunde, f. - hour
Sturm, m. - storm
suchen -to look for, search
Süden, m. -south
Suppe, f. -soup
süss - sweet

t

Tabak, m. - tobacco
Tafel, f. -blackboard, banquet table
Tag, m. -day
täglich - daily
Tal, n. - valley
Tankstelle, f. -gas station
Tante, f. -aunt
Tanz, m. - dance
Tasche, f. -pocket, bag
Taschentuch, n. -handkerchief
Tasse, f. - cup
Tee, m. - tea
Teig, m. - dough
Teil, m. - part
Teller, m. -plate, dish
Teppich, m. -rug
teuer - expensive, dear
Teufel, m. -devil
tief - deep
Tier, n. - animal
Tiergarten, m. -zoo
Tinte, f. -ink
Tisch, m. -table
Tischtuch, n. - tablecloth
Tochter, f. - daughter
Tod, m. - death
Toilette, f. -toilet, W. C. lavatory
Tor, n. - gate; m. -fool
Torte, f. - cake
tot - dead
tragen - to carry, to wear
Träger, m. -portor
Tratte, f. - draft
Treppe, f. - stair
trinken - to drink
Trinkgeld, n. -tip, gratuity
trocknen - to dry
Trottoir, n. - sidewalk
Tuch, n. - cloth
tun - to do
Tür, f. - door

u

übel - ill, bad, evel
über - above, over
übereinstimmen - to agree
übermorgen -day after tomorrow
überqueren - to cross
übersetzen -to translate
Überzieher, m. - overcoat
überzeugen - to convince
Ufer, n. - shore, bank
Uhr, f. - watch, clock
um - around, about
umdrehen (sich)to turn around
umsteigen -to transfer, to change trains

umwechseln - to exchange
umbequem - uncomfortable
und - and
ungefähr - approximately
Unrecht, n. - wrong
unten, unter - below, under
Unterrock, m. - slip
unterschreiben - to sign
Unterschrift, f. - signature
Untersuchung, f. -examination, inquiry
unterzeichnen - to sign
unzufrieden - dissatisfied

V

Vater, m. - father
Ventilator, m. - fan
verbinden -to connect, combine; to bandage
verbieten - to forbid
Vereinigte Staaten-United States
Vergangenheit, f. -past
vergeben - to pardon, forgive
vergessen - to forget
Vergnügen, n. - pleasure
verkaufen - to sell
verlassen - to leave, abandon
verlieren - to lose
Verlust, m. -loss
vermeiden - to avoid
vermieten - to rent
verschieben - to put off, postpone
verschieden -different, varied
Verspätung, f. -delay
versprechen - to promise
verstehen - to understand
Verwandter, -relative
Verzeihung, f. -forgivenness, pardon
viel - much
vielleicht - perhaps
vier - four
Viertel - quarter
vierzehn - fourteen
vierzig - forty
Vogel, m. -bird
Volk, n. -people, nation
voll - full
von - from, of
vor - in front of, before, ago
voraus - in advance
Voranmeldungsgespräch, n. - person-to-person call
Vorbezahlung, f. - advance payment
Vormittag, m. -forenoon
Vorsicht, f. -caution
Vorspeise, f. -appetizer
vorstellen -to introduce; (reflexive); imagine
Vorstellung, f. - performance
vorwärts - forward

W

Wagen, m. -car, wagon, railroad car
wählen -to choose; to vote
wahr - true
während - during, while
Wahrheit, f. -truth
wahrscheinlich - probably
Wald, m. -forest, woods
Wand, f. -wall
Wange, f. -cheek
wann - when
Ware, f. - merchandise
Warenhaus, n. -department store
warm - warm
Warnung, f. - warning
warten - to wait
warum - why
was - what
Waschbecken, n. -sink
Wäsche, f. -laundry, linens
waschen -to wash
Wäscherei, f. -laundry
Wasser, n. -water
Watte, f. -absorben cotton

Wechsel, m. -bank draft, (check), change
wechseln - to change
Weg, m. - way, road
wegen - on account of, because of
wegwerfen - to throw away
weich - soft
Weihnachten - Christmas
weil - because
Wein, m. - wine
weinen - to weep, to cry
weiss - white
weit - far, wide
welcher - which
wenig - little
wenn - if
wer - who
werden - to become
werfen - to throw
Wert, m. -worth, value
weshalb - why
Westen, m. -west
Wetter, n. -weather
wichtig - important
wie - how
wieder - again
wiederholen - to repeat
wiedersehen - to see again
wiegen -to weigh; to rock(cradle)
Wiese, f. -meadow
wieviel(e)-how much(many)
willkommen - welcome
Wind, m. -wind
wir - we
wirklich -really, indeed
Wirtshaus, n. -inn, tavern
wissen - to know
wo - where
Woche, f. -week
wohnen, to live, dwell
Wohnung, f. - apartment
Wolle, f. - wool
wollen - to want
Wort, n. -word
Wörterbuch, n. -dictionary
Wunde, f. -wound
wunderbar - wonderful
wünschen - to wish
Wurst, f. -sausage
würzen - to season(food)

Z

zahlen - to pay
zählen - to count
Zahn, m. -tooth
Zahnarzt, m. - dentist
Zahnbürste, f. - toothbrush
Zahnschmerzen, pl. -toothache
Zehe, f. - toe
zehn - ten
Zeichen, n. - sign
zeigen - to show, indicate
Zeit, f. - time
Zeitschrift, f. -periodical, magazine
Zeitung, f. - newspaper
Zelt, n. - tent
zerbrechen - to break
zerstören - to destroy
ziehen - to pull, draw
ziemlich - rather
Zigarre, f. -cigar
Zigarette, f. - cigarette
Zimmer, n. - room
Zirkus, m. - circus
Zitrone, f. - lemon
Zoll, m. -customs duty
Zollamt, n. - customs house
Zoo - zoo
zu - to, too
zuviel - too much
Zucker, m. - sugar
zuerst - at first
Zufall, m. - coincidence, chance
Zug, m. - train;draft(of air)
zuletzt - finally
zumindest - at least
Zündholz, n. - match

Zunge, f. - tonguc
zurück - back
zurückgeben - to give back
zurückkehren - to turn back,
to return
zurückkommen - to come back,
to return
zwanzig - twenty
zwei - two
Zwirn, m. - thread
zwischen - between
zwölf - twelve

ALPHABETICAL ENGLISH GERMAN VOCABULARY

Note that all the nouns are given in the nominative singular with their respective article, indicating gender. The verbs are given in the infinitive alone, since the principal parts of many common regular as well as irregular verbs are indicated in the grammar section.

a

a, an	ein	ahyn
able	fähig	fae-ig
about (concerning)	über	ue-behr
about(approximately)	ungefähr	oon-geh-faer
above	über	ue-behr
accept	annehmen	ahn-neh-mehn
accident	der Unfall	oon-fahl
ache	der Schmerz	shmehrts
across	gegenüber, hinüber	geh-gehn-ue-behr, hin-ue-behr
address	die Adresse	ah-drehs-eh
adjust	anpassen, richten	shn-pahs-sehn, rih-tehn
admission	der Eintritt	ahyhtrit
afraid (to be)	fürchten, Angst haben	fuerh-tehn, ahngst hah-behn
after	nach	nahh
afternoon	der Nachmittag	nahh-mit-tahg
afterwards	nachher	nahh-hehr
again	wieder	vee-dehr
against	gegen	geh-gehn
ago	vor (bevor)	fohr
two weeks ago	vor zwei Wochen	fohr tsvahy voh-hehn
ahead	vorwärts	fohr-vaerts
air	die Luft	Looft
airfield	der Flugplatz	Floog-plahts
airplane	Flugzeug	Floog-tsoyg
air mail	Luftpost	looft-pohst
airport	der Flughafen	floog-hah-fehn
alarm clock	der Wecker	vehl-kehr
all	alle, alles	ahl-leh, ahl-lehs
allow	erlauben	ehr-lou-behn
almost	beinahe, fast	bahy-nah-eh, fahst
alone	allein	ahl-lahyn
along	entlang	ehnt-lahng

already	schon	shohn
always	immer	im-mehr
am	bin	bin
American	der Amerikaner, die Amerikanerin, amerikanisch	ah-meh-ree-kah-nehr, ah-meh-ree-kah-nehr-in, ah-meh-ree-kah-nish
among	unter	oon-tehr
amount	der Betrag	beh-trahg
and	und	oond
angry (to be)	böse sein	boe-zeh zahyn
animal	das Tier	teer
annoy	belästigen	beh-laes-ti-gehn
another	noch ein	noh ahyn
answer (noun)	die Antwort	ahnt-vohrt
answer (verb)	antworten	ahnt-vohr-tehn
any	etwas	eht-vahs
anybody	irgend jemand	ir-gehd yeh-mahnd
anything	irgend etwas	ir-gehnd eht-vahs
anything else?	noch etwas?	noh eht-vahs
apartment	die Wohnung	voh-noong
appear	erscheinen	ehr-shahy-nehn
appetizer	die Vorspeise	fohr-shahy-zeh
apple	der Apfel	ahp-fehl
approximately	ungefähr	oon-geh-faer
apricot	die Aprikose	ah-pree-koh-zeh
April	der April	ah-pril
are	sind	zind
arm	der Arm	ahrm
armchair	der Sessel	zehs-sehl
around	um	oom
arrival	die Ankunft	ahn-koonft
arrive	ankommen	ahn-kom-mehn
art	die Kunst	koonst
article	der Artikel	ahr-ti-kehl
as	als; wie	ahls, vee
ash tray	der Aschenbecher	ah-shehn-beh-hehr
ask	fragen	frah-gehn
asparagus	der Spargel	shpahr-gehl
aspirin	das Aspirin	ahs-pie-reen
at	bei; um (time)	by, oom
at least	zumindest, mindestens	tsoo-min-dehst, min-dehs-tehns
at once	sofort	zoh-fohrt
attention!	Achtung	ahh-toong
August	der August	ou-goost

aunt	die Tante	tahn-teh
Austrian	der Österreicher, österreichisch	oestehr-rahy-hehr, oe-stehr-rahy hish
automobile	das Auto, der Wagen	ou-toh, vah-gehn
autumn	der Herbst	hehrbst
avoid	vermeiden	fehr-mahy-dehn
awful	schrecklich	shrehk-lih

b

back (noun)	der Rücken	ruek-kehn
back (adv.)	zurück	tsoo-ruek
at the back	hinten	hin-tehn
bacon	der Speck	shpehk
bad	schlecht	shlehht
baggage	das Gepäck	geh-paek
baked	gebacken	geh-bah-kehn
balcony	der Balkon	bahl-kohn
ball (dance and game)	der Ball	bahl
banana	die Banane	bah-nah-neh
bandage (noun)	der Verband	fehr-bahnd
bandage (verb)	verbinden	fehr-bin-dehn
bank	die Bank	bahnk
barber	der Friseur	fri-zoer
bargain (noun)	der Gelegenheitskauf	geh-leh-gehn-hahyts-kouf
basket	der Korb	kohrb
bath, bathe	das Bad, baden	bahd, bah-dehn
bathing suit	der Badeanzug	bah-deh-ahn-tsooh
bathrobe	der Bademantel	bah-deh-mahn-tehl
bathroom	das Badezimmer	bah-deh-tsim-mehr
battery	die Batterie	bah-teh-ree
be (to)	sein	zahyn
beach	der Strand	shtrahnd
bean	die Bohne	boh-neh
beautiful	schön	shoen
beauty salon	der Schönheitssalon	shoen-hahyts-sah-lohn
because	weil	vahyl
become	werden	vehr-dehn
bed	das Bett	beht
bedroom	das Schlafzimmer	shlahf-tsim-mehr
beef	das Rindfleisch	rind-flahysh
beer	das Bier	beer
beet	die rote Rübe	roh-teh rue-beh
before (adv. & prep.)	bevor, vor	beh-fohr, fohr
begin	anfangen, beginnen	ahn-fahng-ehn, beh-gin-nehn

beginning	der Anfang	ahn-fahng
behind	hinter	hin-tehr
believe	glauben	glou-behn
bell (door)	die Klingel	kling-ehl
bellboy	der Hotelpage	hoh-tehl-pah-dsheh
belong	gehören	geh-hoe-rehn
below	unter	oon-tehr
belt	der Gürtel	guer-tehl
best (adj.)	am besten	ahm behs-tehn
bet (verb)	wetten	veht-tehn
better	besser	behs-sehr
between	zwischen	tsvish-ehn
beverage	das Getränk	geh-traenk
big	gross	grohs
bill	die Rechnung; die bank-note(money)	rehh-noong, bahnk-noh-teh
bird	der Vogel	foh-gehl
bitter	bitter	bit-tehr
blade(razor)	die Rasier-klinge	rah-zeer-kling-eh
blank (noun)	das Formular	fohr-moo-lahr
blanket	die Decke	dehl-keh
blood	das Blut	bloot
blouse	die Bluse	bloo-zeh
blue	blau	blou
boardinghouse	die Pension	pehn-zee-ohn
boat	das Boot	boht
body	der Körper	koer-pehr
boiled	gekocht	geh-koht
bone	der Knochen	kno-hehn
book	das Buch	booh
bookstore	die Buchhandlung	booh-hahnd-loong
border	die Grenze	grehn-tseh
born (to be)	geboren (sein)	geh-boh-rehn (zahyn)
borrow	borgen	bohr-gehn
both	beide	bahy-deh
bother (noun)	die Belästigung	beh-laes-ti-goong
bother (verb)	belästigen	beh-laes-ti-gehn
bottle	die Flasche	flah-sheh
box	die Schachtel	shahh-tehl
box office(theater)	die Theaterkasse	teh-ah-tehr-kahs-seh
boy	der Junge, der Knabe	yoong-eh,knah-beh
bra, brassiere	der Büstenhalter	bues-tehn-hahl-tehr
bracelet	das Armband	ahrm-bahnd
brake	die Bremse	brehm-zeh
bread	das Brot	broht

break	brechen, zerbrechen	brehh-ehn, tsehr-brehh-ehn
breakfast	das Frühstück	frue-shtuek
breathe	atmen	aht-mehn
bridge	die Brücke	brue-keh
bring	bringen	bring-ehn
broken	zerbrochen	tsehr-broh-ehn
brother	der Bruder	broo-dehr
brown	braun	broun
brush (noun)	die Bürste	buer-steh
brush (verb)	bürsten	buer-stehn
building	das Gebäude	geh-boy-deh
bulb (electric)	die Glühbirne	glue-bir-neh
burn (verb)	brennen, verbrennen	brehn-nehn, fehr-brehn-nehn
bus	der Autobus	ou-toh-boos
busy	beschäftigt	beh-shaef-tigt
but	aber	ah-behr
butter	die Butter	boot-tehr
button	der Knopf	knopf
buy	kaufen	kou-fehn
by	bei; durch(means)	by, doorh

C

cab	das Taxi	tah-ksee
cabaret	das Kabarett	kah-bah-reht
cabbage	der Kohl	kohl
cable (verb)	telegraphieren	teh-leh-grah-fee-rehn
cake	der Kuchen	koo-hehn
call (noun)	der Anruf	Ahn-roof
call (verb)	rufen, anrufen	roo-fehn, ahn-roof-ehn
calm	ruhig	roo-ig
can (noun)	die Büchse	buek-seh
can (verb)	können	koen-nehn
cancel	abmelden	ahb-mehl-dehn
candle	die Kerze	kehr-tseh
car	das Auto, der Wagen	ou-toh, vah-gehn
card	die Karte	kahr-teh
care (noun)	die Sorge	zohr-geh
careful, carefully	sorgfältig	zohrg-fael-tig
carrot	die Karotte, die gelbe Rübe	kah-rot-teh, gehl-beh rue-beh
carry	tragen	trah-gehn
case, in any case	Fall, auf jeden Fall	fahl, ouf yeh-dehn
cash (noun)	das Bargeld	bahr-gehld

cashier	der Kassierer	kah-seer
castle	das Schloss	shlohs
cat	die Katze	kah-tseh
catch	fangen	fahng-ehn
cathedral	der Dom, Münster	dohn, muen-stehr
Catholic	der Katholik, katholisch	kah-toh-leek, kah-ton-lish
cauliflower	der Blumenkohl	bloo-mehn-kohl
caution	die Vorsicht	fohr-sikt
ceiling	die Decke	deh-keh
center	die Mitte, das Zentrum	mit-teh, tsehn-troom
certainly	gewiss, sicherlich	geh-vis, zi-kehr-lih
certificate	das Zeugniss	tsoyg-nis
chain	die Kette	keht-teh
chair	der Stuhl;der Sessel	shtool, zehs-sehl
change (noun)	die Veränderung, der Wechsel	fehr-den-deh-roong, vehk-sehl.
change(small change)	das Kleingeld	klahyn-gehld
change (verb)	wechseln	vehk-sehln
cheap	billig	bil-lig
check(noun:baggage)	der Gepäckschein	geh-paek-shahyn
check(verb:baggage)	aufgeben	ouf-yeh-behn
checkroom(railway)	die Gepäckaufbe-wahrung	geh-paek-ouf-beh-vah-roong
checkroom(theater)	die Garderobe	gahr-deh-roh-beh
cheek	die Backe, die Wange	bah-keh, vahng-eh
cheese	der Käse	kae-zeh
cherry	die Kirsche	kir-sheh
chest (anat.)	die Brust	broost
chestnut	die Kastanie	kahs-tah-nee-eh
chicken	das Huhn	hoon
child	das Kind	Kind
chin	das Kinn	kin
chocolate	die Schokolade	shoh-koh-lah-deh
choose	wählen, aussuchen	vae-lehn, ous-zoo-hehn
chop (noun)	das Kotelett	kot-leht
Christmas	Weihnachten	Vahy-nahh-tehn
church	die Kirche	kir-heh
cigar	die Zigarre	tsi-gah-reh
cigarette	die Zigarette	tsi-gahr-reht-teh
city	die Stadt	shtaht
city hall	das Rathaus	raht-hous
class	die Klasse	klahs-seh
clean (adj.)	rein, sauber	rahyn, zou-behr

clean (verb)	reinigen, putzen	rahy-ni-gehn, poot-tsehn
cleaner's (dry)	die chemische Reinigung	keh-mish-eh rahy-ni-goong klahr
clear (adj.)	klar	klahr
clear up (sky)	sich aufklären	zih ouf-klae-rehn
climb	hinaufsteigen	hin-ouf-shtahy-gehn
clock	die Uhr	oor
close (adj.)	nahe	nah-eh
close (verb)	schliessen	shlee-sehn
closed	geschlossen	geh-shloh-sehn
closet	der Schrank	shrahnk
cloth	das Tuch, der Stoff (fabric)	tooh, shtohf
clothes	die Kleider	klahy-dehr
cloud	die Wolke	vohl-keh
cloudy	bewölkt	beh-voelkt
coach (horse)	die Kutsche	koot-sheh
coat	der Mantel	mahn-tehl
cocktail	der Cocktail	kok-tehl
coffee	der Kaffee	kahf-feh
coin	die Münze	muen-tseh
coincidence	der Zufall	tsoo-fahl
cold (adj.)	kalt	kahlt
cold(respiratory)	die Erkältung	ehr-kael-toong
cold cuts	der Aufschnitt	ouf-shnit
collar	der Kragen	krah-gehn
color	die Farbe	fahr-beh
comb (noun)	der Kamm	kahm
come, come in	kommen, hineinkommen	koh-mehn hin-ahyn-koh-mehn
come in!	Herein!	heh-ryn
comfortable	bequem	beh-kvehm
company (commercial)	die Gesellschaft	geh-zehl-shahft
compartment	das Abteil	ahb-tahyl
complain	sich beklagen	sih beh-klah-gehn
complaint	die Klage	klah-geh
concert	das Konzert	Kuhn-tsehrt
conductor	der Schaffner (train) Dirigent (music)	shahf-nehr, dee-ree-gehnt
congratulations	die Glückwünsche (pl.)	gluek-wuen-sheh
connected (telephone)	verbunden	fehr-boon-dehn
consist (of)	bestehen (aus)	beh-shteh-ehn (ous)
consul	der Konsul	kohn-sool
continue	fortsetzen	fohrt-zeh-tsehn
convent	das Kloster	kloh-stehr

cooked	gekocht	geh-koht
cool	kühl	kuel
corn (Indian)	der Mais	mah-is
corner	die Ecke	ehl-keh
correct	richtig	rih-tig
cost (noun)	der Preis	prahys
cost (verb)	kosten	kos-tehn
cotton	Baumwolle	boum-voh-leh
cotton(absorbent)	die Watte	vaht-teh
cough (noun)	der Husten	hoos-tehn
count (verb)	zählen	tsae-lehn
country	das Land	lahnd
courtyard	der Hof	hohf
crazy	verrückt	fehr-ruekt
cream(heavy cream)	die Sahne	zah-neh
crossing(railroad)	die Überkreuzung	ue-behr-kroy-tsoong
crystal	das Kristall	kri-stahl
cucumber	die Gurke	goor-keh
cufflinks	die Manschetten-knöpfe	mahn-sheh-tehn-knoe-pfeh
cup	die Tasse	tahs-seh
currency	die Währung	vae-roong
curtain	der Vorhang	fohr-hahng
curve	die Kurve	koor-veh
customs	das Zollamt	tsohl-ahmt
cut (verb)	schneiden	shnahy-dehn
cutlet	das Kotelett	koht-leht

d

daily(by the day)	täglich	taeg-lih
damaged	beschädigt	beh-shae-digt
dance	der Tanz, tanzen	tahnts, tahn-tsehn
danger	die Gefahr	geh-fahr
dark	dunkel	doonk-ehl
darn	stopfen	stopf-ehn
date	das Datum	dah-toom
daughter	die Tochter	toh-tehr
day	der Tag	tahk
dead, death	tot, der Tod	toht, tohd
December	der Dezember	deh-tsehm-behr
deck	das Deck	dehk
deck chair	der Liegestuhl	lee-geh-shtool
declaration (and explanation)	die Erklärung	ehr-klae-roong

deep	tief	teef
deliver, delivery	liefern, die Lieferung	lee-fehrn, lee-feh-roong
definite	bestimmt	beh-shtimt
dentist	der Zahnarzt	tsahn-ahrtst
denture	das Gebiss	geh-bis
depart	abfahren	ahb-fah-rehn
department store	Warenhaus	vah-vehn-hous
departure	die Abfahrt	ahb-fahrt
desk(information)	die Auskunftstelle	ous-koonft-shtehl-leh
dessert	der Nachtisch, das Dessert	nahh-tish, deh-sehrt
detour	der Umweg	oom-vehg
develop	entwickeln	ehnt-vik-kehln
devil	der Teufel	toy-fehl
diaper	die Windel	vin-dehl
dictionary	das Wörterbuch	voer-tehr-booh
defferent	verschieden	fehr-shee-dehn
difficult, difficulty	schwer, die Schwierigkeit	shvehr, shvee-rig-kahyt
dining car	der Speisewagen	vah-gehn shpahy-zeh
dining room	das Speisezimmer, das Esszimmer	shpahy-zeh-tsim-mehr, ehs-tsim-mehr
direction	die Richtung	rih-toong
dirty	schmutzig	shmoots-ig
discount	der Rabatt	rah-baht
dish	das Gericht, der Teller	geh-riht, tehl-lehr
district	das Viertel	feer-tehl
disturb	stören	shtoe-rehn
dizzy	schwindlig	shvind-lig
do	machen, tun	mah-hehn, toon
dock	das Dock	dohk
documents	die Papiere	pah-pee-reh
dog	der Hund	hoond
domestic	heimisch	hahy-mish
door	die Tür	tuer
doorman	der Portier	pohr-tee-eh
double	doppelt	doh-pehlt
double room	das Doppelzimmer	dop-pehl-tsim-mehr
down	unten	oon-tehn
dozen	das Dutzend	doo-tsehnd
draft (bank)	der Wechsel	vehk-sehl
draw (pull)	ziehen	tsie-ehn
drawer	die Schublade	shoob-lah-deh
dress	das Kleid	klahyd

dresser	die Kommode	koh-moh-deh
dressing gown	der Schlafrock	shlahf-rohk
drink (noun)	das Getränk	geh-traenk
drink (verb)	trinken	trink-ehn
drive (car)	chauffieren, fahren	shoh-fee-rehn, fah-rehn
driver	der Fahrer, Chauffeur	fah-rehr, shoh-fuer
drugstore	die Apotheke	ah-poh-teh-keh
drunk	betrunken	beh-troonk-ehn
dry	trocken	troh-kehn
dry cleaning	die chemische Reinigung	keh-mish-eh rahy-ni-goong
duck	die Ente	ehn-teh
during	während	vae-rehn
duty (customs)	der Zoll	tsohl

e

each (one)	jeder	jeh-dehr
ear	das Ohr	ohr
earache	die Ohrenschmerzen	oh-rehn-shmehrts-ehn
early	früh	frue
earring	der Ohrring	ohr-ring
east	der Osten	ohs-tehn
easy	leicht	lahyht
eat	essen	ehs-sehn
egg	das Ei	ahy
eight	acht	ahht
eighty	achtzig	ahht-tsig
either... or	entweder... oder	ehnt-woh-dehr...oh-dehr
electric	elektrisch	eh-lehk-trish
elevator	der Aufzug, Lift	ouf-tsoog, lift
eleven	elf	ehlf
empty	leer	lehr
end (noun)	das Ende	ehn-deh
engine	die Maschine	mah-shee-neh
enjoy	geniessen	geh-nee-sehn
enlargement	die Vergrösserung	fehr-groe-seh-roong
enough	genug	geh-noolg
entrance	der Eingang	ahyn-gahng
envelope	das Kuvert, der Briefumschlag	koo-vehrt, breef-oom-shlahlg
evening	der Abend	ah-behnd
every	jeder, jedes, jede	yeh-dehr, yeh-dehs, yeh-deh
everything	alles	ahl-lehs

everywhere	überall	ue-behr-ahl
examine	untersuchen	oon-tehr-zoo-hehn
excellent	ausgezeichnet	ous-geh-tsahyh-neht
exchange (verb)	umtauschen, umwechseln	oom-tou-shehn, oom-vehk-sehln
excursion	der Ausflug	ous-floog
excuse (verb)	(sich) entschuldigen	zih ehnt-shool-di-gehn
exit	der Ausgang	ous-gahng
expect	erwarten	ehr-vahr-tehn
expensive	teuer	toy-ehr
explain (and declare)	erklären	ehr-klae-rehn
express (train)	der Schnellzug	shnehl-tsoog
extraordinary	ausserordentlich	ou-sehr-or-dehnt-lih
eye	das Auge	ou-geh
eyebrow	die Augenbraue	au-gehn-brou-eh
eyeglasses	die Brille	bril-leh
eyelash	die Wimper	vim-pehr

f

face	das Gesicht	geh-ziht
fall	fallen	fahl-lehn
false	falsch	fahlsh
family	die Familie	fah-mee-lee-eh
famous	berühmt	beh-ruemt
far	weit	vahyt
fast	schnell	shnehl
father	der Vater	fah-tehr
fear	die Angst, Angst haben	ahngst, ahngst hah-behn
February	der Februar	feh-broo-ahr
feel like	Lust haben	loost hah-behn
feel	fühlen	füe-lehn
feet	Füsse	füe-seh
festival	das Fest	fehst
fever	das Fieber	fee-behr
few	einige, wenige	ahy-ni-geh, veh-ni-geh
fifteen	fünfzehn	fuenf-tsehn
fifty	fünfzig	fuenf-tsig
fig	die Feige	fahy-geh
fill	füllen, ausfüllen	fue-lehn, ous-fu-lehn
filling (tooth)	die Plombe	plom-beh
film	der Film	film
find	finden	fin-dehn
fine (adj.)	fein, hübsch, schön	fahyn, huebsh, shoen

fine (noun)	die Strafe	shtrah-feh
finger	der Finger	fing-ehr
finished	fertig, beendet	fehr-tilg, beh-ehnd-eht
fire (noun)	das Feuer	foy-ehr
first	erst	ehrst
first aid	erste Hilfe	chr-steh Hil-feh
fish	der Fisch	fish
fit	passen	pahs-sehn
five	fünf	fuenf
fix (verb)	reparieren	reh-pah-ree-rehn
flashlight	die Taschenlampe	tah-shehn-lahm-peh
flat tire	die Reifenpanne	rahy-fehn-pahn-neh
flight	die Flucht	flooht
flight(airplane)	der Flug	floog
floor	der Boden	boh-dehn
flower	die Blume	bloo-meh
fluid (noun)	die Flüssigkeit	flues-sig-kahyt
fog	der Nebel	neh-behl
follow	folgen	gohl-gehn
food	das Essen	ehs-sehn
foot	der Fuss	foos
for	für	fuer
forbidden	verboten	fehr-boh-tehn
forehead	die Stirn	shtir-neh
foreign	ausländisch	ous-laend-ish
forest	der Wald	vahld
forget	vergessen	fehr-gehs-sehn
fork	die Gabel	gah-behl
form(document)	das Formular	fohr-moo-lahr
formerly	früher	frue-ehr
forty	vierzig	feer-tsig
forward (adv.)	vorwärts	fohr-vaerts
fountain	der Brunnen	broon-nehn
four	vier	feer
free	frei	frahy
Friday	der Freitag	frahy-tahg
fried	gebraten	geh-brah-tehn
friend	der Freund(masc.) die Freundin(fem.)	fruynd, froyn-din
friendly	freundlich	froind-lih
from	von	fohn
from it	davon	dah-fohn
front	vorn, vor	fohrn, fohr
fruit	das Obst, die Frucht	ohbst, frooht

full	voll	fohl
furnished	möbliert	moe-bleert
further	weiter	vahy-tehr

g

gallery (art)	die Gemäldegallerie	geh-mael-deh-gah-leh-ree
game	das Spiel	shpeel
garage	die Garage	gah-rah-dsheh
garden	der Garten	gahr-tehn
garlic	der Knoblauch	knohb-louh
garter	das Strumpfband	shtroomf-bahnd
gasoline	das Gasolin	gah-zoh-leen
gas station	die Tankstelle	tahnk-shtehl-leh
gate	das Tor	tohr
general delivery	postlagernd	pohst-lah-gehrnd
gentleman	der Herr	hehr
German	der Deutsche, deutsch	doyt-sheh, doytsh
get (obtain)	bekommen	beh-kohm-ehn
get off (train, etc.)	aussteigen	ous-shtahy-gehn
get up	aufstehen	ouf-shteh-ehn
gift	das Geschenk	geh-shehnk
girdle	der Hüfthalter	hueft-hahl-tehr
girl	das Mädchen	maed-hehn
give	geben	geh-behn
glad	froh	froh
gladly	gerne	gehr-neh
glass	das Glas	glahs
glasses (eye)	die Brille, Augengläser	bril-leh, ougehn-glae-zehr
glove	der Handschuh	hahnd-shoo
go	gehen	geh-ehn
go away	weggehen	wehlg-geh-ehn
go down	hinuntergehen	hin-oon-tehr-geh-ehn
go home	nach Hause gehen	nahh hou-zeh geh-ehn
go in	hineingehen	hin-ahyn-geh-ehn
go out	hinausgehen	hinous-geh-ehn
go up	hinaufgehen	hin-ouf-geh-ehn
gold	das Gold	gold
good	gut	goot
goose	die Gans	gahns
gradually	allmählich	ahl-mae-lih
grapefruit	die Pampelmuse	pahm-pehl-moo-zeh
grapes	die Trauben (pl.)	trou-behn

grass	das Gras	grahs
grateful	dankbar	dahnk-bahr
gravy	die Sosse, die Sauce	zoh-seh
gray	grau	grou
green	grün	gruen
greeting	der Gruss	groos
guide	der Führer	fue-rehr
guide book	der Reiseführer	rahy-zeh-fue-rehr
gum (chewing)	der Kaugummi	kou-goom-mee
gums	das Zahnfleisch	tsahn-flahysh
guy	der Kerl	kehrl

h

hail (noun; weather)	der Hagel	hah-gehl
hair	das Haar	hahr
haircut	der Haarschnitt	hahr-shnit
hairpin	die Haarnadel	hahr-nah-dehl
hair tonic	das Haarwasser	hahr-vahs-sehr
half	halb, die Hälfte	hahlb, haelf-teh
ham	der Schinken	shink-ehn
hammer	der Hammer	hahm-mehr
hand	die Hand	hahnd
handbag	die Handtasche	hahnd-tahsh-eh
handkerchief	das Taschentuch	tah-shehn-tooh
hanger (coat)	der Kleiderbügel	klahy-dehr-bue-gehl
happen	geschehen	geh-sheh-ehn
happy	glücklich	gluck-lih
harbor	der Hafen	hah-fehn
hard (difficult)	schwer	shvehr
hard (physically)	hart	hahrt
hard-boiled	hart gekocht	hahrt geh-koht
hardly	kaum	koum
hat	der Hut	hoot
have	haben	hah-behn
head	der Kopf	kopf
headache	das Kopfweh	kopf-veh
health	die Gesundheit	geh-zoond-hahyt
hear	hören	hoe-rehn
heart	das Herz	hehrts
heat	die Hitze, heizen	hi-tseh, hahy-tsehn
heaven	der Himmel	him-mehl
heavy	schwer	shvehr
heel (of foot)	die Ferse	fehr-zeh
heel (of shoe)	der Absatz	ahb-zahts

hell	die Hölle	hoel-leh
help	Hilfe, helfen	hil-feh, hehl-fehn
here	hier	heer
high	hoch	hohh
highway	die Autobahn	ou-toh-bahn
him	ihn, ihm	een, eem
hip	die Hüfte	huef-teh
hire	mieten	meet-ehn
his	sein	zahyn
hold	halten	hahl-tehn
hole	das Loch	loh
home (noun)	das Heim	hahym
hook	der Haken	hah-kehn
hope	hoffen	hof-fehn
horn (auto)	die Hupe	hoo-peh
horse	das Pferd	pfehrd
hospital	das Krankenhaus, das Hospital	krahnk-ehn-hous, shpi-tahl
hostel (youth)	die Jugendherberge	yoo-gehnd-hehr-behr-geh
hot	heiss	hahys
hotel	das Hotel	ho-tehl
hour	die Stunde	shtoon-deh
house	das Haus	hous
how	wie	vee
how far	wie weit	vee vahyt
how long	wie lang	vee lahng
how many, how much	wieviele, wieviel	vee-fee-leh, vee-feel
human being	der Mensch	mehnsh
hundred	hundert	hoon-dehrt
hunger	der Hunger	hoong-ehr
hurry	sich beeilen	zih beh-ahy-lehn
husband	der Ehemann, der Gatte	eh-eh-mahn

i

I	ich	ih
ice	das Eis	ahys
ice cream	das Gefrorene	geh-froh-reh-neh
identification card	der Ausweis	ous-vahys
if	wenn, falls	vehn, fahls
ill	krank	krahnk
illness	die Krankheit	krahnk-hahy
immediately	gleich, sofort	glahyh, zoh-fort

important	wichtig	vih-tig
imported	importiert	im-pohr-teert
impossible	unmöglich	oon-moeg-lih
in	in	in
in advance	im voraus	im vohr-ous
included	einbegriffen	ahyn-beh-grif-fehn
indigestion	die Magenverstimmung	mah-gehn-fehr-shtim-moong
indisposed	unwohl	oon-vohl
information	Auskunft	ous-koonft
injection	die Einspritzung	ahyn-shpri-tsoong
ink	die Tinte	tin-teh
inquire	um Auskunft bitten	oom ows-koonft bit-tehn
insect	das Insekt	in-sehkt
inside	drinnen	drin-nehn
instead	anstatt	ahn-shtaht
insurance	die Versicherung	fehr-zih-eh-roong
insure	versichern	fehr-sih-ehrn
interest	das Interesse, interessieren	in-teh-rehs-seh, in-teh-rehs-sie-rehn
interrupt	unterbrechen	oon-tehr-brehh-ehn
interpreter	der Dolmetscher	dol-meht-shehr
intersection	die Kreuzung	kroy-tsoong
into	hinein	hin-ahyn
introduce	vorstellen, einführen	vohr-shtehl-hehn, ahyn-fue-rehn
invitation	die Einladung	ahyn-lah-doong
iodine	das Jod	yohd
iron (metal)	das Eisen	ahy-zehn
iron (for pressing)	das Bügeleisen	bue-gehl-ahy-zehn
is	ist	ist
it	es	ehs

J

jacket	die Jacke	yahk-keh
jam	die Marmelade	mahr-meh-lah-dah
January	der Januar	yah-noo-ahr
jeweler	der Juwelier	yoo-veh-leer
jewelry	die Juwelen, der Schmuck	yoo-veh-lehn, shmook
Jewish	jüdisch	yue-dish
journey	die Reise	rahy-zeh
juice	der Saft	zahft

July	der Juli	yoo-lee
June	der Juni	yoo-nee
just (adj.)	gerecht	geh-rehht

k

keep	behalten	beh-hahl-tehn
key	der Schlüssel	shlues-sehl
kilogram	das Kilo	kee-loh
kilometer	der Kilometer	kee-loh-meh-tehr
kind (adj.)	freundlich, gütig	froynd-lih, gue-tig
kind (noun)	die Art, die Sorte	ahrt, zor-teh
kiss	der Kuss, küssen	koos, kues-sehn
knee	das Knie	knee
knife	das Messer	mehs-sehr
knock (verb)	klopfen	klohp-fehn
know	kennen, wissen	kehn-nehn, vis-sehn

l

label	das Etikett, der Zettel	eh-ti-keht, tseht-tehl
lace	die Spitze	shpitse
ladies' room	die Damentoilette	dah-mehn-toh-ah-leht-teh
lady	die Dame	dah-meh
lamb	das Lamm	lahm
lamp	die Lampe	lahm-peh
land	das Land, landen	lahnd, lahn-dehn
language	die Sprache	shprah-keh
large	gross	grohs
last (adj.)	letzte	lehts-teh
last (verb)	dauern	dou-ehrn
late	spät	shpaet
laugh (verb)	lachen	lah-hehn
laundry	die Wäsche, die Wäscherei	vaesh-eh, vaesh-eh-ahy
lavatory	der Waschraum	vahsh-roum
laxative	das Abführmittel	ahb-fuer-mit-tehl
lead (verb)	führen	fue-rehn
lean	lehnen, sich anlehnen	leh-nehn, zih ahn-leh-nehn
learn	lernen	lehr-nehn
least (at)	wenigstens, mindestens, zumindest	veh-nig-stehns, min-dehs-tehns, tsoo-min-dehst

leather	das Leder	leh-dehr
leave (behind)	zurücklassen	tsoo-ruek-lahs-sehn
leave (depart)	abreisen	ahb-rahy-zehn
left(opp. of right)	links	links
leg	das Bein	bahyn
lemon	die Zitrone	tsi-troh-neh
lemonade	die Limonade	li-moh-nah-deh
lend	leihen, borgen	lahy-ehn, bor-gehn
length	die Länge	laeng-eh
lens	die Linse	lin-zeh
less	weniger	veh-ni-gehr
let	lassen	lahs-sehn
letter	der Brief	breef
letterbox	der Briefkasten	breef-kahs-tehn
lettuce	der Kopfsalat	kopf-zah-laht
library	die Bibliothek	bib-li-oh-tehk
lie (down)	sich niederlegen	zih nee-dehr-leh-gehn
life	das Leben	leh-behn
lifeboat	das Rettungsboot	reht-toongs-boht
life-preserver	der Rettungsgürtel	reht-toongs-guer-tehl
lift (verb)	heben	heh-behn
light(adj.)	hell, leicht	hehl, lahyht
light (noun)	das Licht	liht
lighter(cigarette)	das Feuerzeug	foy-ehr-tsoyg
lightning	der Blitz	blits
like (prep.)	wie, als	vee, ahls
like (verb)	mögen, gerne haben	moe-gehn, gehr-neh hah-behn
limit	die Grenze	tseh
line	die Linie	lee-nee-eh
linen	das Leinen	lahy-nehn
lip	die Lippe	lip-peh
lipstick	der Lippenstift	Lip-pehn-shtift
liqueur	der Likör	li-koer
liquor	der Schnaps	shnahps
listen (to)	zuhören	tsoo-hoe-rehn
little	klein, wenig	ahyn, veh-nig
live (verb)	leben, wohnen(dwell)	leh-behn, voh-nehn
liver	die Leber	leh-behr
living room	das Wohnzimmer	vohn-tsim-mehr
lobby	die Vorhalle	fohr-hahl-leh
lobster	der Hummer	hoom-mehr
lock	das Schloss	shlohs
long	lang	lahng
long distance call	das Ferngespräch	fehrn-geh-shpraeh

look	schauen, sehen, aussehen	shou-ehn, zeh-ehn, aus-zeh-ehn
lose	verlieren	fehr-lee-rehn
lost and found office	das Fundbüro	foond-bue-roh
lounge	die Diele	dee-leh
love	die Liebe (n.) lieben (v.)	lee-beh, lee-behn
low	niedrig	nee-drig
luck	das Glück	gluek
lunch (noun)	das Mittagessen	mit-tahk-ehs-sehn
lung	die Lunge	loong-eh

m

magazine	die Zeitschrift	tst-shrift
maid (chamber)	das Zimmermädchen, das Dienstmädchen	tsim-mehr-maed-hehn, deenst-maed-hehn
mail	die Post	pohst
mailbox	der Briefkasten	breef-kahs-tehn
main street	die Hauptstrasse	houpt-shtrahs-seh
make	machen	mahh-ehn
man	der Mann	mahn
management	die Leitung	lahy-toong
many	viele	fee-leh
map	die Landkarte	lahnd-kahr-teh
March	der März	maerts
market	der Markt	mahrkt
match	das Streichholz, das Zündholz	shtrahyh-hohlts, tsuend-hohlts
motor	der Motor	moh-tohr
mountain	der Berg	behrg
mouth	der Mund	moond
mouthwash	das Mundwasser	moond-vahs-sehr
move (verb)	bewegen;umziehen	beh-veh-gehn, oom-tsee-ehn
much	viel	feel
museum	das Museum	moo-zeh-oom
mushroom	der Pilz	pilts
must	müssen	mues-sehn
mutual	gegenseitig	geh-gehn-zahy-tig
my	mein	mahyn

n

nail	der Nagel	nah-gehl

nail file	die Nagelfeile	nah-gehl-f-fahy-leh
nail polish	der Nagellack	nah-gehl-lahk
name	der Name	nah-meh
named (to be)	heissen	hahy-sehn
napkin	die Serviette	zer-vi-eht-teh
narrow	eng	ehng
nationality	die Nationalität	nah-tsee-oh-nah-li-taet
naturally	natürlich	nah-tuer-lih
nauseated	Brechreiz haben	brehh-rahyts hah-behn
near	nahe	nah-eh
nearly	beinahe	bahy-nah-eh
necessary	notwendig, nötig	noht-vehn-dilg, noe-tig
neck	der Hals	hahls
necktie	die Kravatte, der Schlips	krah-vaht-teh, shlips
need (verb)	brauchen	brou-hehn
needle	die Nadel	nah-dehl
neither...nor	weder...noch	veh-dehr...nohh
nerve	der Nerv	nehrf
never	niemals, nie	nee-mahls, nee
new	neu	noy
newspaper	die Zeitung	tsahy-toong
newsstand	der Zeitungsstand	tsahy-toongs-shtahnd
next	nächst, neben	naehst, neh-behn
night	die Nacht	nahht
night club	das Nachtlokal	nahh-loh-kahl
nightgown	das Nachthemd	nahht-hehmd
night life	das Nachtleben	nahht-leh-behn
nine	neun	noyn
nineteen	neunzehn	noin-tsehn
ninety	neunzig	noyn-tsig
no	kein, nein	kahyn, nahyn
nobody	niemand	nee-mahnd
noise	der Lärm, das Geräusch	laerm, geh-roysh
noisy	lärmend	laer-mehnd
none	kein	kahyn
nonesense	der Unsinn	oon-zin
no one	niemand	nee-mahnd
noon	der Mittag	mit-tahg
north	der Norden	nohr-dehn
nose	die Nase	nah-zeh
not	nicht	niht
nothing	nichts	nihts
notice (verb)	bemerken	beh-mehr-kehn

novel (noun)	der Roman	roh-mahn
November	der November	noh-vehm-behr
now	jetzt, nun	yehtst, noon
number	die Nummer	noom-mehr
nurse	die Pflegerin, die Krankenschwester	pfleh-geh-rin, krahnk-ehn-shvehs-tehr
nut (edible)	die Nuss	noos

O

o'clock	Uhr	oor
occupied	besetzt	beh-zehtst
October	der Oktober	ohk-toh-behr
oculist	der Augenarzt	ou-gehn-ahrtst
of	von	fohn
of course	natürlich	nah-tuer-lih
off	aus; weg; ab	ous, vehg, ahb
office	das Büro	bue-roh
often	oft	oft
oil	das Öl	oel
old	alt	ahlt
olive	die Olive	o-lee-veh
omelet	das Omelett	om-lett
on	auf	owf
one	ein	ahyn
once	einmal	ahyn-mahl
onion	die Zwiebel	tsvee-behl
only	nur	noor
open (adj.)	offen (adj.), öffnen (v.)	of-fehn, oef-nehn
opera	die Oper	oh-pehr
opposite	gegenüber	beh-gehn-ue-behr
optician	der Optiker	ohp-ti-kehr
or	oder	oh-dehr
orange	die Orange, die Apfelsine	o-rahng-dsheh, ahp-fehl-zee-neh
order	die Bestellung, bestellen	beh-shtehl-loong, beh-stehl-lehn
other	andere	ahn-deh-reh
otherwise	sonst	zuhust
our, ours	unser	oon-zehr
out	aus, hinaus	ous, hin-ous
outlet (electric)	der Steckkontakt	stehk-kohn-tahkt
outside	draussen	drou-sehn
over	über, vorüber, vorbei	ue-behr, fohrue-behr, fohr-by

overcoat	der Überzieher	ue-behr-tsee-ehr
overnight	übernacht	ue-behr-nahht
owe	schulden	shool-dehn
own (verb)	besitzen	beh-zit-sehn
oyster	die Auster	ous-tehr

P

pack (verb)	packen	pahk-kehn
package	das Paket	pah-keht
page	die Seite, das Blatt	zahy-teh, blaht
pain (noun)	der Schmerz	shmehrts
painting	das Gemälde	geh-mael-deh
pair	das Paar	pahr
pajamas	der Pyjama	pi-dshah-mah
pants	die Hose	hoh-zeh
paper	das Papier	pah-peer
parasol	der Sonnenschirm	son-nehn-shirm
parcel	das Paket	pah-keht
pardon	verzeihen, entschuldigen	fehr-tsahy-ehn, ehnt-shool-di-gehn
park (verb)	parken	pahr-kehn
part (noun)	der Teil	tahyl
pass (a place)	vorbeigehen	fohr-bahy-geh-ehn
passenger	der Passagier	pahs-sah-dsheer
passport	der Pass	pahs
past (noun)	die Vergangenheit	vehr-gahng-ehn-nahyt
pastry	das Gebäck	geh-baek
pastry shop	die Bäckerei, die Konditorei	baek-keh-rahy, kon-dee-toh-rahy
pay (verb)	zahlen, bezahlen	tsah-lehn, beh-tsah-lehn
pea	die Erbse	ehrp-seh
peach	der Pfirsich	pfir-zih
pear	die Birne	bir-neh
pedestrian	der Fussgänger	foos-gaeng-ehr
pen	die Feder	feh-dehr
pencil	der Bleistift	blahy-shtift
people	die Leute, das Volk	loy-teh, fohlk
pepper	der Pfeffer	pfehf-fehr
percent	das Prozent	proh-tsehnt
performance	die Vorstellung	fohr-stehl-loong
perfume	das Parfüm	pahr-fuem
perhaps	vielleicht	fee-vahyht
permanent wave	die Dauerwelle	dou-ehr-vehl-leh
permit (noun)	der Erlaubnisschein	ehr-loub-nis-shahyn

personal	persönlich	pehr-zoen-lih
perspire	schwitzen	shvit-sehn
petticoat, slip	der Unterrock	oon-tehr-rok
photograph (noun)	die Photographie, das Foto	foh-toh-grah-fee, foh-toh
physician	der Arzt	ahrtst
piano	das Klavier	klah-veer
picture	das Bild, das Gemälde	bild, geh-mael-deh
pie	die Torte	tor-teh
piece	das Stück	shtuek
pier	der Landungsplatz, der Pier	lahn-doongs-plahts, peer
pill	die Pille	pil-leh
pillow	das Kissen	kis-sehn
pink	rosa	roh-zah
pipe (smoking)	die Pfeife	pfahy-feh
pitcher	der Krug	kroog
pity, what a ...!	wie schade!	vee shah-deh
pin	die Nadel	nah-dehl
pineapple	die Ananas	ah-nah-nahs
place (noun)	der Platz, der Ort, die Stelle	plahts, ohrt, shtehl-leh
plane (air)	das Flugzeug	floog-tsoyg
plate	der Teller	tehl-lehr
platform (railway)	der Bahnsteig	bahn-shtahyk
play (theater)	das Theaterstück	teh-ah-tehr-shtuek
play (verb: game or instrument)	spielen	shpee-lehn
pleasant	angenehm	ahn-geh-nehm
please	bitte	bit-teh
pleasure	das Vergnügen	fehr-gnue-gehn
plum	die Pflaume	pflou-meh
pocket	die Tasche	tah-sheh
pocketbook (handbag)	die Handtasche	hahnt-tah-sheh
poison	das Gift	gift
police	die Polizei	poh-li-tsahy
policeman	der Polizist, der Schutzmann	poh-li-tsist, shoots-mahn
polite	höflich	hoef-lih
poor	arm	ahrm
pork	das Schweinefleisch	shvahy-neh-flahysh
port (harbor)	der Hafen	hah-fehn
porter	der Gepäckträger	geh-paek-trae-gehr
portion	die Portion	pohr-tsee-ohn

possess	besitzen	beh-zitsehn
possible	möglich	moeg-lih
post card	die Postkarte	pohst-kahr-teh
post office	das Postamt	pohst-ahmt
postage	das Porto	pohr-toh
potato	die Kartoffel	kahr-toh-fehl
pour	giessen, schütten	gee-sehn, shuet-tehn
powder	der Puder	poo-dehr
prefer	vorziehen	fohr-tsee-ehn
prepare	vorbereiten	fohr-beh-rahy-tehn
prescription	das Rezept	reh-tsehpt
present	die Gegenwart	geh-gehn-vahrt
press (iron)	bügeln	bue-gehln
pretty	hübsch	huepsh
price	der Preis	prahys
priest	der Priester	prees-tehr
probably	wahrscheinlich	vahr-shahyn-lih
program	das Programm	proh-grahm
promise	versprechen	vehr-sprehh ehn
properly	richtig	rih-tilg
provide	besorgen	beh-zohr-gehn
public	öffentlich	oef-fehnt-lih
pull (verb)	ziehen	tsee-ehn
purchase (noun)	der Einkauf	ahyn-kouf
pure	rein	rahyn
push (verb)	stossen	shtohs-sehn
put	legen	leh-gehn

q

quality	die Qualität	kvah-li-taet
quarter	das Viertel	feer-tehl
quick, quickly	schnell	shnehl
quiet	ruhig, still	roo-ig, shtil
quite	ziemlich, ganz	tseem-lih, gahnts

r

rabbi	der Rabbiner	rah-bee-nehr
radiator (car)	der Kühler	kue-lehr
radiator (room)	der Heizkörper	hahyts-koer-pehr
radio	das Radio	rah-dee-doh
railroad	die Eisenbahn	ahy-zehn-bahn
railroad station	der Bahnhof	hahn-hohf
rain (noun)	der Regen, regnen	feh-gehn, rehg-nehn

raincoat	der Regenmantel	reh-gehn-mahn-tehl
raise (verb)	heben	heh-behn
rate (exchange)	der Kurs	koors
rather	lieber, eher, ziemlich	lee-behr, eh-ehr, tseem-lih
rayon	die Kunstseide	koonst-zahy-deh
razor	das Rasiermesser	rah-zeer-mehs-sehr
razor, safety	der Rasierapparat	rah-zeer-ah-pah-raht
razor blade	die Rasierklinge	rah-zeer-kling-eh
reach (verb)	erreichen, reichen	ehr-rahy-hehn, rahy-hehn
read	lesen	leh-zehn
ready	bereit, fertig	beh-ryt, fehr-tig
real	echt	ehht
really	wirklich	virk-lih
receipt	die Quittung	kvit-toong
receive	bekommen, empfangen	beh-koh-mehn, ehm-pfahng-ehn
recommend	empfehlen	ehm-pfeh-lehn
record(phonograph)	die Schallplatte	shahl-plaht-teh
recover (get back)	zurückbekommen	tsoo-ruek-beh-kohm-mehn
recover (health)	sich erholen	zih ehr-hoh-lehn
red	rot	roht
refuse (verb)	verweigern	fehr-vahy-gehrn
regards	die Grüsse	grues-seh
registered (mail)	eingeschrieben	ahyn-geh-shree-behn
regular(ordinary)	gewöhnlich	geh-voen-lih
remain	bleiben	blahy-behn
remedy	das Heilmittel	hahyl-mit-tehl
remember	sich erinnern	zih ehr-in-nehrn
rent (noun)	die Miete, mieten	mee-teh, mee-tehn
repair	reparieren, die Reparatur	reh-pah-ree-rehn, reh-pah-rah-toor
repeat	wiederholen	vee-dehr-hoh-lehn
reply (noun)	die Antwort, antworten	ahnt-vort, ahnt-vor-tehn
reservation(hotel)	die Vorbestellung	fohr-beh-shtehl-loong
reserve	reservieren, belegen	reh-zehr-vee-rehn, beh-leh-gehn
rest (verb)	sich ausruhen	zih ous-roo-ehn
restaurant	das Restaurant	rehs-toh-rahnt
return (give back)	zurückgeben	tsoo-ruek-geh-behn
return (go back)	zurückkehren, zurückgehen	tsoo-ruek-keh-rehn, tsoo-ruek-geh-ehn
rib	die Rippe	rip-peh
ribbon	das Band.	bahnt

rice	der Reis	rahys
rich	reich	rahyh
right (opposite of left)	rechts	rehhts
right, to be	recht haben	rehht hah-behn
right (correct)	richtig	rih-tig
ring (noun)	der Ring	ring
ring (verb)	läuten, klingeln	loy-tehn, kling-ehln
rise	aufstehen	ouf-steh-ehn
river	der Fluss	floos
road	die Strasse	shtrah-seh
roast (noun)	der Braten	brah-tehn
rob	(be) rauben	(beh) rou-behn
robe	der Schlafrock	shlahf-rohk
roll (bread)	das Brötchen, die Semmel	broet-hehn, zehm-mehl
roll (of film, etc.)	die Rolle	roh-leh
roof	das Dach	dahh
room	das Zimmer	tsim-mehr
root	die Würzel	voor-tsehl
rope	der Strick	shtrik
round	rund	roond
round trip	Hin-und Rückfahrt	hin oont ruek-fahrt
row (theater)	die Reihe	rahy-eh
rubber	der Gummi	goom-mee
rubbers	die Überschuhe, die Galoschen	ue-behr-shoo-eh, gah-losh-ehn
rug	der Teppich	tehp-pih
run (verb)	rennen, laufen	rehn-nehn, lou-fehn
running water	das fliessendes Wasser	flee-sehn-dehs vahs-sehr

S

safe	der Geldschrank, das Safe	gehlt-shrahnk, sehf
safety pin	die Sicherheitsnadel	sih-ehr-hahys-nah-dehl
safety razor	der Rasierapparat	rah-zeer-ahp-pah-raht
sail (verb)	segeln	zeh-gehln
salad	der Salat	zah-laht
sale	der Verkauf, der Ausverkauf	fehr-kouf, ous-fehr-kouf
salt	das Salz	zahlts
same	dasselbe	dahs-zehl-beh
sand	der Sand	zahnt
sandal	die Sandale	sahn-dah-leh

sandwich	das belegte Brot	beh-lehg-tehs broht
satisfied	zufrieden	tsoo-free-dehn
Saturday	der Samstag, der Sonnabend	zahm-stahg, zohh-ah-behnd
saucer	die Untertasse	oon-tehr-tahs-seh
sausage	die Wurst	voorst
say	sagen	zah-gehn
scarf	das Halstuch,	hahls-tooh
school	die Schule	shoo-leh
scissors	die Schere	sheh-reh
sea	das Meer	mehr
seam	die Naht, der Saum (hem)	naht, zoum
search (for)	suchen	zoo-hehn
seasickness	die Seekrankheit	zeh-krahnk-kahyt
season	die Jahreszeit, die Saison	yah-rehs-tsahyt, seh-zohn
seasoned (food)	gewürzt	geh-vuertst
seat	der Platz, der Sitz	plahts, zits
second	zweite	tsvahy-teh
secretary	die Sekretärin, der Sekretär	seh-kreh-tae-rin, seh-kreh-taer
see	sehen	zeh-ehn
seem	scheinen	shahy-nehn
select (verb)	auswählen	ous-vae-lehn
sell	verkaufen	fehr-kou-fehn
send	schicken	shik-kehn
sender (mail)	der Absender	ahb-zehn-dehr
serve	be (dienen)	beh-dee-nehn
set	setzen, stellen	zeh-tsehn, shtehl-lehn
several	einige, mehrere	ahy-nee-geh, meh-reh-reh
sew	nähen	nae-ehn
shade (window)	die Jalousie	Dshah-loo-zee
shaddow	der Schatten	shaht-tehn
shampoo	das Haarwaschmittel	hahr-vahsh-mit-tehl
shave (verb)	(sich) rasieren	zih rah-zee-rehn
shaving brush	der Rasierpinsel	rah-seer-pin-zehl
shaving cream	der Rasierkrem	rah-sedr-krehm
she	sie	zee
sheet	das Leintuch, das Betttuch	lahyn-tooh, beht-tooh
shining	leuchtend	loyh-tehnd
ship (noun)	das Schiff	shif
shipment	die Sendung	sehn-doong
shirt	das Hemd	hehmt

shoe	der Schuh	shoo
shoelaces	die Schnürsenkel	shnuer-zehnk-ehl
shop	das Geschäft	geh-shaeft
shopping	einkaufen	ahyn-kouf-ehn
short	kurz	koorts
shorts (underwear)	die Unterhosen (pl.)	oon-tehr-hoh-zehn
shoulder	die Schulter	shool-tehr
show (verb)	zeigen	tsahy-gehn
shower (bath)	die Dusche, die Brause	doo-sheh, brou-zeh
shrimp	die Krabbe, die Garnele	krahb-beh, gahr-neh-leh
shut	schliessen	shlee-sehn
shutter	der Fensterladen	fehn-stehr-lah-dehn
sick	krank	krahnk
sickness	die Krankheit	krahnk-hahyt
side	die Seite	zahy-teh
sidewalk	der Bürgersteig, das Trottoir	buer-gehr-shtahyg, trot-toh-ahr
sightseeing	die Stadtbesichtigung	sutaht-beh-sih-ti-goong
sign (noun)	das Schild, das Zeichen	shild, tsahy-hehn
sign (a letter)	unterzeichnen	oon-tehr-tsahyh-nehn
significant	bedeutend	beh-doy-tehn
silk	die Seide	zahy-deh
silver	das Silber	zil-behr
similar	ähnlich	aen-lih
simple	einfach	ahyn-fahh
sing	singen	zing-ehn
single room	das Einzelzimmer	ahyn-tsehl-tsim-mehr
sink (noun)	das Waschbecken	vahsh-behk-kehn
sister	die Schwester	shvehs-tehr
sit	sitzen	zit-sehn
size	die Grösse	grohe-seh
skin	die Haut	hout
skirt	der Rock	ro-hk
sky	der Himmel	him-mehl
sleep	schlafen	shlah-fehn
sleeve	der Ärmel	aer-mehl
slip (petticoat)	der Unterrock	oun-tehr-rohk
slippers	die Pantoffeln (pl.)	pahn-toh-fehln
slow	langsam	lahng-sahm
small	klein	klahyn
smoke (verb)	rauchen	rou-hehn
snow (noun)	der Schnee, schneien	shneh, shnahy-ehn

soap	die Seife	zahy-feh
socks	die Socken (pl.)	zoh-kehn
sofa	das Sofa	zoh-fah
soft	weich	vahyh
soiled	schmutzig	shmootsig
sole (shoe)	die Sole	zoh-leh
someone	jemand	yeh-mahnd
something	etwas	eht-vahs
sometimes	manchmal	mahnh-mahl
son	der Sohn	zohn
song	das Lied	leeu
soon	bald	bahld
sorrow	Leid	lahyd
soup	die Suppe	zoop-peh
sour	sauer	zou-ehr
south (noun)	der Süden	zue-dehn
souvenir	das Andenken	ahn-dehnk-ehn
space	der Raum	roum
spare tire	der Ersatzreifen	ehr-sahts-rahy-fehn
sparkplug	die Zündkerze	tsuend-kehr-tseh
speak	sprechen	shpreh-hehn
special	besondere	beh-zohn-deh-reh
specially	besonders	beh-zohn-dehrs
speed limit	die Geschwindigkeits-grenze, die Höchst-geschwindigkeit	geh-shvin-dig-kahyts-grehn-tseh, hoehst-geh-shvin-dig-kahyt
spend (time)	verbringen	fehr-bring-ehn
spend (money)	ausgeben	ous-geh-behn
spinach	der Spinat	shpi-naht
spit	ausspucken	ous-shpook-ehn
spoon	der Löffel	loef-fehl
sprain (noun)	die Verrenkung	fehr-rehnk-oong
spray (verb)	spritzen	shprit-sehn
spring(mechanical)	die Feder	feh-dehr
spring (season)	der Frühling	frue-ling
square (adj.)	viereckig, quadratisch	feer-ehk-kig, kvah-drah-tish
stairs	die Treppe	trehp-peh
stamp (postage)	die Briefmarke	breef-mahr-keh
stand (verb)	stehen	suteh-ehn
star	der Stern	shtehrn
starch (noun)	die Stärke, stärken	shtaer-keh,shtaer-kehn
start (verb)	anfangen	ahn-fahng-ehn
stateroom	die Kabine	kah-bee-neh

station(railroad)	der Bahnhof, die Bahn-station	bahn-hohf, bahn-shtah-tsee-ohr
stationmaster	der Stationsvorstand	shtah-tsyohns-fohr-shtahnt
stationery store	das Papierwaren-geschäft	pah-peer-vah-rehn-geh-shaeft
stay (noun)	der Aufenthalt	ouf-ehnt-hahlt
stay (verb)	bleiben	blahy-behn
steak	das Steak	stehk
steal	stehlen	shteh-lehn
steel	der Stahl	shtahl
steep	steil	shtahyl
steering wheel	das Steuerrad	shtoy-ehr-rad
steward	der Steward	shtoo-ahrt
stewardess	die Stewardess	shtoo-ahr-dehs
stockings	die Strümpfe (pl.)	shtruem-pfeh
stomach	der Magen	mah-gehn
stop(noun:bus or car)	die Haltestelle	hahl-teh-shtehl-leh
stop (verb)	halten; aufhören	hahl-tehn, ouf-hoe-rehn
store	das Geschäft	geh-shaeft
story	die Geschichte	geh-shih-teh
straight	gerade	grah-deh
strap	der Riemen	ree-mehn
straw	das Stroh	shtroh
strawberry	die Erdbeere	ehrd-beh-reh
street	die Strasse	shtrah-seh
streetcar	die Strassenbahn	shtrah-sehn-bahn
string	die Schnur	shnoor
strong	stark	shtahrk
style	der Stil, Model	shteel, Moh-dehl
sudden, suddenly	plötzlich	ploets-lih
sugar	der Zucker	tsook-ehr
suit (noun)	der Anzug; das Kostüm	ahn-tsook, kos-tuem
suitcase	der Handkoffer	hahnd-kof-fehr
summer	der Sommer	zom-mehr
sun	die Sonne	zoh-neh
sun glasses	die Sonnenbrille	zoh-nehn-bril-leh
Sunday	der Sonntag.	zohh-tahg
sunny	sonnig	zoh-nig
supper	das Abendessen	ah-behnt-ehs-sehn
sure	sicher	zih-ehr
surprise (noun)	die Überraschung	ue-behr-rahsh-oong
surprise (verb)	überraschen	ue-behr-rahsh-ehn
suspenders	die Hosenträger	hoh-zehn-trae-gehr

sweater	der Pullover, der Sweater, Wolljacke	pool-loh-vehr, sveh-tehr, vohl-yah-keh
sweet	süss	zues
swell (verb)	schwellen	shvehl-lehn
swim (verb)	schwimmen	shvim-mehn
swimming pool	das Schwimmbassin	shvim-bahs-sehn
switch (electric)	der Schalter	shahl-tehr

t

table	der Tisch	tish
tailor	der Schneider	shnahy-dehr
take (a person)	führen	fue-rehn
take	nehmen	neh-mehn
take off (garment)	ausziehen	ous-tsee-ehn
taken (occupied)	besetzt; belegt	beh-zehtst, beh-lehkt
talk	sprechen, reden	shpreh-ehn, reh-dehn
tall	gross	grohs
tan (color)	hellbraun	hehl-broun
tangerine	die Mandarine	mahn-dah-ree-neh
tape (adhesive)	das Heftpflaster	hehft-pflahs-tehr
taste (noun)	der Geschmack, schmecken	geh-shmahk, shmehk-kehn
tax	die Steurer	shtoy-ehr
taxi	das Taxi	tahk-si
tea	der Tee	teh
teaspoon	der Teelöffel	teh-loof-fehl
telegram	das Telegramm	teh-leh-grahm
telegraph (verb)	telegrafieren	teh-leh-grah-fee-rehn
telephone (noun)	das Telefon, der Fernsprecher	teh-leh-fohn, fehrn-shprehh-ehr
telephone (verb)	telefonieren	teh-leh-foh-nee-rehn
tell	sagen, erzählen	zah-gehn, ehr-tsaelehn
temporarily	vorübergehend	foh-rue-behr-geh-ehn
ten	zehn	tsehn
terminal (bus, etc.)	die Endstation	ehnt-shtah-tsee-ohn
than	als	ahls
thank (verb)	danken	dahnk-ehn
thank you	danke schön	dahn-keh shoen
that (conjunction)	dass	dahs
that (demonstrative)	dieser, jener	dee-zehr, yeh-nehr
the	der, die, das	dahr, dee, dahs
theater	das Theater	teh-ah-tehr
their (s)	ihr	eer

them	sie, (dir. obj.) ihnen	(ind. obj.) zee, ee-nehn
then	dann	dahn
there	da; dort	dah, dort
there is (are)	es gibt	ehs gibt
these	diese	dee-zeh
they	sie	zee
thick	dick	dik
thief	der Dieb	deeb
thigh	der Schenkel	shehnk-ehl
thing	das Ding, die Sache	ding, zah-heh
think	denken	dehnk-ehn
thirsty	durstig	door-stig
this	dies	dees
thoroughfare	die Durchfahrtstrasse	doorh-fahrt-strah-seh
thread	der Faden	fah-dehn
throat	der Hals	hahls
through	durch	doorh
thumb	der Daumen	dou-mehn
thunder	der Donner	dohn-nehr
thunderstorm	das Gewitter	geh-vit-tehr
Thursday	der Donnerstag	dohn-nehrs-tahk
ticket (theater)	die Eintrittskarte	ahyn-trits-kahr-teh
ticket (railway)	die Fahrkarte	fahr-kahr-teh
tight	eng	ehng
time	die Zeit	tsahyt
timetable	der Fahrplan	fahr-plahn
tip (gratuity)	das Trinkgeld	trink-gehld
tire(automobile)	der Reifen	rahy-fehn
tired	müde	mue-deh
toast (bread)	der Toast	tohst
tobacco	der Tabak	tah-bahk
today	heute	hoy-teh
toe	die Zehe	tseh-eh
together	zusammen	tsoo-sahm-mehn
toilet	die Toilette, das Klosett	too-ah-leht-teh, kloh-zeht
toilet paper	das Klosettpapier	kloh-zeht-pah-peer
tomato	die Tomate	toh-mah-teh
tomorrow	morgen	mohr-gehn
tongue	die Zunge	tsoong-eh
tooth	der Zahn	tsahn
toothache	die Zahnschmerzen (pl.)	tsahn-shmehr-tsehn
toothpaste	die Zahnpaste	tsahn-pahs-teh
top (on)	oben	oh-behn

touch (verb)	berühren, anfassen	beh-rue-rehn, ahn-fahs-sehn
tourist	der Tourist	too-rist
toward	nach, gegen	nahh, geh-gehn
towel	das Handtuch	hahnd-tooh
town	die Stadt	shtaht
traffic	der Verkehr	fehr-kehr
train	der Zug	tsoog
transfer	das Umsteigebillet	oom-shtahy-geh-bil-yeht
translate	übersetzen	ue-behr-zeh-tsehn
travel	reisen	rahy-zehn
traveler	der Reisende	rahy-zehn-deh
tree	der Baum	boum
trip	die Reise, die Fahrt	rahy-zeh, fahrt
trolley car	die Strassenbahn, die Trambahn	shtrah-sehn-bahn, trahm-bahn
trouble (to be in trouble)	in Verlegenheit sein	in fehr-leh-gehn-hahyt zahyn
trousers	die Hosen	hoh-zehn
truck	der Lastwagen	lahst-vah-gehn
true	wahr, richtig, treu	vahr, rih-tig, troy
trunk (baggage)	der Koffer	koh-fehr
try	versuchen, anprobieren	fahr-soo-hehn, ahn-proh-bee-rehn
Tuesday	der Dienstag	deens-tahk
turn (road)	die Biegung	bee-goong
turn (verb)	umdrehen, wenden	oom-dreh-ehn, vehn-dehn
tuxedo	der Smoking	smoh-king

U

ugly	hässlich	haes-lih
umbrella	der Regenschirm	reh-gehn-shirm
uncle	der Onkel	ohn-kehl
uncomfortable	unbequen	oon-beh-kvehm
under	unter	oon-tehr
undershirt	das Unterhemd	oon-tehr-hehmt
understand	verstehen	fehr-shteh-ehn
underwear	die Unterwäsche	con-tehr-vae-sheh
unfinished	unvollendet	oon-fohl-ehn-deht
unfortunately	leider	lahy-dehr
United States	die Vereinigten Staaten	fehr-ahy-nig-tehn shtah-tehn
university	die Universität	oo-ni-vehr-zi-taet

until	bis	bis
up	oben, auf, hinauf	oh-behn, ouf, hin-ouf
use (verb)	gebrauchen, benützen	geh-brou-hehn, beh-nuet-sehn

V

valise	der Handkoffer	hahnd-koh-fehr
valuables	die Wertsachen(pl)	vehrt-zah-hehn
value	der Wert	vehrt
veal	das Kalbfleisch	kahlb-flahysh
vegetables	das Gemüse	geh-mue-zeh
very	sehr	zehr
vest	die Weste	vehs-teh
vicinity	die Umgebung	oom-geh-boong
view	die Aussicht	ous-ziht
village	das Dorf	dohrf
vinegar	der Essig	ehs-sig
visit (noun)	der Besuch, besuchen	beh-zooh, beh-zoo-hehn
voyage	die Reise	rahy-zeh

W

waist	die Taille	fah-lee-eh
wait	warten	vahr-tehn
waiter	der Kellner	kehl-nehr
waiting room	der Wartesaal, das Wartezimmer	vahr-teh-zahl, vahr-teh-tsim-mehr
waitress	die Kellnerin	kehl-neh-rin
wake up	aufwachen	ouf-vahh-ehn
walk (take a)	spazieren gehen	shpah-tsee-rehn geh-ehn
wall	die Mauer, Wand	mou-ehr, vahnd
want	wünschen, wollen, mögen	vuen-shehn, voh-lehn, moe-gehn
war	der Krieg	kreeg
warm	warm	vahrm
wash (verb)	waschen	vah-shehn
washroom	das Waschzimmer	vahsh-tsim-mehr
watch (verb)	zuschauen	tsoo-shou-ehn
watch out	aufpassen	ouf-pahs-sehn
watch (noun)	die Uhr	oor
water	das Wasser	vahs-sehr
wave (verb)	winken	vink-ehn
way	der Weg	vehg

way back	der Rückweg	ruek-vehg
we	wir	veer
weak	schwach	shvahh
wear	tragen	trah-gehn
weather	das Wetter	veht-tehr
Wednesday	der Mittwoch	mit-voh
week	die Woche	voh-heh
weigh	wiegen	vee-gehn
weight	das Gewicht	geh-viht
welcome	willkommen	vil-koh-mehn
world	die Welt	vehlt
worry (verb)	sich sorgen	zih zohr-gehn
worse	schlechter	shlehh-tehr
worth (to be)	wert sein	vehrt zahyn
wound	die Wunde	voon-deh
wrap up	einpacken	ahyn-pahk-kehn
wrist	das Handgelenk	hahnd-geh-lehnk
wrist watch	die Armbanduhr	ahrm-bahnd-oor
write	schreiben	shrahy-behn
write down	aufschreiben	ouf-shrahy-behn
wrong	falsch, verkehrt	fahlsh, fehr-kehrt

X

X-ray photograph	die Röntgenaufnahme	roent-gehn-ouf-nah-meh

Y

year	das Jahr	yahr
yellow	gelb	gehlb
yes	ja	yah
yesterday	gestern	gehs-tehrn
yet	noch; doch	nohh, dohh
you	sing: Sie	
	Du	
	pl.: Ihr	
	Sie	
young	jung	yoong
youth hostel	die Jugendherberge	yoo-gehnd-hehr-behr-geh

Z

zipper	der Reissverschluss	rahys-fehr-shloos
zoo	der Zoo, der Tiergarten	tsoh, teer-gahr-tehn